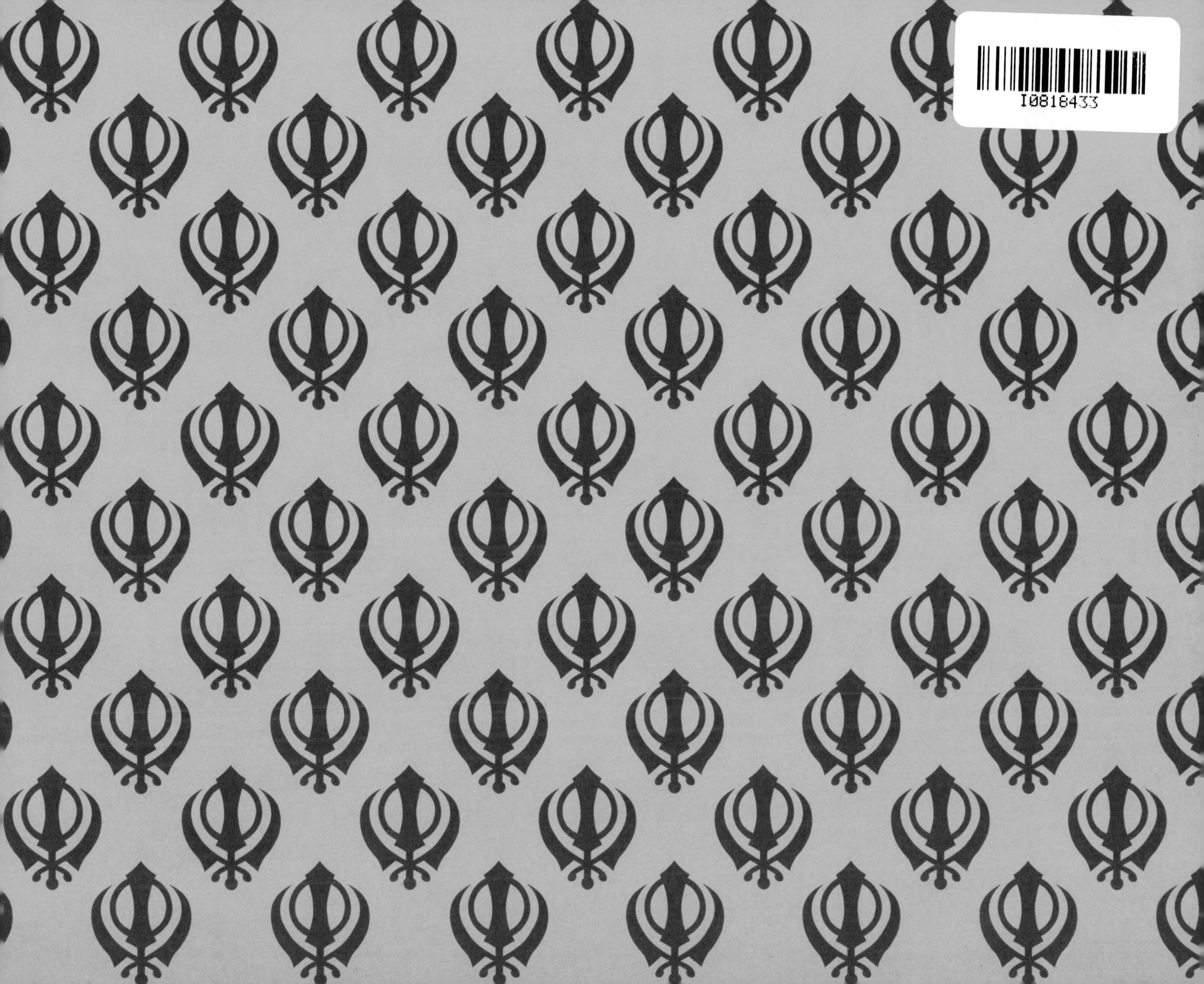
I0818433

An illustration based on the folio of an original manuscript that bears the Nisan of Guru Gobind Singh.

GURDWARAS

ABODES OF THE GURU

Roopinder Singh
Illustrated by Allan Quesada

First published in 2025 in the Philippines by Gentry Press OPC

Gentry Press OPC
Unit L2-026, Silver City 1, Central Avenue corner
Julia Vargas Avenue, Ortigas East, Barangay Ugong,
Pasig City, 1604, Metro Manila, Philippines
phl@gentrypress.com

Gentry Press Private Limited
C - 20, G Block Road, G Block BKC,
Bandra Kurla Complex, Bandra East,
Mumbai, Maharashtra, 400051, India
ind@gentrypress.com

www.gentrypress.com

ISBN: 978-621-96687-9-8

The Cataloging in Publication data of this book is available at the National Library of the Philippines

Printed in China

The Editorial Team

Publisher Rajiv Daswani
Author Roopinder Singh
Editor Kuljit Bains
Illustrator Allan Quesada
Art Director Danyel Santos

Gentry Press is committed to a sustainable future for our business, our readers and our planet. This book is made from Forest Stewardship Council™ certified paper.

Publisher's Note

In a world where race, religion, and ideology often separate us, *Gurdwaras: Abodes of the Guru* offers a quiet yet powerful reminder of our shared humanity. Religion, while sometimes used to divide, can also be a profound force for unity.

This book embodies the spirit of collaboration across those very lines. Written by a Sikh, beautifully illustrated by a Roman Catholic, designed by a member of the Iglesia ni Cristo (Church of Christ), and published by a Hindu, it symbolises harmony and shared reverence.

As you turn the pages, may you not only appreciate the beauty of the Gurdwaras themselves but also recognise the more profound beauty of human connection—the potential for unity within our diversity. It demonstrates that while our practices and beliefs may differ, the values of compassion, community, and devotion are universal. This book is born from the contributions of different faiths. It is a testament to what can be achieved when we come together rather than remain apart.

To the Sikh scholars
I was blessed to have as my parents.

Giani Gurdit Singh
1923-2007

Inderjit Kaur
1923-2022

Contents

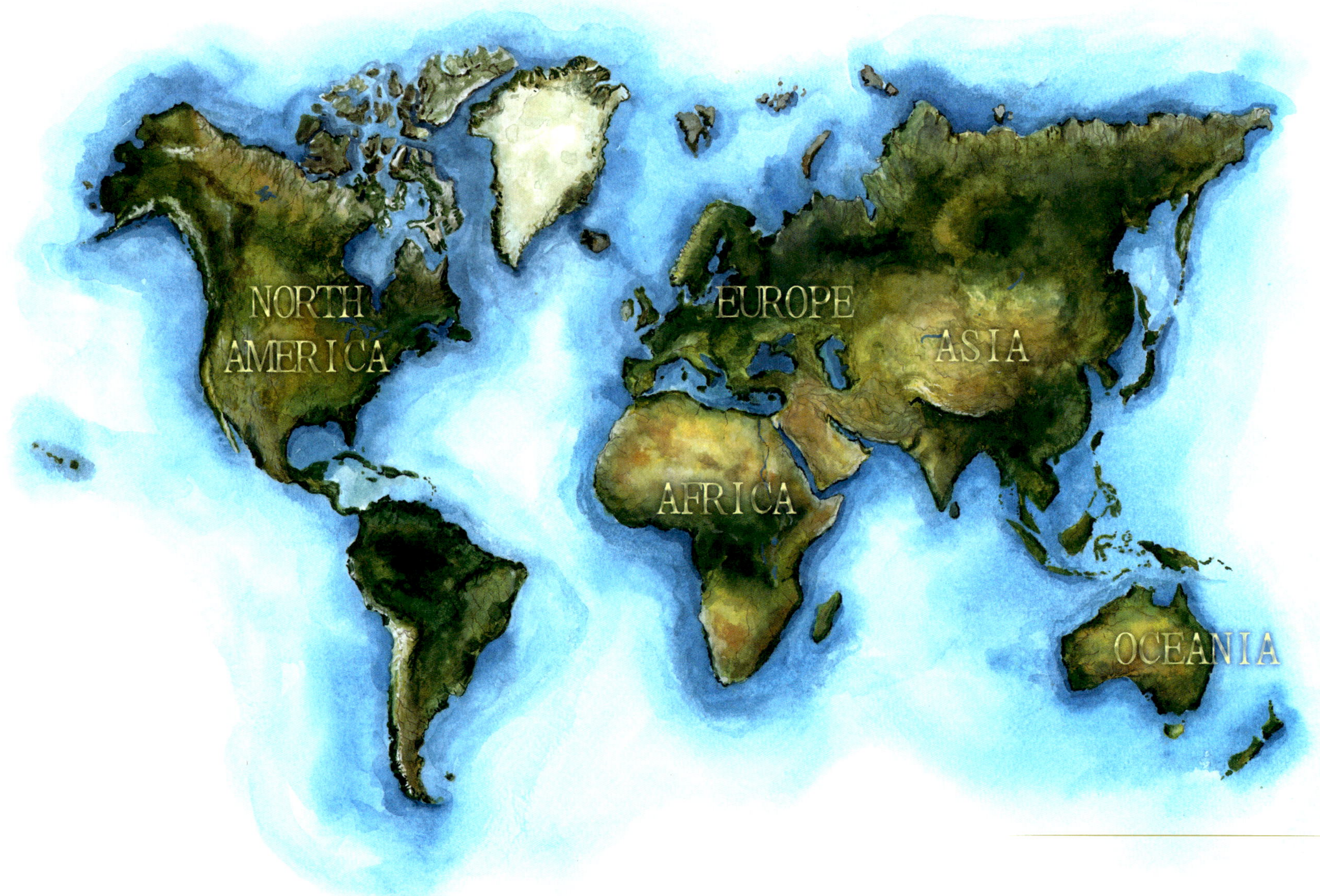

Asia and the Middle East

Europe

North America

Africa

Oceania

Foreword

His Excellency Dr Manmohan Singh
Former Prime Minister of India

The Gurdwara is a material expression of the spiritual, devotional and social aspects of the Sikh way of life. Sikhs seek spiritual solace and society of the like-minded in this place of prayer, even as they find wisdom and guidance in Guru Granth Sahib, which is central to all Gurdwaras. Guru Granth Sahib opens with Mool Mantra, the Primal Creed, wherein Guru Nanak makes a definitive statement about the unity of God and brotherhood of mankind.

The Sikh ethos is manifested through various activities that take place in a Gurdwara—such as the recitation of Gurbani from Guru Granth Sahib, *kirtan*, *katha*, *sewa*, and *langar*. Since their inception, Gurdwaras have been open to all and have been involved in various kinds of community outreach. The way the Sikh community contributed by organising food and "oxygen *langar*s" for the affected during the Covid 19 pandemic is still fresh in peoples' minds.

I am pleased to note that this book has international scope and an international audience in mind. It offers details about Gurdwaras around the world which have historical and social significance. Harmandir Sahib in Amritsar was designed by Guru Arjan Dev, and Sikh architecture has been heavily influenced by this holy shrine. We see representations of Sikh culture in the murals that adorn historical Gurdwaras. We also see many expressions of local sensibilities and community vision. The Gurdwaras abroad tell the story of how the enterprising Sikh diaspora has spread to distant lands and made a mark in different walks of life. Gurdwaras bring people together. I remember how moved my wife Gursharan, and I, felt when we went to Darbar Sahib Gurdwara in Kartarpur, Pakistan, which is featured in the book. The artist Allan Jay Quesada has captured the spirit of the Gurdwaras with his beautiful watercolours.

Roopinder Singh is well-positioned to write on Gurdwaras due to his deep understanding of Sikh heritage and history. He was associated for many years with The Tribune, Chandigarh, and has authored several well-received books. I am glad that this book is dedicated to Roopinder's parents, the late Giani Gurdit Singh and Mrs Inderjit Kaur, both esteemed scholars with whom I have had a personal association.

I hope that this book on Gurdwaras will serve as a gateway to the world of the Sikh ethos.

Manmohan Singh

Manmohan Singh

Preface

URU NANAK and his successor Gurus rejected the notion of their followers renouncing the world and exclusively seeking the spiritual, even as they also dismissed the idea of living without spiritual and ethical moorings. The Gurus expected the Sikhs to be moral in their conduct, to put in an honest day's labour, and to share the fruit of that work with others. The followers were also encouraged to congregate with like-minded individuals to meditate and pray.

Giani Gurdit Singh and Prof Inderjit Kaur, my parents, ensured my brother and I received early exposure to Sikh values and practices. They are no longer with us. We marked 2023 as the year of their birth centenary, and I respectfully dedicate this book to them. Both were scholars who won many laurels and positions in life, which they lived steeped in the Sikh ethos. My mother encouraged me to write this book.

Our parents took us to Gurdwaras, and we even spent many a night in them. My father, a leader of the Singh Sabha Centenary Movement from the 1970s, preferred to stay in Gurdwaras, as there he could freely meet with people who might be uncomfortable in parlours, or drawing rooms. Even when he visited us in New York City in the 1980s, he spent a few days at a Gurdwara! An affinity and a natural curiosity in my mind for Gurdwaras was thus a natural outcome.

The Sikhs are expected to move fluidly between the overlay of social reality and spiritual consciousness in Gurdwaras. Both are expressions of the aspirations of local people who contribute to raise a Gurdwara and play a major role in its running.

Devotees meditate and listen to *kirtan*, as they sit facing the mesmerising reflection of Harmandir Sahib in the ripples of Amrit Sarovar.

Harmandir Sahib embodies the essence of Sikh spiritual architecture. Devotees shed their egos and worldly worries at the entrance as they walk down the stairs to reach the *parkarma* around the *sarovar* in which the sanctum sanctorum is located.

Out of the numerous Gurdwaras around the world, the 51 in this book have been selected for their impact on the community and for what they represent; but by no means are they the chosen ones. These Gurdwaras are from all over the world, and I could not visit all of them. Generous people, friends, and those who became friends in the process, helped gather the necessary information on many of the Gurdwaras, and I am deeply grateful to them. One person has written this book, but it took so many to put it together. While I am thankful for their help, any mistakes that may have crept in would be entirely mine.

I am grateful to Dr Manmohan Singh, who was Prime Minister of India from 2004 to 2014, for writing the Foreword to the book on 4 July 2024. As he navigated a life full of many challenges and remarkable achievements, he was guided by his Sikh heritage and values. Unfortunately, we lost him on 26 December 2024 and I regret that the person I admired so much will not see the book in its final form.

I leaned heavily on the scholarship of many writers who have worked before me on this subject, and their books are acknowledged in the Bibliography. I was also informed by what I learned from my parents, and indeed, my mother persuaded me to work on this book rather than any other and helped me with the initial phase before she passed on in January 2022.

Sometimes, the same word is spelt differently. Indeed, many scholars have advanced good reasons for differences in spelling, but in the absence of a stylesheet that is approved by appropriate bodies and institutions, I have adopted the conventional spellings and honorifics used in India. In some cases, the names and spellings used by respective Gurdwaras on the signboards have been adopted.

While I wrote the book, Rajiv Daswani, the publisher, enlisted Allan Jay Quesada, an architect and an accomplished artist from the Philippines, to paint these Gurdwaras. Allan used watercolours for every illustration in the book and captured the unfamiliar Gurmukhi text diligently. Of course there are some variations, as are expected in paintings. To visit the Gurdwaras featured in the book, they travelled from Manila to India and certain other countries. The credit for how the book looks goes to Rajiv, who had a specific vision for it right from the start and ensured it was executed. And while I'm pleased with the result, the last word, dear reader, is yours.

Roopinder Singh

Gurdwaras and the Sikhs

URDWARAS are more than mere soaring edifices for spiritual congregants; they are also structural expressions of devotion, gathering places for like-minded individuals, and focal points of social and material support where people can come find spiritual guidance and wisdom enshrined in the teachings of the Gurus and chosen saints, as found in Guru Granth Sahib, a compilation of 5,894 divine *shabads*. Through these *shabads*, they learn about the mysterious world of the Creator, *Akal Purkh*, and His Creation.

The tradition of a Gurdwara, where Sikhs congregate to listen to *shabad kirtan* and pray together, goes back to Guru Nanak Dev (1469–1539). Local people would assemble where the Guru was, to listen to him. During his *Udasis*, or spiritual journeys, his followers would gather at a common dwelling to sing the *bani*[1] they had learnt and recite God's praises, even after he left.

In Kartarpur, a village he founded in the 1520s during the dusk of his life, the Guru distilled, consolidated, and formalised his life's spiritual journey and held regular *diwans* for the followers who lived there at the Gurdwara, or "the abode of the Guru". The word Gurdwara appears thrice in Guru Nanak's *bani*, and *dharamsal* only once, as Prof. Gurinder Mann pointed out while discussing the importance of Kartarpur in understanding the institution[2].

However, the traditional stream of scholarship uses the word *dharamsal*, literally the 'abode of truth', for the early Gurdwaras. The *bani* of Guru Nanak and his successors—Guru Angad Dev, Guru Amar Das, and Guru Ram Das—was recited and sung in *dharamsals*. Guru Arjan Dev (1563-1606) compiled the bani of his predecessors, his own, and the wisdom of 15 *bhagats*, Hindu and Muslim, whose teachings were in harmony with his, and his predecessors', beliefs. The Guru installed this compendium of teachings in Harmandir Sahib in 1604. As copies of the manuscript were made and disseminated, the *dharamsals* where they were installed were called Gurdwaras, abode of the Gurus' word.

Guru Granth Sahib, the living Guru, is central to every Gurdwara and the primary focus has always been on the spiritual aspect. Even as it has remained conceptually the same—the venue where the Sikhs congregate to pray—the Sikhs' place of worship has been variously called Gurdwara, *dharamsal*, *dera*, and *takht*, and this reflects the evolution of its functions and role.

The Gurus held that the spiritual is not divorced from the obligations of an individual to society, and incorporated practices that reflected the egalitarian values they expected their followers to inculcate. As the focal point of Sikh interaction, Gurdwaras serve as places for congregations to assemble as a *sangat*, pray, partake of the *langar*, and perform *sewa*[3].

Guru Nanak established a *sangat* of his followers wherever he went. Sikh *sangats* were to be found in places visited by Guru Nanak and his successors. The word is still used in the name of some Gurdwaras, both in India and abroad.

Seeking the true meaning of the *shabads* contained in Gurbani, and reflecting on the meaning of these spiritual compositions, is at the core of a Sikh's religious quest and ethical understanding. The *sangat* comes to Gurdwaras to recite and listen to Gurbani rendered in the form of *kirtan*, to hear it expounded through *katha*, to interact with each other, and to hear lectures and sermons.

Guru Nanak's principle that all humans must be treated equally has guided all Gurdwaras from their inception. Indeed, the four doors of Harmandir Sahib signify that they are open to seekers coming from all directions and faiths. It is common for non-Sikhs to pay obeisance at Gurdwaras and listen to *kirtan*, especially on special occasions like Gurpurbs and various festivals.

Langar is intertwined with the concept of Gurdwara and has proved a potent instrument in ensuring egalitarian conduct and mutual respect. Everyone is expected to sit in *pangats*, or rows. This arrangement ensures that all break bread together without distinction of caste, creed, or religion. Many of those who partake of *langar* in a Gurdwara are not Sikhs and are welcomed with open arms.

People preparing and serving food are often volunteers performing *sewa*. Tasks such as serving food in the *langar*, cleaning shoes at the *jora ghar*, attending to

1 The Guru's divine compositions.
2 The New York-based scholar recently shared his thoughts with the author. He is working on an academic paper on this subject that will be published soon.
3 Devoted service.

Gurdwaras showcase artistry and devotion that makes the place sacred. This close-up shows the intricate lotus petal details adorning the domes of Harmandir Sahib.

other maintenance tasks at the Gurdwara, and participating in the *kar sewa* to build Gurdwaras, all stem from the overwhelming urge to perform *sewa*. The spirit of *sewa*, or selfless service, empowers these pursuits by quelling selfish impulses and inculcating humility.

Hundreds of thousands of devotees participated enthusiastically in the 1973 *kar sewa* at Harmandir Sahib. The sight of women in their Sunday best lined up to gather and carry away pans of silt from the Amrit Sarovar became a visual metaphor for the importance and significance of doing Gurus' work. Their husbands were not so striking in their apparel, but the crowd included people who ordinarily would never have allowed their hands to be soiled literally covered in mud. There are pictures of bejewelled Maharajas of yore mingling with those who were then their subjects, all performing *kar sewa* together.

Gurdwaras are diverse in their form and dimensions. Most of them are influenced by the architecture of Harmandir Sahib, originally built by Guru Arjan Dev between 1588 and 1601. While Harmandir Sahib's predominance in Sikh sacral architecture is undisputed, tradition does not allow it to be replicated. The aspirations, artistic sensibilities, and requirements of local *sangats* are reflected in the structures, even as they are informed by the grammar of the architectural conventions of Harmandir Sahib.

Looking at the glorious Harmandir Sahib today, it is difficult to imagine that this preeminent Gurdwara has faced existential threats over the centuries and, indeed, was rebuilt and restored by Sikhs as soon as they were able to return to Amritsar after having to strategically evacuate the city on several occasions.

In the second half of the 18th century, the Sikh *misls*, a confederation of warriors, established reputation as a formidable fighting force in northwestern India. As they consolidated their power, they built Gurdwaras at sites connected to Gurus and events in Sikh history. The successful attack on Delhi, which took them to the Red Fort on 11 March 1783, empowered the Sikhs to build Gurdwaras at sites of historical importance in Delhi. These Gurdwaras continue to flourish till date.

(left) Nishan Sahib, the tall triangular Sikh religious flag seen in all Gurdwaras.

(right) A rich geometric design is executed in *gach* and *tukri* work in the ceiling above Harmandir Sahib's *parkash asthan*.

Sikh *misls*, and later Maharaja Ranjit Singh and other Sikh rulers, gave land and *jagirs* (land grants) to Gurdwaras. Nankana Sahib, the birthplace of Guru Nanak, received the largest grant from Maharaja Ranjit Singh[4]. Besides gilding Harmandir Sahib, he played an important role in establishing and helping Gurdwaras across India. While prominent, he wasn't the only one. Land grants from the state treasuries of various Sikh rulers were often given to Gurdwaras and religious institutions of other faiths.

At that time, most Gurdwaras were administered by hereditary priests. Over a period, many became indolent and even corrupt.[5] In 1873, the Singh Sabha Movement fuelled the Gurdwara Sudhar Lehar, which led to the enactment of the Sikh Gurdwara Act of 1925. The Shiromani Gurdwara Parbandhak Committee (SGPC), instituted under this Act, is elected through adult franchise under government supervision. This kind of democratic governance is a unique ecclesiastical feature of Sikh religious administration. While the SGPC has control only over certain historical Gurdwaras, it provides the required leadership in Sikh religious affairs.

4 Earlier, Rai Bular Bhatti, the medieval feudal chief and contemporary of Guru Nanak, donated much land to mark the Guru's birthplace.
5 Most of the Gurdwaras were managed by ascetic Udasis, followers of Sri Chand.

Artisans often used semi-precious stones to adorn marble in geometric, abstract, arabesque, botanical, and other designs. Such details are seen in Harmandir Sahib and other Gurdwaras, even some contemporary ones.

IKH history has been a tumultuous journey. Forced displacement has been a regular feature since the time of the Gurus. The reasons for this included military invasions, tyrannical regimes, political upheaval, or socio-economic impetus, as Sikhs sought better prospects in distant lands.

The biggest disruption of the last century was caused by the Partition of India and the creation of Pakistan in 1947. The Sikh sacred geography was split perilously as many historical and significant Gurdwaras became part of the Muslim-majority Pakistan, inaccessible to Sikhs in India. Many non-Muslims, especially Sikhs and Hindus, who had to migrate from the newly created Pakistan to India, found themselves rendered refugees who had to build life anew. In their quest for a fresh start in distant cities, existing Gurdwaras offered the necessary support. In time, as Sikhs settled down in various towns in India after Partition, more Gurdwaras were built.

As we will see, a few small enclaves of Sikhs still exist in the Islamic Republic of Pakistan, but most of the Gurdwaras there are not functional. Yet, the 2019 opening of the Kartarpur Corridor from Gurdwara Darbar Sahib, near Lahore in Pakistan, to Gurdwara Dera Baba Nanak in Gurdaspur district of Punjab, India, shows what can be achieved and the goodwill it generates.

Gurdwaras have played a significant role in providing spiritual and material support to the Sikh diaspora, the spread of which was triggered by the fall of Maharaja Ranjit Singh's empire in 1849. The British Imperial Service incorporated Sikhs as soldiers and policemen and sent them to Burma, British Malaya (Malaysia and Singapore), Hong Kong, and the Philippines.

Along with those directly employed by the British, others also sought their fortune and soon set up Gurdwaras and trade associations. Gurdwaras helped early Sikh immigrants find work in foreign lands such as the USA and Canada. Their skills and hardiness were prized, and the British colonial authorities took them to lay and run railroads in Africa and even as far off as Argentina. They built the Panama Canal, worked as lumberjacks in Canada, and became farmers in America. The UK has many Sikhs, as does Australia. They are in significant numbers in Europe, too.

Except for the historical Gurdwaras in India and Pakistan, all Gurdwaras are administered by committees chosen by local *sangats*, who look to the SGPC for guidance in religious matters. It is fair to say that there is no populated continent without Sikh presence and, consequently, without Gurdwaras. Where there are people, there is also politics, but that is not in the purview of this book.

Bhai Kahan Singh, in his venerable *Mahan Kosh* (published in 1930), writes: "The Gurdwara is the centre of learning for students, preacher for seekers of spiritual knowledge, hospital for the sick, storehouse of food for the hungry, an iron fortress for protecting the chastity of women, and resting place for the pilgrims."

As we observe modern-day Gurdwaras, we can see a reflection of their historical purpose. These places of prayer now offer medical clinics, where volunteer doctors give their time and expertise to help those in need.

Additionally, they have schools providing secular and religious education to Sikh children. In times of social unrest, Gurdwaras have been seen as sanctuaries of safety.

For Sikhs living outside Punjab or India, these Gurdwaras are a vital connection to their homeland and its people. They are the centres for spiritual, political, social, and sometimes economic life of the Sikhs.

The grandeur of these Gurdwaras extends beyond their physical attributes, as they reflect the community's history and aspirations and serve as the focal point of spiritual and cultural life for devotees.

Asia and the Middle East

PUNJAB is the cradle of the Sikh faith, and, therefore, it is central to Sikh sacred geography. Guru Nanak was born in Punjab, as were almost all Gurus that succeeded him. People of this region were the privileged ones who directly interacted with them and adopted their teachings. Significant Gurdwaras associated with the Gurus came up in the area that constituted the larger pre-Partition (1947) Punjab. Guru Nanak undertook four spiritual journeys between 1500 and 1524, covering 28,000 kilometres. Guru Tegh Bahadur also travelled widely outside Punjab, as did Guru Gobind Singh, who was born in Patna. Gurdwaras mark their presence in many places spread across the Indian subcontinent, and even beyond it. The carving out of various nation-states has put certain impediments in the followers' access to some of the historical Gurdwaras, but in most cases ways have been found to overcome the hurdles. The importance of the region to Sikh sacred geography is, thus, undisputed.

Sikhs left the Indian subcontinent in significant numbers as a result of their recruitment in the British Indian Army around the 1860s, which took them to China (Shanghai and Hong Kong) and South-East Asia (the British territories of Burma and Malaya). In time, they were also absorbed into the civilian police forces of the region. Many Gurdwaras of the time received direct support from the British authorities.

Triggered by various socio-economic factors, other immigrants, too, went to these lands and found support even as they established themselves as professionals and business people. They also spread to other countries, including Thailand, Singapore, the Philippines, Indonesia, and Fiji.

Sikhs had a small but early presence in Afghanistan, which was, however, reduced to a mere token strength by the 2020s. In World War II, they fought in the Gulf countries but did not settle down there. The oil boom in the area in the 1970s brought in immigrants in larger numbers. Since then, there has been an ebb and flow of Sikh numbers in the region, governed mainly by the demand for particular skills at various times. Overall, the region's emergence as an economic powerhouse attracted more Sikhs in various professions.

PAKISTAN
UNITED ARAB
EMIRATES
BANGLADESH
CHINA
INDIA
THAILAND
PHILIPPINES
MALAYSIA
SINGAPORE
Asia

Harmandir Sahib

AMRITSAR, PUNJAB, INDIA

SPIRITUALITY, history, heritage, and architecture come together to create an ethereal vision of white marble, topped with golden domes reflected in the water surrounding it—a sight that never fails to mesmerise visitors and devotees alike. Harmandir Sahib[6] is the most enduring symbol of Sikh devotion that attracts people from all over the world. The most outstanding architectural monument of the Sikh faith, it has the essence of Sikh spiritual architecture.

Harmandir Sahib is the most outstanding architectural monument of the Sikh faith. It showcases the essence of Sikh spiritual architecture.

The site of Amritsar, where Harmandir Sahib is located, was identified by Guru Amar Das. He asked his disciple Ram Das, who became his successor and the fourth Guru, to develop the Amrit Sarovar and the surrounding town. Work began on both in 1570 and took seven years to complete. Fifth Guru Arjan Dev planned the building of Harmandir Sahib, and he invited the Lahore-based Sufi divine Hazrat Mian Mir[7] to lay the foundation stone. Baba Budha[8] and other prominent Sikhs, who supervised various aspects of the construction work, assisted the Guru, as the *sangat* contributed the labour and their mite.

6 Spellings vary; Harmandar Sahib and Harimandir Sahib are also used.
7 A contemporary Sufi Muslim saint who lived in Lahore, he commanded great respect.
8 Bura Randhawa, a significant person in Sikh history, was often called Baba Budha or "wise old man". He was a close confidant of the first six Gurus and was a repository of knowledge and Sikh tradition.

ਜੋ ਮਾਗਹਿ ਠਾਕੁਰ ਅਪੁਨੇ ਤੇ ਸੋਈ ਸੋਈ ਦੇਵੈ ॥

Divine music permeates the souls of the devotees who throng the Golden Temple throughout the day.

Guru Arjan entrusted Bhai Gurdas with the duty of scribing the *Adi Granth* under his supervision. He incorporated compositions of Guru Nanak, Guru Angad, Guru Amar Das and Guru Ram Das, along with his own hymns. He also selected certain Hindu and Islamic saints, whose teachings were in consonance with those of the Gurus, for inclusion. Guru Ram Das installed the *Adi Granth* in the newly built temple in 1604.

Devotees walk down a flight of steps to get to the level of Harmandir Sahib, signifying humility and shedding of one's ego. The edifice plays a vital role in concretising the conceptual premises—four doors opening in the cardinal directions instead of one imposing entrance signal openness to all. The white building stands out in a pond of water, much like a lotus, a symbol of purity. The same lotus motif is used in various forms, including the inverted shape on the dome, to reinforce the element. Indeed, there are several books on the architecture of Harmandir Sahib.

Harmandir Sahib faced many challenges after Guru Arjan built it, including attacks and destruction. It became the target of Mughal satraps like Massa Ranghar, who took charge of Harmandir Sahib in 1740 and defiled it till two Sikhs killed him.[9] Six years later, Lakhpat Rai, a *diwan* of Lahore, desecrated the *sarovar*. The most destructive actions were those of the Afghan invader Ahmed Shah Durrani,[10] who attacked the spiritual centre of the Sikhs multiple times. After that, the most important shrine of the Sikhs suffered significant damage in 1984,[11] which scarred the Sikh psyche.

Sikh confederacies arose, and the Mughal empire weakened. Improving and embellishing the premises of Harmandir Sahib became an expression of rising Sikh power. This process got a further fillip when, in 1808, Maharaja Ranjit Singh gained control over Amritsar. He executed significant renovations, including the gilding, which would give Harmandir Sahib the epithet Golden Temple. Electricity first came in 1898.[12] During the British Raj, the government took control, but Sikh reformers eventually replaced its managers and took control.

9 Ballads about Bhai Mehtab Singh and Bhai Sukha Singh are sung to date, remembering their daring assault.
10 Widely known as Ahmed Shah Abdali, he founded the Durrani dynasty and is regarded as the founder of Afghanistan.
11 In 1984, Akal Takht, near Harmandir Sahib, suffered much damage in Operation Bluestar, the Army assault on the Golden Temple ordered by then Prime Minister Indira Gandhi.
12 Maharaja Bikram Singh of Faridkot funded the endeavour.

Gilded fluted domes adorn the roof of Harmandir Sahib and are topped with the *kalash*, or the pinnacle, with a *chhatri* at the top of the larger one.

Darshani Deori, with its over 20-foot-high arch and heavily embellished doors, stands at its shore end. As you enter, you see the western facade of Harmandir Sahib, approachable through a 202-foot-long vaulted causeway that leads to the entrance and connects with the 13-foot-wide circumambulatory path around the main shrine.

At the eastern end, opposite the main entrance, the cuboid shape of the structure has been extended by adding a hexagonal prism. Here, devotees walk down the steps of Har ki Pauri[13] to the *sarovar* and take palmfuls of Amrit. Granthi Singhs read Guru Granth Sahib continuously in the building above the steps.

Harmandir Sahib is a three-storeyed building. It is made of brick masonry and lime mortar, using Nanakshahi bricks[14] and other traditional materials. Embellishments came later, as Sikh confederacies arose. The artisans often used semi-precious stones like onyx, mother-of-pearl, lapis lazuli, and carnelian to adorn marble. They executed designs in a range that includes geometrics, abstracts, arabesques, flowers, foliage, fish, animals, and a few human figures. *Pietra dura* or *jaratkari* work still stands strong, centuries after its creation.

Gold gilding on copper panels starts around the first floor and goes to the top. Etched in bas-relief are various inscriptions and some pictures. The skill of the artisans is quite evident, as is their mastery over the medium. The gilding withstood the vagaries of weather for about 150 years before it required refurbishing.

13 Literally, the steps of God.
14 Kiln-burnt clay tile about 5.6 inches long, 3.8 inches wide and an inch thick.

An artistic representation of the bass-relief sculpture panel at the entrance of Harmandir Sahib.

(left) A rich geometric design is executed in *gach* and *tukri* work in the ceiling above Harmandir Sahib's *parkash asthan*.

(right) Pietra dura, or *jaratkari*, work featuring semi-precious stones on marble depicting two birds, two fish and two elephants in a geometric arrangement on a wall of Harmandir Sahib.

When we look at the western facade, we see the top decorated with repeated cusped arches and the corners with *chhatris*. A four-foot parapet is lowered in the centre to allow an unobstructed view of the low-fluted elliptical golden dome. The flutes end with the inverted lotus base and are topped with the pinnacle, or the *kalash*, with a delicate *chhatri* at the top. Gilding covers the dome and domelets.

The interior of the *parkash asthan* is richly embellished with *gach*[15] and *tukri*[16] work. The combination of gold and brilliant colours creates a vibrant atmosphere as devotees view the double-storeyed dome in the centre of the sanctum sanctorum through the 17-foot opening. The mezzanine is open to devotees, and the frescos here reflect the artistic talent of the *naqqash* or the multitude of artists from different schools of art.

15 A paste of crushed gypsum and water etched in designs, predominantly floral or geometric, applied on walls and ceilings. Once it sets, it is filled with colours and covered with gold leaf.
16 Glass or mirror pieces, shaped and cut to specifications, inlaid into *gach*.

The Dukh Bhanjani Beri dates to the time of Guru Ram Das, when Harmandir Sahib was built. *Dukh Bhanjani* is translated as "eradicator of suffering", and it is sacred to devotees.

The *sarovar*, or the sacred tank, which is 490 feet by 510 feet at the level of the marble-tiled *parkarma*, surrounds Harmandir Sahib. It gets water from a canal via a desilting station, supplemented by tube wells. A state-of-the-art filtration plant was installed in 2004, which also adds oxygen to the water through aeration ducts. Taking a holy dip in the holy *sarovar* ranks high in the spiritual acts of Sikhs.

At the *sarovar* edge of the *parkarma* on the eastern side is the Dukh Bhanjani Beri (jujube) tree that dates back to the time of Guru Ram Das, when Harmandir Sahib was built. Dukh Bhanjani is translated as "eradicator of suffering", and devotees consider it sacred and believe in its curative power.

After paying obeisance, most devotees visit the *langar* hall to partake of the food or perform *sewa*, often both. Volunteers, who need to book their place months in advance, perform various duties at the *langar* hall, where over a hundred thousand people are served daily.

Trained musicians sing the daily *kirtan*[17] in the appropriate *ragas*. It is performed from about 2 am to 10 pm. Thus, divine music permeates the souls of the devotees who throng the Golden Temple throughout the day. Only *kirtan* and no other activity like *katha* is allowed in Harmandir Sahib.

Harmandir Sahib is among the most visited places in the world, with over a hundred thousand visitors daily, the number even doubling during festivals. Yet every visit is unique and memorable for those who pay obeisance at this shrine to the one Almighty.

17 The recitation of holy hymns.

Akal Takht Sahib

AMRITSAR, PUNJAB, INDIA

MPOSING because of its impact on Sikh history and architecture, Akal Takht Sahib is the primary seat of authority for the Sikhs. All disputes are resolved there; those who bring laurels to the religion are honoured, and those who allegedly violate the religious code of conduct are given a hearing—and punished, if necessary.

Akal Takht Sahib is the primary seat of authority for the Sikhs.

The Sikhs recognise the close relationship between the spiritual and the temporal. The placement of Akal Takht Sahib near Darshani Deori, the inner entrance of Harmandir Sahib, is significant. It acknowledges the close yet distinct spheres that *Miri* and *Piri*, the worldly and the spiritual domains of life, occupy.

The institution is housed in a building originally called Akal Bunga. Nowadays, the term Akal Takht Sahib is used for both. Guru Hargobind laid the foundation stone of what was then called Thara Sahib on 14 June 1606. Bhai Buddha and Bhai Gurdas, among the most pious of the Sikhs, constructed the raised platform about 3.5 metres high, where the Guru was anointed and given the two swords of *Miri* and *Piri*. He sat there to hear his Sikhs and to guide them, and watched martial arts. Ceremonies were held there. The Guru issued the first *Hukamnama*, his epistle to his Sikhs, enjoining them to bring weapons and horses as offerings, from here. Till today, a *Hukamnama* issued from Akal Takht Sahib is an imperative considered binding on the Sikhs.

In time, the raised platform became a building called Akal Bunga. After the Gurus, it was here that disputes were settled, religious edicts issued, and matters of grave importance to the community discussed; indeed,

Sangat paying obeisance and listening to *kirtan* in the sanctum sanctorum of Akal Takht Sahib.

for three centuries, Akal Bunga was central to Sikh discourse. Sikhs would gather at least every Diwali in the area in front of the Bunga building, where issues of interpretation of Guru Granth Sahib, disputes between Sikhs or institutions, including *misls*, and matters of conduct would be discussed. Unanimous decisions were considered the Guru's direction, Gurmatas. Political decisions were also taken at Akal Takht Sahib for a long time, but Maharaja Ranjit Singh's rule led to this practice taking a back seat. However, religious matters were another aspect altogether. In one instance, even the Maharaja submitted himself to the authority of then Akal Takht Sahib Jathedar Akali Phula Singh.

As Akal Takht Sahib and Harmandir Sahib became the seat of Sikh piety, they also became targets of Imperial Mughal forces and invaders such as Ahmed Shah Durrani. During one of his attacks, the 30 Sikhs posted there fought to the last man against the invading army. "They had neither the fear of slaughter nor the dread of death."[18]

After the attack, the Sikhs regrouped, and at the Baisakhi festival that they celebrated in Amritsar in 1765, they resolved to take over Lahore, even as they stood in front of the ruins of Akal Bunga, the ground floor of which was rebuilt by 1774. The rest of the floors were added as time passed, with the help of Sikh *misls* and Maharaja Ranjit Singh, who had the top three storeys constructed. His famous general, Hari Singh Nalwa, executed the gold leaf dome from his personal funds.

Akal Takht Sahib was severely damaged in the 1984 assault on the Golden Temple by the army. There was a tremendous loss of life and the Indian government had it rebuilt by Baba Santa Singh, a Nihang chief. However, the Sikhs, in keeping with the tradition that only pious voluntary labour should be used for building Akal Takht, demolished the structure and rebuilt it into what stands today. The traditional design has been retained even as specific changes have been made to accommodate more pilgrims and for other requirements.

18 Jadunath Sarkar, *Fall of the Mughal Empire*, quoting the eye-witness Qazi Nur Muhammad, who accompanied Durrani in 1764.

The ground floor has a circular projecting bow at the centre that becomes the ceremonial platform on the first floor of the building, from which the Jathedar of Akal Takht Sahib pronounces his verdict and announces the *Hukamnamas*. The parapet is lower in the middle, and the centre has a gap so the disciples can receive the *Hukamnamas*. Traditionally, *dhadi jathas*, or groups of bards, sing ballads evoking history and heritage for impromptu audiences sitting in the open area in front of Akal Takht. These singers play the *sarangi*[19] and *dhads*[20] as they recite *vaars*, or ballads. These traditional folk singers have a special place in Sikh ethos as they reinforce the message of the Gurus and Gurbani.

The first floor is accessible through stairs on the sides of the building. Mirror work and gold embellishments are used on the ceiling. A room on the left from the entrance is called Kotha Sahib. This was the place where Guru Arjan Dev rested. When the Guru compiled the *Adi Granth*, he had it placed here ceremonially, and the Guru himself slept on the floor.

Every morning at 4 a.m., Guru Granth Sahib is taken from Akal Takht Sahib to Harmandir Sahib. The golden palanquin is ceremonially carried by devotees, with continuous chanting of hymns and trumpeters heralding the procession. At 11 p.m., it is time for Guru Granth Sahib to be brought back to Akal Takht Sahib for *sukhasan*, or repose. There is always a large gathering of devotees on both these occasions.

The Takht also has a significant collection of weapons of the Gurus and important Sikh martyrs. These are ceremoniously displayed on special occasions.

Akal Takht Sahib is preeminent of the five *takhts* of the Sikhs. It is here that all important decisions are taken, and edicts on religious conduct issued. The two Nishan Sahibs[21] seen at the side of the building signify its importance and authority—both spiritual and temporal.

19 A short-necked string instrument played with a bow.
20 A percussion instrument common in Punjab.
21 The 101-foot flagpole represents *Piri* and the 100-foot flagpole is for *Miri*, thus placing the spiritual at a higher plane than temporal authority.

A *granthi* Singh reads from Guru Granth Sahib at Akal Takht Sahib.

Takht Sri Kesgarh Sahib

ANANDPUR SAHIB, PUNJAB, INDIA

SITUATED atop a hillock, the grand edifice of Takht Sri Kesgarh[22] Sahib marks the birthplace of the Khalsa. In 1699, on Baisakhi Day that heralds the dawn of a new solar year in many of the traditional Indian calendars, Guru Gobind Singh held a massive congregation, and administered Amrit to the first five Sikhs, thus ordaining the Khalsa. In turn, the Guru received the *Amrit* from them, and thus "the Guru also became a follower".[23]

The imposing Takht Sri Kesgarh Sahib complex dominates the horizon when seen from the approach road.

Anandpur Sahib was called Chak Nanaki. Guru Gobind Singh's father, Guru Tegh Bahadur, founded the city in 1665 and named it after his mother. Guru Gobind Singh moved there from Patna when he was five years old. He received traditional education and was trained in the art of warfare there. The Takht is near the site of the old Kesgarh Fort, where the Baisakhi congregation was held.

Historical shrines at Anandpur Sahib were under the care of the local Sodhi family, which traces its descent back to the Gurus. In the 1920s, in common with other historical Gurdwaras, the Shiromani Gurdwara Parbandhak Committee took over the shrines and the responsibility for their upkeep.

Only a little remains of the old fort. The Gurdwara is built around a basic complex constructed between 1936 and 1944. It has undergone many renovations and additions subsequently.

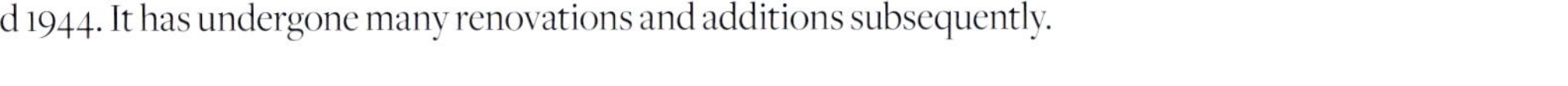

22 It is also spelt Keshgarh.
23 Bhai Gurdas Chote or II, a prominent poet of Guru Gobind Singh's *darbar*, describes the Guru thus.

Ragi Singhs recite *kirtan* at Takht Sri Kesgarh Sahib.

The lower levels of the multi-storeyed complex have a *langar* hall, residential rooms for pilgrims and staff, shops, a bank office, a shoe storage room, etc. There is also a *sarovar* at a lower level.

Atop the hillock is Takht Sahib, the Gurdwara with a large courtyard. Located higher and approached by climbing stairs is the main building that houses the sanctum sanctorum.

Celebrations to mark the tercentenary of the Khalsa in 1999 drew hundreds of thousands of pilgrims. Naturally, this triggered a major makeover at Takht Sri Kesgarh Sahib, the birthplace of the Khalsa, and the town of Anandpur Sahib, all buildings of which were painted white.

Rich in history, the Takht is also rich in relics. Among the weapons of Guru Gobind Singh are a *khanda*[24] that was used to prepare *Amrit*[25] in 1699, a *katar*[26] of the Guru, and a *saif*[27] that was given to Guru Gobind Singh by Bahadur Shah I and is believed to have been owned by Imam Hazrat Ali. It has verses from the Holy Quran inscribed, along with the names of Hazrat Ali, his wife, and their two sons.

Two different spears, a *karpa barcha*[28] used in the battles around Anandpur fort, and a *nagni barcha*[29] used by Bhai Bachitar Singh to tackle a rampaging war elephant, are also preserved there.

Weapons of Guru Gobind Singh, taken away by the British from Maharaja Ranjit Singh's treasury, were returned to India in 1966, and are now kept at the Takht. They include swords of the 10th Guru, the *Shamshir-e-Tegh*,[30] and *Dagh-e-Aine*,[31] as well as a golden *chakra*[32] inscribed with couplets from the *Japji Sahib* that was worn by the Guru on his turban, and a rhinoceros-skin battle shield.

A trove of relics was received from the descendants of Maharaja of Nabha some years ago. They are now housed at Takht Sahib. A turban of Guru Gobind Singh and his short comb with hair entangled, given to Pir Budhu Shah at Sadhora, are of particular significance. Guru Hargobind's massive *tega*, or broadsword, a sword that belonged to Guru Tegh Bahadur, and Guru Gobind Singh's sword given to Baba Phul of Bhai Rupa are also significant attractions among the newer acquisitions.

24 A double-edged broadsword.
25 Literally, divine nectar, first prepared by Guru Gobind Singh to ordain the Khalsa, or the pure.
26 A short thrust dagger.
27 A curved sword.
28 A heavy spear with a broad base.
29 A serpentine or corkscrew-shaped long spear.
30 A sword designed for downward thrust, also known as the Kora sword.
31 A close-combat weapon designed to break open armour/helmets.
32 A quoit typically worn over a turban.

The intangible heritage of Anandpur Sahib is being a literary and spiritual base. Guru Gobind Singh was well versed in Indian classical languages—Sanskrit, Persian and Arabic—and Braj, a language used for religious literature in northern India. Like his predecessors, he encouraged literary discourse, and during his sojourn here, poets, bards, musicians and literary luminaries flocked to be in his congregations. History mentions the 52 poets[33] he patronised, and the many classical texts translated and made available to ordinary people.[34] Anandpur Sahib emerged as a literary hub and the Guru's *darbar* held sessions of poetry and music and martial arts demonstrations/training.

The *nagara*, or war drum, being sounded at Takht Sri Kesgarh Sahib.

In 1684, he wrote his only major work in Punjabi, *Chandi di Var*. During his two decades in these foothills, he also wrote *Jaap Sahib*, *Akal Ustat*, and *Sawaya*. The Sirsa river, which flows into the mighty Satluj, was in spate when the Guru evacuated Anandpur Sahib in 1705. Crossing the river caused a tremendous loss of life. The precious manuscripts that were being transported on pack animals were also lost. We find various references in *Gurpartap Suraj Parkash* about *Vidya Sagar Granth*, a massive compendium weighing over 300 kg, which was lost while the Guru's party was crossing the Sirsa river.

The literature of Anandpur gave strength at a time when it was needed. The translations of major religious texts of other faiths, and Guru Gobind Singh's commentary raised the consciousness of the Sikhs.

Anandpur Sahib is now a major centre of pilgrimage. Takht Sri Kesgarh Sahib is naturally the focus. However, the importance of other Gurdwaras around it must be kept in mind.

Those associated with Guru Tegh Bahadur include Guru ka Mahal, which was his residence, and those connected with him—Damdama Sahib, where the Guru addressed congregations; Bhora Sahib, where he meditated; Thara Sahib, where Kashmiri Pandits were given refuge; and Sisganj, where the Ninth Guru's head was cremated, have their special significance.

Akal Bunga is where the young Guru Gobind Singh addressed the Sikhs after his father's cremation, while Gurdwara Mata Jit Kaur is dedicated to Guru Gobind Singh's wife.

Also of note is the new Virasat-e-Khalsa Museum opened in 2011 to commemorate the 300 years of the Khalsa.

33 The poets who translated Sanskrit texts to common languages like Braj and Punjabi include Amrit Rai, Ani Rai, Siam, Sainapati, Alam, Tahikan, Daya Singh, Sukha Singh and Dharam Singh.

34 Giani Gurdit Singh, *Anandpur de Sahit nu Den* (Punjabi), Punjab Government, 1968.

Takht Sri Damdama Sahib

TALWANDI SABO, PUNJAB, INDIA

A SHORT motorable distance from the ancient town of Bathinda is Talwandi Sabo, where Takht Sri Damdama Sahib is located. Local tradition maintains that Guru Nanak Dev visited it during the second of his four spiritual journeys, Udasis.

Guru Tegh Bahadur camped here in the 1670s. Manji Sahib marks the spot where he sat and addressed congregations, and where Sikhs performed *kirtan*. When his successor, Guru Gobind Singh, evacuated Anandpur Sahib after battles there and around the area, this jungle fastness became his headquarters and a place of repose, hence the name Damdama Sahib. He spent nine months here in 1706, during which time Sikhs of the region travelled over rugged terrain to be with their Guru as he regrouped his forces.

This spot in the desert became known as *Guru ki Kashi*—a centre of Sikh learning. It bloomed with intellectuals and learned men. The manuscript of the *Adi Granth* was lost when the Guru, his family and Sikhs crossed the Sirsa River in spate. However, Guru Gobind Singh dictated the compositions contained in the *Adi Granth* from memory.[35] He thus prepared the manuscript anew, which Bhai Mani Singh scribed.

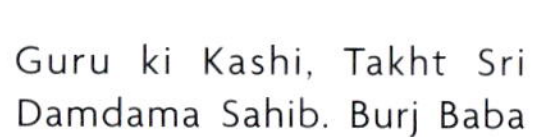

Guru ki Kashi, Takht Sri Damdama Sahib. Burj Baba Deep Singh is seen on the left.

35 Guru Arjan Dev, the fifth Guru, originally compiled the *Adi Granth* in 1604 at Amritsar. There are no *banis* (hymns) of the 6th, 7th, and 8th Gurus. The 9th Guru, however, wrote extensively.

The imposing interior of Takht Sri Damdama Sahib.

At Damdama Sahib, Guru Gobind Singh added 115 *slokas* (verses) of Guru Tegh Bahadur to this volume. Prominent Sikhs, including the scholar warrior Baba Deep Singh,[36] assisted Bhai Mani Singh in scribing the most important manuscript of the Sikhs. The Guru mandated him to look after the affairs of the Sikhs and spread the message of Sikhism. The site where Guru Gobind Singh held his daily assemblies is where Takht Sri Damdama Sahib's present building stands.

After Baba Deep Singh's death, the care of the Damdama Sahib shrine passed on to Misl Shaheedan, and since the 1830s, the Shahzadpur Sardars, who trace their descent from Baba Deep Singh, looked after it. The SGPC took it over from Captain Ranjit Singh of Shahzadpur in 1963.

Kar sewa volunteers, under the supervision of Sant Sewa Singh, constructed the building in the 1970s, and the basic structure stands, although renovations and additions have taken place. Gurdwaras, towers, *bungas* and *sarovars* remind us of various historical events.

Nanaksar Sarovar commemorates the visit of the first Guru; Gurusar Sarovar was dug under the directions of Guru Tegh Bahadur, and Akalsar Sarovar is associated with Guru Gobind Singh. Most pilgrims take a sip of water from this *sarovar*, which they believe safeguards them from disease.

Guru Granth Sahib is placed atop a 6-foot *takht* (throne) in the Takht Sahib building. A spacious hall with high ceilings provides the area for pilgrims to sit. White marble cladding and extensive mirror art dominate the structure, with magnificent chandeliers providing light.

The manuscript of the *Adi Granth* scribed by Baba Deep Singh is kept here. He then made copies of it and sent those to the other takhts. The 'contents' segment of the manuscript is 29 leaves, and the *Gurbani* verses are written on 707 leaves.

36 A scholar who was also a warrior of renown, Baba Deep Singh (1682 -1757) fell in battle defending Harmandir Sahib.

From Takht Damdama Sahib, the Guru issued his *Hukamnamas*[37] to far-flung Sikh *sangats*. A seal, preserved in the main Gurdwara, reads: "Akal Sahai Guru Gobind Singh ji ki Jagha: Takht Damdama Sahib ji".[38] Talwandi Sabo became a centre of Sikh learning. It has maintained its character ever since and there are significant institutions devoted to teaching nuances of Sikh spiritual practices.[39]

In Gurdwara Likhansar, there is an area where pilgrims, especially children, are encouraged to write in the Gurmukhi script in sand. The 10th Guru reportedly said: "Whoever writes the thirty-five letters of the Gurmukhi script here will be blessed with a sharp mind." This is where Guru Gobind Singh had reed pens dropped in the *sarovar* after they had been used to inscribe Gurbani. It is also where he declared that Damdama Sahib would be a nodal centre of Sikh scholarship.

Guru Gobind Singh entrusted the affairs of Damdama Sahib to the care of Baba Deep Singh, who constructed a 60-foot tower called Burj Baba Deep Singh. As the Jathedar of Damdami Taksal, he spent his time in scholastic endeavours, leading Sikhs of the area, till he left to fight the forces of Ahmed Shah Durrani that invaded Harmandir Sahib. The 75-year-old scholar-warrior died in the battle of Amritsar, heroically fighting against all odds to break the enemy siege of Harmandir Sahib and free the holy shrine.

Historical artefacts at the Takht include a sword of Guru Gobind Singh and a *tega* (curved double-edged sword) of Baba Deep Singh. A muzzle-loading gun presented to Guru Gobind Singh can also be seen, along with a seal (described earlier) and a mirror presented to Guru Gobind Singh by Sikhs from Delhi. Devotees seeking relief from facial palsy sit in front of it. Baba Deep Singh's manuscript of Guru Granth Sahib is also kept with great reverence.

While Damdama Sahib at Talwandi Sabo was always considered a very important shrine, its formal induction as the fifth Takht took place only on November 18, 1966. The recognition followed the recommendation of a sub-committee formed by the Shiromani Gurdwara Parbandhak Committee on 30 July 1960 to examine the matter. In its 183-page report, the committee presented a forceful argument that was accepted by the SGPC as also by the Government of India.[40]

As nature and scholarship bloom at Takht Sri Damdama Sahib, the blessings of Guru Gobind Singh are evident.

The mirror in this enclosure was presented to Guru Gobind Singh. It is believed to have curative powers for those suffering from facial palsy.

37 Literally, commands in letters.
38 "May the Almighty Bless You. Guru Gobind Singh Ji's Place: Takht Damdama Sahib Ji."
39 The SGPC runs the Guru Kashi Gurmat Institute.
40 Giani Gurdit Singh, the author's father, played a significant role. Later, he was honoured at Takht Sri Damdama Sahib by the Shiromani Gurdwara Parbandhak Committee on February 24, 1993.

ਅਬਰੇ ਰਹਿਮਤ ਬਾਰ ਗੁਰੂ ਗੋਬਿੰਦ ਸਿੰਘ
THIS SACRED BELONGS TO SHRI GURU GOBIND SINGH JI AS PER ITS
RELIGOUS BELIEVES BY OBSERVING NEARLY THIS MIRROR CONTINUOSLY
FOR THREE DAYS PARALYSED FASCES CARE CURED
NOTE ONE CAN OBSERVE ONCE A DAY TIMINGS: 8 00AM TO 600 PM DAILY
ਅਬਰੇ ਰਹਿਮਤ ਬਾਰ ਗੁਰੂ ਗੋਬਿੰਦ ਸਿੰਘ

Takht Sri Harimandir Ji

PATNA, BIHAR, INDIA

Guru Nanak stayed in the ancient town of Patna for about three months during his spiritual journey. Among his followers was a jeweller Salis Rai, whose house became a place where seekers of spiritual wisdom would gather to listen to the founder of Sikhism. After the Guru left, the congregations continued, and the place came to be known as *dharamsal*.[41] Salis Rai's employee Bhai Adrakha, a devoted follower of the Guru, was given the charge of the *dharamsal*.

The grand edifice of Takht Sri Harimandir Ji.

When Guru Tegh Bahadur came to Patna on his tour of the East, he was greeted warmly by descendants of Adrakha. Escorting the Guru, they went in a procession to what is now known as Gurdwara Chhoti Sangat. He lived here with his family for a while. Mata Gujri, his wife, stayed with her brother Kirpal Chand and some devoted Sikhs. The Guru travelled further east and was in Assam when his son Guru Gobind Singh was born in Patna on 22 December 1666. The young Gobind Rai spent his childhood in the city.

41 A place of spiritual learning, a common term used before the word Gurdwara became more prevalent. The term is now more often used for guest houses that focus on religious pilgrims.

Guru Granth Sahib is placed in the sanctum sanctorum, where Guru Gobind Singh was born.

Takht Sri Harimandir Ji stands where Guru Gobind Singh was born. Naturally, the physical building has changed since it was initially built in 1665 by Raja Fateh Chand Maini. The 18th-century writer Mullah Ahmed Bukhari recorded that "the Sikhs have a public edifice and call it Harimandir".[42] The Orientalist Charles Wilkins visited the site too and recorded his impressions, both of meeting the Sikhs present there, as well as the building and its interior.[43]

After a fire damaged the building at the beginning of the 19th Century, Maharaja Ranjit Singh initiated reconstruction in 1839. In 1934, an earthquake left a wide swath of destruction in Bihar, and a portion was broken, which was rebuilt. The building that stands to date was built by the *sangat* from 1954 to 57. However, renovations and additions were made in the years preceding Guru Gobind Singh's 350th birth anniversary celebration in 2017.

Historically, a series of priests, some hereditary, took care of the Gurdwara. The British East India Company directly assumed control for a while. However, following the Religious Endowments Act of 1863, it divested direct supervision, and Mahant Ganda Singh took charge on 11 March 1865. In 1930, the priests were ousted after protests by Sikh devotees, and an SGPC-supported takeover took effect.[44] In time, the control was passed to a committee appointed by the District Judge of Patna. Since 1956, a committee of representatives of specified Sikh bodies and some nominees of the Patna District Court formed the management.

Takht Patna Sahib is an oasis of serenity in the city's busy, crowded area. The tall marble-clad five-storeyed building is imposing, topped by a ribbed dome shaped like a lotus and smaller cupolas around it.

The gilded *deori*[45] has "Takht Sri Harimandir Sahib Ji Patna Sahib" embossed on its golden panel. The pillars have lovely polychrome marble inlay at the base, topped with embossed gold panels with stylised botanical engravings with flower arrangements, fruit, etc.

The sanctum sanctorum, where Guru Granth Sahib is placed, is where Guru Gobind Singh was born. A likeness of the 10th Guru, painted in a historical style, is visible there. A passage has been provided around it to allow the pilgrims to circumambulate. The enormous hall is two storeys high. Guru Granth Sahib rests on a seat under a golden canopy in the centre. In the foreground are two golden canopies on each side, one with the *Dasam Granth* and one with Guru Granth Sahib.

Within its compound, the Gurdwara has a well that dates back to the time of Mata Gujri, the wife of Guru Tegh Bahadur. It still provides water.

---

42 *Mir'at ul-Ahwal-i Jahan Numa* by Ahmad Behbahani (1819).

43 An official of the East India Company, he is famous for translating the Gita into English for the first time. After visiting Sri Takht Harimandir Sahib, he wrote a note to the Asiatic Society from Benares on 1 March 1781. It was published in the Asiatick Researches or Transactions of the Society in 1788.

44 A fascinating eye-witness account of this confrontation is given in *Guru Tirath Cycle Yatra: 11 March 1930-26 June 1934* by Bhai Dhana Singh Chahal Patialvi, a former chauffeur of the Maharaja of Patiala who undertook a cycling tour of Indian Gurdwaras.

45 The entrance gateway.

Guru Tegh Bahadur and Guru Gobind Singh spent a lot of time at Patna Sahib. Consequently, there is a rich collection of the Gurus' relics there. Takht Sahib has the *kharawan* of both the Gurus, a small sword carried by the young Guru Gobind Singh, four arrows he used to target pots as a child, and a dagger.

Of particular significance are *Hukamnamas*, including the one that bears Guru Gobind Singh's *nisan*.[46] Several weapons of the Guru and his robe are also housed at Takht Sahib.

Visitors can stay the night as accommodation is provided. The *langar* hall is spacious, and there is also a museum that visitors can explore.

The city of Patna has an abundance of historical Gurdwaras. A short distance from Takht Sri Harimandir Sahib is Gurdwara Sri Kangan Ghat Sahib, where the young Gobind Rai threw away his gold bracelets in a visible renunciation of materialism.

Maini Sangat, or Gurdwara Sri Bal Lila Maini Sahib, is also located nearby, approachable through a narrow lane. This is where Raja Fateh Chand Maini, a local chief, lived. His childless queen was especially fond of the child Gobind Rai and gave him and his friends boiled and salted grams. Even today, this is the *parshad*[47] at the Gurdwara, which has a historical manuscript of Guru Granth Sahib and a *kimkhwab*[48] attire of the 10th Guru.

Gurdwara Pehla Bara, also known as Gurdwara Sri Gau Ghat Sahib, was Bhai Jaita Mal's house. Guru Nanak Dev and Guru Tegh Bahadur are both associated with it. Heritage items of importance here include a *rabab* of Bhai Mardana, the grindstone used by Mata Gujri, and wooden pillars referred to as Tham Sahib.

Gurdwara Sri Guru ka Bagh Sahib marks the site where Guru Tegh Bahadur first met his son. He was received at a garden that belonged to the local grandees, Nawab Rahim Bakhsh and Nawab Karim Bakhsh. The nobles gifted the *bagh* to the Guru, which became the centre for the *sangat* to meet.

History and heritage make Takht Sri Harimandir Sahib Ji the preeminent Sikh institution in eastern India.

The *kharawan*, traditional flat wooden sandals with a toehold, of Guru Tegh Bahadur and Guru Gobind Singh are placed in an ornate box and shown to the *sangat*.

46 Autograph/seal/signature of the Guru.
47 The devotional food offering made at the Gurdwara is later distributed to the devotees.
48 *Kimkhwab*, which is a Persian word for 'little dream', is a silk brocade-like fabric richly embroidered with gold and/or silver threads worn by royalty.

Takht Sachkhand Sri Hazur Abchalnagar

NANDED, MAHARASHTRA, INDIA

ONE OF the five *takhts* of the Sikhs and the final resting place of Guru Gobind Singh, Takht Sachkhand Sri Hazur Abchalnagar Sahib is steeped in history and a repository of local traditions that have been maintained over the centuries, drawing droves of devotees. It has certain unique rites and norms which have been shaped by its geography and the Udasi tradition.

In 1708, Guru Gobind Singh set up his camp on the left bank of the Godavari river, about 500 metres from the waterfront, outside Nanded[49] in what is today Maharashtra state, so that his 300 or so warriors would not inconvenience the local people. He called it Abchalnagar. Soon, the word spread, and followers of Guru Nanak Dev, who had visited the town two centuries ago, flocked to attend the congregations and listen to the discourses of the Tenth Guru. In this area, he met Madho Das, an ascetic who would become the Guru's warrior Sikh, Banda Bahadur.

Guru Gobind Singh was cremated at this spot in 1708. Sikhs raised a stone platform at the site and slowly developed the area around it. There were instances of hostilities with the locals. The walls of the area were raised to deter marauders, wells were dug to supply water, and accommodations were built to house the faithful. The platform was the sanctum sanctorum, where Guru Granth Sahib was installed and read aloud by Udasis.[50] Also placed there were artefacts related to the Guru, including his weapons. By 1710, a simple structure stood there, raised by Nihang Singhs.

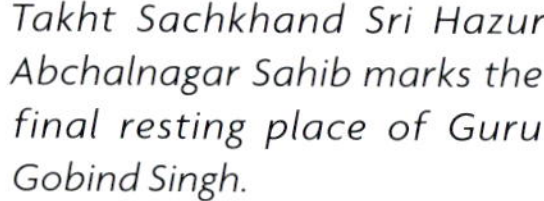

Takht Sachkhand Sri Hazur Abchalnagar Sahib marks the final resting place of Guru Gobind Singh.

49 Literally, Steadfast City. It is a district headquarters located in the Marathwada region of Maharashtra.
50 Udasis follow the teachings of Baba Sri Chand, the eldest son of Guru Nanak Dev. They were appointed custodians of Gurdwaras, especially when ruling authorities targeted the Sikhs.

The richly embellished sanctum sanctorum is where Guru Gobind Singh was cremated.

Raja Chandu Lal, a Punjabi[51] who had served in the court of Maharaja Ranjit Singh, rose to prominence in the Hyderabad State. Weathering the courtiers' prejudice against his religion, he also earned the trust of the Nizam and important East India Company officials. He headed the state's administration for four tumultuous decades. Having been instrumental in bringing a contingent of Maharaja Ranjit Singh's army to Hyderabad, he incorporated some of them into what became known as *Jamat-e-Sikhan*, as policemen, tax collectors, and bodyguards. He also contributed heavily to the maintenance of Hazoor Sahib, including assigning the revenue of some villages for the upkeep of the shrine.

When Maharaja Ranjit Singh sent the Sikh soldiers to serve in Hyderabad, he also sent along selected artisans and workers from Lahore in 1832. The construction of the Takht, and historic buildings associated with it, including the Ramgarhia Bunga and Bara Dari, can be traced back to this period. The work continued at a good pace till Maharaja Ranjit Singh's death in 1839. Even after that, support from his successors and Chandu Lal continued. The Takht building was crowned with a magnificent dome and executed in the style of Sikh architecture seen in the important Gurdwaras of Punjab at the time.

The Government of India's plan to celebrate the 300th anniversary of the Gurgaddi Divas of Guru Granth Sahib in 2008 led to a massive expansion of the infrastructure, in various forms, at the Takht, with funds raised from the *sangat* and facilities provided by various government schemes under the leadership of then Prime Minister Manmohan Singh.

The management went into overdrive. The expanded facilities catered to pilgrims from India and abroad, and also provided help during the Covid lockdown when around 2,500 pilgrims were stuck at the Gurdwara. However, some historical structures, including the Baba Wassan Singh Bunga, Ramgarhia Bunga and the Bara Dari, were razed to make room for the expansion.

51 He was Prime Minister of Hyderabad State twice, in 1808 for some time, and then from 1832 to 1843. He was considered a *sehajdhari* Sikh.

As you enter, you walk through a gate crowned by two crossed swords and the *khanda-chakkar* with the *Ek Onkar* symbol in the centre. The gateway opens into a vast area with gardens, fountains, and marble floors. On the sides are buildings used for administrative purposes and as *dharamsalas* for the devotees. There are two tall Nishan Sahibs; the one near the Takht building is where Guru Gobind Singh used to tie his horse.

The sanctum sanctorum of the Gurdwara is Angitha Sahib, built over the spot where Guru Gobind Singh was cremated. Only the head priest is allowed to enter Angitha Sahib. The weapons of Guru Gobind Singh are kept there, as is a portrait of the Guru, executed in the Deccan style of miniature painting, which is considered contemporary. The gateway is covered with gold sheets, atop which rests a large painting of the Guru by the largely Amritsar-based artist Hari Singh (1894-1970). In 2018 the original wooden frame, which had become warped, was replaced by an ornate frame embedded with semi-precious stones, commissioned by a UAE-based Sikh.

Golden embellishments are extensively used. Several miniature portraits of Gurus are embedded among the traditional plates in the inner chamber of Takht Sahib. Also are to be seen two *palkis*—Guru Granth Sahib is resplendent in one and the *Dasam Granth* in the other. Weapons of Guru Gobind Singh are ceremoniously displayed in the evening before *sukhasan*. Some weapons of other prominent Sikhs, such as Baba Phula Singh Nihang and Maharaja Ranjit Singh, are also displayed.

The in-house facilities for stay and *langar* are extensive and attract many pilgrims to pay obeisance at the Takht in central India.

The *gajgah* of Guru Gobind Singh. This steel frontal headpiece, worn by Guru Gobind Singh, is preserved at Takht Sachkhand Sri Hazur Abchalnagar Sahib.

Gurdwara Baba Atal Sahib

AMRITSAR, PUNJAB, INDIA

A TOWERING tribute to a Guru's son, a monument to the commitment to non-interference with the Divine Will and penance for having done so, and a father's wish to commemorate his devoted and brilliant boy, Gurdwara Baba Atal is all that and more.

The 30-metre-high Baba Atal is a monument to the piety and atonement of the young Baba Atal Rai.

The octagonal nine-storeyed tower close to Harmandir Sahib in Amritsar stands out because of its unique architecture and history. Gurdwara Baba Atal Sahib commemorates Guru Hargobind's son, Atal Rai. Born on 23 October 1619, he was a precocious, profoundly spiritual, and reflective child. Atal was nine years old when he was told that his playmate, Mohan, had died because a snake had bitten him at night.

Atal went to Mohan's house and found the boy's parents and relatives crying and lamenting the loss of the young child. "Mohan, why are you sleeping so soundly? It is not the time for you to sleep," said Atal, touching his friend's body with a stick. The young Mohan sat up. Even as the playmates went out to play, the town was abuzz with the news about Atal's miracle.

Guru Hargobind was annoyed when he heard about this since the Will of God must prevail. Only God can decide who lives and dies; if humans perform such miracles, they interfere with the Divine Will.

Beautifully carved silver doors open to allow devotees to pay obeisance to Guru Granth Sahib.

Atal was a sensitive and pious soul. His father's reprimand made him realise he had done something very wrong. Atal thought about his ancestors, who had even allowed themselves to be tortured rather than perform a miracle that would save them. He respectfully bowed to his father and took his leave.

Then he went to the holy *sarovar* at Harmandir Sahib for *ishnaan*, a purifying bath ritual. Later, reciting Gurbani, he lay down on the bank of Kaulsar and left his body on 23 October 1628. Guru Hargobind ordered his disciples to build a *samadhi* to commemorate the short life of Atal Rai. The *samadhi* eventually became a Gurdwara.

The current tower dates to the time of the rise of Sikh chiefs in the 1760s. They set up *misls*, or independent political units. The Bhangi Misl contributed significantly to the expansion of Amritsar, and Jassa Singh of the Ahluwalia Misl focused on the restoration of Harmandir Sahib and its construction in its present form after Ahmed Shah Durrani's forces demolished the most sacred place of the Sikhs.

The octagonal tower comprises two similarly shaped structures, outer and inner. It is topped with a golden dome, and a narrow staircase runs through it, allowing access to the top. The exterior structure rises to the sixth floor, and the interior continues for another three storeys.

The east-facing entrance has embossed doors. The other entrances face the cardinal directions. Guru Granth Sahib rests in a richly decorated canopy. However, the surrounding space is narrow, thus restricting the number of devotees at a time.

Frescos that depict Sikh historical personalities and events are of particular significance, and Gurdwara Baba Atal has a rich collection adorning its interior. Frescos on the life of Guru Nanak as recreated from the *Janamsakhis*[52] have a predominant place, with panels depicting Bibi Nanki, the birth of his son Sri Chand, and episodes from Guru Nanak's four Udasis, his spiritual journeys. There are also frescos depicting the life of Baba Atal, showing the house of Mohan and other vignettes of his life. Also seen are depictions of 18th-century heroes and martyrs such as Baba Deep Singh, Baba Uday Singh, Baba Bachittar Singh, Baba Naudh Singh, and Baba Hanuman Singh.

52 Literally, the "life stories" of Guru Nanak Dev. They are said to have been written after his death. They concentrate on his childhood and his four spiritual journeys, or Udasis. They tend to be hagiographic, even as scholars glean historical events from them.

Painted frescos at Baba Atal depict important events from Sikh history.

The artwork was carried out at different times by various artists and supported by patrons, some of whose names are inscribed. There is a vivid description of how the artwork was executed at Baba Atal at the beginning of the 20th century: "The inside walls of several of the storeys are covered with painted frescoes. And on the floor, true fresco painting upon wet plaster was actually going on. Small boys were grinding the colours. An artist of skill and invention was covering the surface with scenes of crowded life illustrating sacred stories."[53]

Lack of upkeep and aggressive restoration measures have resulted in damage, as did some ill-conceived attempts to cover the rich works of artistic heritage by installing tiles and plaster over them. This is most visible on the ground floor. However, public pressure put a stop to these measures, leaving the first floor intact. The higher storeys of Gurdwara Baba Atal have unadorned white walls.

Tradition holds that a spiritual journey to Amritsar is incomplete without paying obeisance at Baba Atal, the tallest Gurdwara in the holy city. "*Baba Atal Pakian Pakaian Ghal*" is a popular saying in which the devotees request Baba Atal to send cooked food. Local devotees bring cooked food to be distributed among visitors, a custom unique to this Gurdwara.

The top of the 30-metre building makes for a vantage point that gives a unique bird's-eye view of Harmandir Sahib, its surrounding areas, and the city of Amritsar. It is a monument to the piety and atonement of the young Baba Atal Rai.

53 *Through India and Burma with a Pen and a Brush*, by A H Fisher (1911).

Gurdwara Baoli Sahib

GOINDWAL SAHIB, PUNJAB, INDIA

EVERYONE is directed to partake of the *langar* first and then pay obeisance at Gurdwara Baoli Sahib in Goindwal Sahib. Guru Angad Dev directed his follower Amar Das to set up a new religious establishment here, and his devoted Sikh carried out the Guru's will.

When asked by Guru Angad Dev to help inhabit the area on the right bank of the Beas river and live there, Amar Das followed his Guru's instructions. He, however, continued his practice of taking fresh water from the river and carrying it to Khadur Sahib, where the Guru lived, so that he could bathe with it. He would recite *Japji Sahib* as he walked to his Guru's abode.

In 1552, Guru Angad Dev chose Amar Das, who had devoted 11 years of service to the Guru, instead of his sons, as his successor. He bade him to live in Goindwal. The 73-year-old Guru Amar Das developed it into a major centre of spiritual pilgrimage. The Guru had a *baoli*, or stepwell, constructed. Completed in 1559, it has 84 steps, symbolically linked with the Indic tradition's reincarnation cycle of 8.4 million lives. The Guru welcomed men and women of all castes and creeds and asked them to take water from the well, thereby washing away their social barriers and exposing the pure soul.

Guru Amar Das developed Goindwal Sahib into a major centre of spiritual pilgrimage. He had a *baoli*, or stepwell, constructed (foreground, left).

While the exterior is stark, the interior is colourfully decorated and has ample space for devotees.

At any given time, devotees can be seen reciting *Japji Sahib* and walking down the steps that have a partition to segregate men and women.

The entrance to Baoli Sahib, with its gold-covered dome, stands east of the main Gurdwara, which is resplendent with a white dome. The mural at the entrance depicts the 10 Gurus and prominent Sikh personalities, including Guru Amar Das's sons, Bhai Mohan and Bhai Mohari, on the left edge and the scholar Bhai Gurdas on the right. Jutting out to the right of the entrance is Thara Sahib, a small square marble platform with a canopy supported by four columns. This marks the place where Guru Amar Das sat while he supervised the digging of the *baoli*. A squat structure covered with a low dome which stands at a distance, visible towards the back of the main Gurdwara and the Baoli Sahib entrance, marks the well. Near the Gurdwara, there is the entrance to the 84 steps that lead to the well.

The two-storeyed Gurdwara is made in the traditional architectural style. As one enters, one sees the *parkash asthan* with a golden *palki* and Guru Granth Sahib placed in the centre. The simplicity of the room accentuates the sanctum sanctorum. The central dome stands out in pure white against a cerulean sky.

Guru Amar Das emphasised on the institution of *langar* and insisted that everyone who came to meet him should eat at the *langar* with the *sangat* before they joined the congregation. Tradition holds that even when Emperor Akbar came to meet the Guru, he partook of *langar* before the meeting. He was so impressed by the institution that he gifted a grant in the name of Bibi Bhani, the Guru's daughter, to support the tradition of *langar*.

Today, a massive *langar* hall serves the *sangat* on festivals and other important occasions. The tradition of marking celebrations, like Maghi, Diwali and Baisakhi, with *sangat* from all over, goes back to Guru Amar Das. The Guru strengthened Goindwal Sahib's position by binding his Sikhs with shared spiritual and everyday worldly activities.

The frescos at the entrance of Baoli Sahib depict the 10 Gurus and prominent Sikh personalities. This closeup shows the first three Gurus.

The Guru asked women to discard the *purdah* system of veiling themselves and introduced new ceremonies to mark birth and death. The Guru was particularly against the practice of *sati*, or the immolation of widows at the pyre of their husbands. Scholars note that he even asked Emperor Akbar to ban this terrible practice.

Guru Ram Das, too, wrote at Gurdwara Baoli Sahib, composing *Anand Sahib*, the *path* recited before every celebration, and even death. *Anand Sahib* is part of the daily prayers of Sikhs, and it is recited while preparing *Amrit* and before every prayer. The hymn comprises 40 stanzas, often shortened to six—the first five and the last.[54]

The centre of Sikh spiritual endeavour, Goindwal was the place where the Guru introduced institutions and practices that consolidated the Sikh faith and gave the followers the structure with which they went about their lives, in the pursuit of worldly duties, along with the spiritual underpinnings that the Guru desired them to adhere to.

As you walk into Gurdwara Darbar Sahib, and view Gurdwara Baoli Sahib, you connect with this very significant aspect of the development of the Sikh faith. The devotees that visit Goindwal Sahib on various Gurpurbs and festivals have steadily grown to a massive number, and an enormous new *langar* hall has been built within the Gurdwara complex to accommodate them. The first centre of pilgrimage for the Sikhs is well prepared to receive devotees.

54 *Anand* means bliss; the *bani* is sung during the Sikh wedding ceremony called *Anand Karaj*, a blissful event.

Gurdwara Darbar Sahib

TARN TARAN, PUNJAB, INDIA

ICTURE a dark night, a pristine white Gurdwara, its golden dome reflected in the gentle waves of a massive *sarovar*, and the presence of thousands of devotees; what you have is a sense of the celebrations at the historic Gurdwara Darbar Sahib Sri Guru Arjan Dev Ji on every new moon night.

When we behold the beautiful Gurdwara in daytime, our eye is drawn to its reflection in the *sarovar* that was built at the direction of Guru Arjan Dev, the fifth Guru who bought this land in 1590 and had the largest *sarovar* of its kind dug.

The venerated Baba Budha, who had the honour of anointing five successors of Guru Nanak, performed the *ardas* here. Manji Sahib marks the spot where Guru Arjan Dev sat while supervising the excavation of the *sarovar*. It is also where his successor, Guru Hargobind, stayed a night. *Guru ka Khu*, or the Guru's well, provided water for the Guru and the *sangat*.

The massive *sarovar* was dug over a period of six years, a task completed on 19 March 1596. The Guru called it Tarn Taran, literally to swim and help others swim across. The Guru also built the city, that took the name of the *sarovar*, on the Delhi-Lahore highway, about 24 km from Amritsar. He had bought village common land for digging the pond in a natural dip. The *sarovar* is rectangular and measures 300 square metres.

Darbar Sahib is a magnificent three-storeyed building. A two-storeyed archway marks the entrance from the *parkarma*.

ਸਤਿਨਾਮੁ
ਵਾਹਿਗੁਰੂ

Guru Granth Sahib is placed under a golden canopy. The interior of the congregation hall is embellished with rich blue and red stucco work, with mirror inlays and golden corners.

Once the *sarovar* was dug, the construction of the main shrine, Darbar Sahib, situated on the southeast corner of the *sarovar*, started. Meanwhile, Nuruddin, a local warlord, assisted by his son Amiruddin, confiscated the bricks meant for this construction and diverted further production from the kiln to the site of the *sarai* he was making. Additional development work at Tarn Taran was suspended until 1768, when Budh Singh Faizullapuria (Singhpuria) took over and demolished Nuruddin's *sarai* and brought the bricks back for use in the Gurdwara complex.

Sikh chiefs Budh Singh and Jassa Singh Ramgharia joined hands to have the building of Darbar Sahib Gurdwara constructed. It was further embellished by Maharaja Ranjit Singh, who paid obeisance here in 1802 and had the construction of the *parkarma*, the circumambulatory passage, completed. He also donated gold to embellish the building.[55] At this time, the Maharaja also ceremoniously exchanged turbans with Fateh Singh Ahluwalia, Jassa Singh Ahluwalia's grandnephew, as a token of lasting friendship.

Later, Kanwar Nau Nihal Singh, the Maharaja's grandson, donated gold, but the political instability that followed Maharaja Ranjit Singh's death hampered the work.[56] In time, more buildings were added, and various people, rulers and common folk contributed to the renovation at different times.

The Darshani Deori, or the main entrance, is an impressive structure with projected balconies. In 2019, some volunteers partially demolished this two-century-old archway in an ill-advised attempt to renovate it. However, public protests stopped the demolition, and it stands today as a slightly battered and proud expression of heritage.

Darbar Sahib is now a magnificent three-storeyed marble-clad building. A two-storeyed archway marks the entrance from the *parkarma*. The front facade is gilded in metalwork covered with gold leaf. Sitting atop the front facade are small golden domes with pinnacles, and at the corners, larger, golden *chhatris*, square chambers with domes. Naturally, the largest golden dome sits atop the Darbar Sahib building. The other sides are not as extensively covered with gold gilding as the front. Each has a gold panel with a stylised rendering of a vignette of Sikh heritage, and projected balconies relieve the facade.

55 Maharaja Ranjit Singh donated gold in large quantities to Harmandir Sahib, Amritsar; Gurdwara Darbar Sahib, Tarn Taran; and the Kashi Vishwanath Temple, Varanasi.

56 The gold leaf exterior work was done in the last quarter of the 19th century under the leadership of Sant Sham Singh of Amritsar.

A bas-relief panel depicting the 10 Gurus and their followers, Bala and Mardana.

As we enter the Gurdwara, we see the rich blue and red stucco work, with mirror inlays and golden corners. The two-storeyed congregation hall has a gallery overlooking it. At its edge are archways overlooking the hall, richly decorated with stucco work. White marble walls at the lower level provide the contrast that sets off the splendour of the decorative work. Indeed, the quality of artistry and the style reminds the visitor of Harmandir Sahib at Amritsar, although the scale here is smaller.

Guru Granth Sahib is placed under a golden canopy that was donated by Kanwar Nau Nihal Singh. The sound of *kirtan*, which carries across the extensive complex, adds to the sense of serenity that is experienced at this *sarovar*.

The back of Darbar Sahib has Har-ki-Pauri, or marbled steps, that lead to the *sarovar*. Tradition holds that this is where Guru Arjan Dev dug the *sarovar* for the first time. The *sarovar* was originally rainfed. In 1883, Raja Raghubir Singh of Jind had a channel dug from a canal 5 km (3 miles) away to the *sarovar* to bring fresh water. As the need arose, this channel was paved and repaved.

In 1841, Kanwar Nau Nihal Singh started the construction of a four-storeyed 155-ft Akal Bunga tower. Maharaja Sher Singh provided the finishing touches. The exposed red bricks contrast with the white plastered balconies at various levels, and the white dome stands out against the blue sky.[57] Amidst the chanting of hymns by devotees every morning Guru Granth Sahib is carried in a ceremonial procession from there to Darbar Sahib, and in the evening brought back for the night.

57 Four towers were envisaged; however, only one was built.

The four-storeyed 155-ft Akal Bunga tower was built by Kanwar Nau Nihal Singh in 1841 at the edge of the 300 square-metre *sarovar*.

After the eclipse of the Sikh empire, under the British Raj, the Deputy Commissioner of Amritsar appointed the manager of the shrine, who largely left the priests unsupervised, which resulted in laxity, and many malpractices and neglect of the institution followed. The revivalist Singh Sabha Movement[58] and reformist Gurdwara Sudhar Movement[59] significantly impacted the Sikhs of Tarn Taran. The mismanagement and misconduct of the local managers led to a confrontation in which Sikh reformers were attacked, and two were killed on 25 January 1921. Subsequently, the management was ousted, and the control of the Gurdwara shifted to the reformists.

Guru ka Khuh, or Guru's well, is to be seen near the Gurdwara. Guru Arjan Dev had set up a lepers' asylum in the Gurdwara's vicinity. It is widely held that the water in the *sarovar* has healing properties, and pilgrims perform the ritual bath in the *sarovar* to cure themselves.

The digging of the *sarovar* began on the *amawas*, or new-moon night, of 1500 Bikrami,[60] and it was finished in 1653 Bikrami.[61] Since then, thousands of visitors have been gathering every *amawas* to mark the occasion. A dip in the *sarovar* at this time has a special significance.

The reflection of Darbar Sahib gently shimmering in the waters of the *sarovar*, with mellifluous *kirtan* rendered from early morning to late evening, all combine to soothe the souls of the pilgrims who visit this sacred institution.

58 The first Singh Sabha was founded in 1873 in Amritsar. The Singh Sabha Movement sought to revive the fundamental practices of Sikhism in a pure form and to counter the proselytising supported by British colonial officials. The Gurdwara Reform Movement drew heavily on the Singh Sabha Movement.

59 Literally, the Gurdwara Reform Movement, it sought to change the way Gurdwaras were administered. In 1925, the colonial government adopted the Sikh Gurdwara Bill, thereby empowering the Shiromani Gurdwara Parbandhak Committee (SGPC) to manage the historical Sikh Gurdwaras.

60 1443 A.D.

61 1596 A.D.

Gurdwara Darbar Sahib (Angitha Sahib)

KHADUR SAHIB, PUNJAB, INDIA

THE HEADQUARTERS of Guru Angad Dev—where he led the followers of Guru Nanak, created literature, worked further on the Gurmukhi script, scribed Gurbani and took forward the message of Guru Nanak—Khadur Sahib has a special place in the history of the Sikhs.

Gurdwara Darbar Sahib (Angitha Sahib) marks the spot where Guru Angad was cremated by his successor, Guru Amar Das.

Eight of the 10 Gurus visited Khadur Sahib. When Guru Nanak anointed Guru Angad Dev as his successor at Kartarpur, he told him to move to his village, Khadur, about 75 km from the town that Guru Nanak had founded. Guru Angad Dev spent 13 years there, from 1539 to 1552.

Khadur Sahib became the focus of Sikh activities. Guru Angad held regular congregations there, consolidating and expanding Guru Nanak's mission. He developed the Gurmukhi script, which was used to write the verses composed by Guru Nanak and his successors.

Guru Angad's daughter Bibi Amro was married to a person from Basarke village.[62] Her husband's uncle, Amar Das, drawn to a hymn of Guru Nanak that she sang, sought to be introduced to Guru Angad, following which he devoted himself to the *sewa* of the Guru for the next 12 years.

62 It is about 40 km from Amritsar.

ਗੁਰਦੁਆਰਾ ਸ੍ਰੀ ਦਰਬਾਰ ਸਾਹਿਬ (ਅੰਗੀਠਾ ਸਾਹਿਬ, ਸ੍ਰੀ ਗੁਰੂ ਅੰਗਦ ਦੇਵ ਜੀ)

The sanctum sanctorum is in the enormous main hall with room for a substantial congregation.

At the Guru's bidding, Amar Das lived in the newly founded Goindwal Sahib, on the banks of the river Beas, 8 km away as the crow flies. Every day he would draw water from the river in a pitcher and walk to Khadur Sahib with it so that the Guru could have fresh water to bathe. At times it would be pitch dark as he walked, and the path was not without obstacles. An incident where he stumbled on a weaver's wooden peg is widely narrated. The peg can be seen even now. Amar Das would spend the day in Khadur Sahib and return to Goindwal Sahib at night.

Khadur Sahib emerged as a literary centre where oral traditions gained a written form. Guru Nanak's compositions were put in a single volume. Under Guru Angad's supervision, devotees compiled accounts of Guru Nanak's travels. The Gurmukhi script was taught to more and more people, including children of the followers who lived in Khadur Sahib. Literature in Gurmukhi was created and from here it spread out to other Sikh spiritual centres. Punjabi in Gurmukhi script is now a recognised official language in India, Canada, and the UK. It is the official language of Punjab and is also taught in schools in other Indian states where Punjabis are in large enough numbers.

Guru Angad encouraged physical fitness along with spiritual and literary aspects of life, which were naturally in focus. Wrestling matches were regularly held at Gurdwara Mal Akhara Sahib.

The most impressive and prominent among the six historical Gurdwaras in the town is Gurdwara Darbar Sahib (Angitha Sahib). It marks the spot where Guru Angad was cremated by his successor, Guru Amar Das.

The Gurdwara is in brilliant white, with a gold steeple. The marble-clad building is embellished with *pietra dura* work with floral and geometric designs. From the front, two of the four cupolas are visible at the corners, and at the centre is a triple-arched, domed *chhatri* with the words *Sat Nam Waheguru* inscribed on it. Some arched windows of the facade also have inscriptions with the words *Sat Nam* and *Waheguru* in Gurmukhi and verses from Sikh historical tradition.

At a lower level, the words "Gurdwara Sri Darbar Sahib, Khadur Sahib, Amritsar" are inlaid in the Roman and Devnagri scripts on the marble strip.[63] The marble cladding on the sides of the Gurdwara is unembellished.

63 The Gurmukhi text at the centre, above the entrance, is longer, with "Angitha Sahib Sri Guru Angad Dev Ji" added in brackets.

The main hall is enormous and has room for a substantial congregation. Most of the ceiling is white, which maintains the restrained design. Floral borders and a medallion at the centre provide a vibrant relief. A golden *palki* with Guru Granth Sahib in it marks the sanctum sanctorum. The weaver's peg, on which Amar Das stumbled, is now wrapped in a cloth, and placed under another canopy.

Just beside the main entrance is Bibi Amro's Khuh (well). She had asked her father to have a well dug to take care of the needs of pilgrims. The Guru's blessing provided sweet water in an area where the water was brackish.

The Gurus who have historical linkages with Khadur Sahib are Guru Nanak Dev, who visited the place five times; Guru Angad Dev and Guru Amar Das, who lived there for extended periods; Guru Ram Das and Guru Arjan Dev, who halted there en route to Amritsar; Guru Hargobind, who stayed there with his family after the marriage of his daughter, Bibi Veero, at Jhabal; and Guru Har Rai, who camped there with his 2,200 followers. Guru Teg Bahadur, too, visited Khadur Sahib.

Within the Gurdwara complex is a multimedia museum. It shows vignettes of Sikh history and is a major draw for the pilgrims. Many paintings, executed in a realistic style, depict important events associated with the Sikh historical tradition.

Major Gurdwaras in the city are built around Angitha Sahib. They are Gurdwara Mall Akhara, Gurdwara Mai Bharai, Gurdwara Tap Asthan, Gurdwara Japiana Sahib, and Gurdwara Tharra Sahib, where Baba Budha anointed Guru Amar Das as the third Guru.

The beautifully manicured garden attests to the horticultural heritage of the place, as does the banyan tree at the edge of the Gurdwara. It is said to be five centuries old. In recent years, various initiatives to plant trees have come from Khadoor Sahib, which provides eco-inspiration to Punjab.

The silver door is framed by a marble arch tastefully decorated with intertwined vines and the *khanda-chakkar* design executed in *pietra dura*.

Gurdwara Paonta Sahib

SIRMAUR, HIMACHAL PRADESH, INDIA

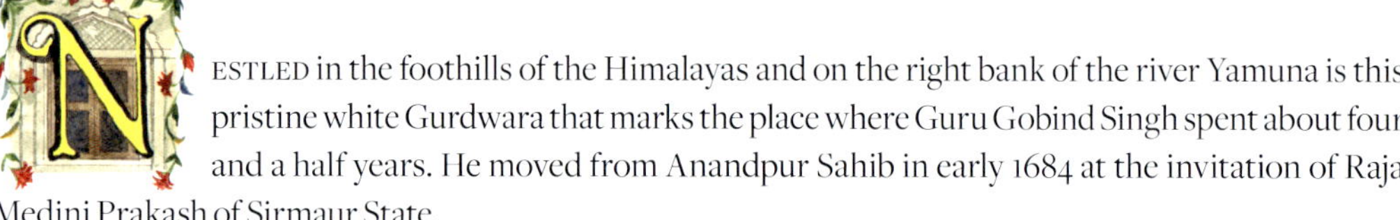

NESTLED in the foothills of the Himalayas and on the right bank of the river Yamuna is this pristine white Gurdwara that marks the place where Guru Gobind Singh spent about four and a half years. He moved from Anandpur Sahib in early 1684 at the invitation of Raja Medini Prakash of Sirmaur State.

Guru Gobind Singh created literary works, patronised poets, and honed the warrior-like skills of his Sikhs at Paonta Sahib.

The Guru founded the town of Paonta, which is now in Sirmaur district of Himachal Pradesh. For his camp, he picked a scenic site on the bank of the Yamuna. His Sikhs constructed a fortified *haveli*, and such was their zeal that it was completed in 12 days. The Guru pursued literary interests here, even as he motivated his followers to hone their martial skills by training with various weapons and practising manoeuvres.

Paonta Sahib is where the Guru patronised 52 poets and writers whose compositions were recited in *kavi darbars*, and it is here that he composed *Jap Sahib*, *Savaiyya* and *Chandi-di-Var*. Much of the *Dasam Granth* was written at Paonta Sahib. Besides, the poets were asked to translate traditional Vedic texts into commonly understood languages. Poetry competitions were held, and the winners were richly rewarded.

ੴ ਇਨ ਹੀ ਕੀ ਕ੍ਰਿਪਾ ਕੇ ਸਜੇ ਹਮ ਹੈ ਨਹੀ ਮੋਸੋ ਗਰੀਬ ਕਰੋਰ ਪਰੇ ॥ ੴ

Guru Granth Sahib is kept under the marble *palki* in the sanctum sanctorum.

The Guru was around 18 years old when he arrived at Paonta Sahib, and his time there was significant. Besides the considerable literary accomplishments that took place under his tutelage, he also focused on developing the fighting skills of his followers. They would soon be tested in the nearby area of Bhangani when the Sikhs faced a combined force of Hill Rajas, who were defeated. His eldest son Ajit Singh was also born there.

Passing through a market, you see the arched main entrance with "Gurdwara Sri Paonta Sahib Patshahi 10" written in Devnagri, English, and Gurmukhi on an illuminated sign. Under it can be seen a traditional marble plaque with "*Sach Khand Wase Nirankar*"[64] engraved on it in Gurmukhi. This demarcates the Gurdwara's three-acre complex[65] on the banks of the Yamuna.

The door to Darbar Hall of the main Gurdwara complex has the words "*Kurban jayee us vela suhavee jit tumre duarey aaya*"[66] etched in black on marble. The hall has a high ceiling painted light blue and white. Most of the embellishments are through mirror work, and it has a large, strategically placed chandelier to light up the area. The white marble *palki* is richly carved, and the wall behind it has a display cupboard with Guru Gobind Singh's weapons, including swords, maces, *chakras*, arrows, and matchlock guns. Reed pens used by the Tenth Guru are also reverentially preserved.

The Sahibzada Ajit Singh Library and Museum on the premises has Sikhism-related books and artefacts. The walls are covered with over a hundred paintings and prints related to Sikh history.

Also, within the compound is Gurdwara Dastar Asthan, which marks the place where Guru Gobind Singh organised turban-tying competitions for Sikhs, and where he presented robes of honour to warriors after the battle of Bhangani. Turban tying is an art that is still taught there, and the competitions too continue. It is also where the Guru embraced Pir Buddhu Shah[67] and bestowed honours upon him, including his *kangha* with hair in it.[68] Talab Asthan is where pay was disbursed to the Guru's soldiers.

64 *Sach Khand*: the abode of the Formless God.
65 It is recorded that the shrine had 120 acres of land attached to it at one point.
66 'I am grateful for that blessed moment which brought me to Your door.'
67 Badr ud Din (1647-1704): a Muslim saint, an admirer and ally of Guru Gobind Singh who supported the Guru in the Battle of Bhangani with his followers and family members. He was later executed by the Mughals.
68 The *kangha* was given by the descendants of Pir Budhu Shah to the Maharaja of Nabha, and it is now at Takht Sri Kesgarh Sahib.

The weapons of Guru Gobind Singh and other artefacts are prominently displayed, as are reed pens that he used.

Gurdwara Kavi Darbar Asthan is marked by a richly carved entrance. This is where the 52 poets patronised by the Tenth Guru assembled and presented their compositions. This was also the literary centre where the Guru composed his divine *bani*, and where translations of religious and cultural texts from Sanskrit and Persian were presented to the Guru. A small Gurdwara called Kalpi Rishi Asthan marks the place where the revered saint, who had a long association with Sikh Gurus, breathed his last. Guru Gobind Singh had met the Rishi and brought him ceremoniously to this spot. The Gurdwara has a golden *palki*, and Guru Granth Sahib is continually recited there. Gobind Ghat has steps that lead down to the Yamuna.

Bhai Bishan Singh was given the responsibility of looking after the fortified *haveli* by the Guru, and his successor, Baba Kapur Singh, with the support of Sikh *misls*,[69] built the Gurdwara in 1823. In time, hereditary *mahants* took over the Gurdwara and treated it as their personal property till a group of Nihang Sikhs challenged them in 1964. A legal tussle followed, and in 1970, a court appointed an 11-member committee to run the affairs of the Gurdwara. A few years later, the services of Baba Harbans Singh of Delhi were tapped to extensively renovate the Gurdwaras in the complex through *kar sewa*.

Gurdwara Paonta Sahib has rooms for pilgrims, and *langar* is served daily. Sikhs come in large numbers for Gurpurbs. The annual fair of Hola Mahalla is held with great enthusiasm, while the annual *kavi darbar* showcases the literary tradition of the place where Guru Gobind Singh is said to have spent the happiest period of his life.

69 Sahib Singh Sandhawalia provided the necessary funds.

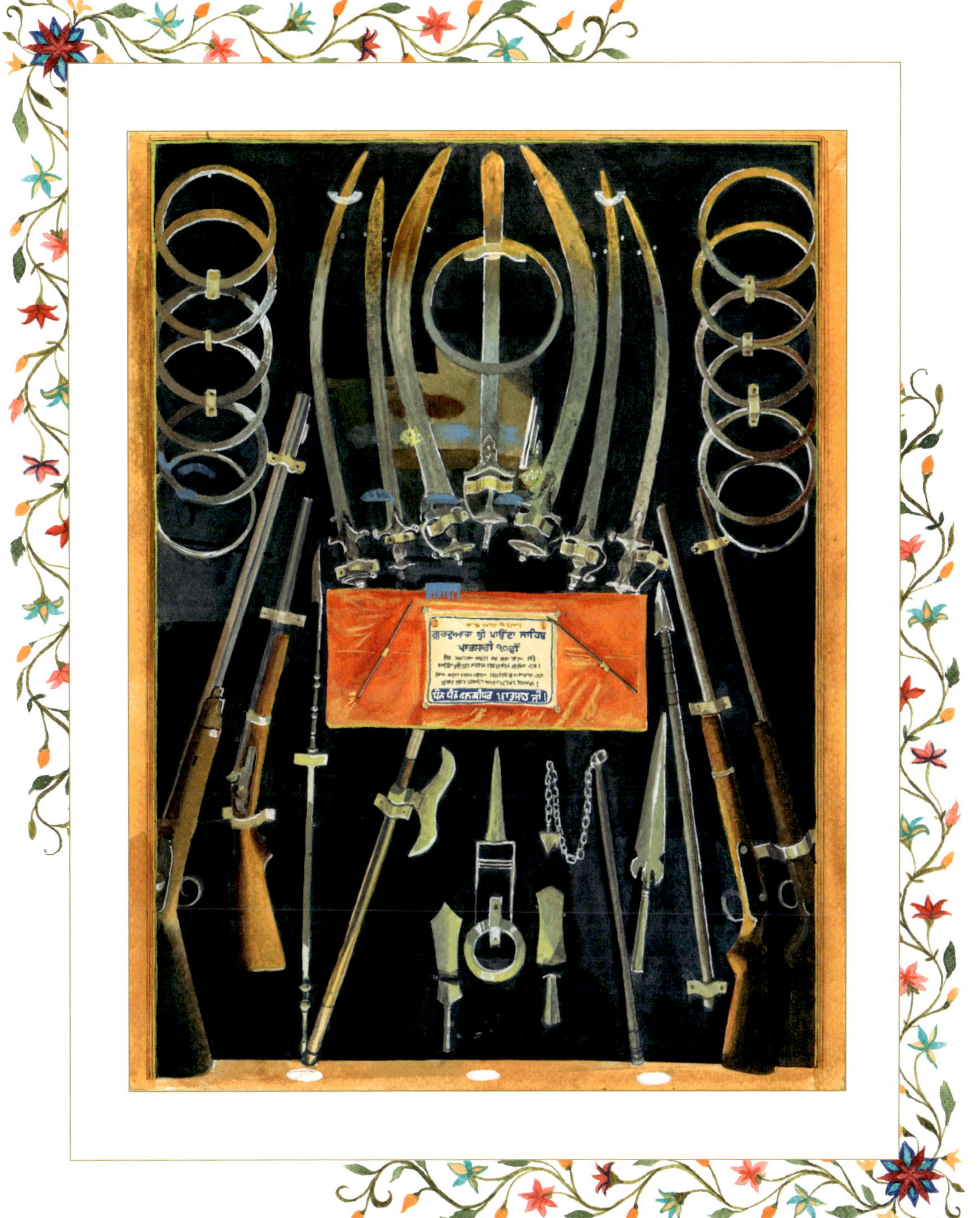
ਗੁਰਦੁਆਰਾ ਸ੍ਰੀ ਪਾਉਂਟਾ ਸਾਹਿਬ
ਪਾਤਸ਼ਾਹੀ ੧੦ਵੀਂ

Gurdwara Nada Sahib

PANCHKULA, HARYANA, INDIA

The Battle of Bhangani was fought between the armies of the Hill Rajas headed by Raja Bhim Chand and Guru Gobind Singh's forces. The Rajas had the support of Mughal army, and the Guru had a volunteer force, which included non-Sikhs, even *sadhus*, who fought with great valour. The two forces fought near Paonta Sahib, culminating in the Guru's victory. In keeping with the tradition set by his great-grandfather, Guru Hargobind, the Tenth Guru did not hold on to any territory after the battle.

The Guru's forces rested at the place where the Gurdwara Sahib Patshahi 10 Nada Sahib, popularly known as Gurdwara Nada Sahib, stands for a few days during his journey from Paonta Sahib to Anandpur Sahib. The area was a jungle and sparsely inhabited. Among those living in the neighbourhood were relatives of Makhan Shah Labana. Nadu Shah, a local Labana Sikh, attended to the Guru and served him and his companions with great devotion and zeal. The Guru blessed him and said that one day, that very area would be known by his name, and it would thus be immortal. The Guru continued his journey and eventually reached Anandpur Sahib via Dhakoli, Ropar, and Kiratpur Sahib.

The imposing Gurdwara Nada Sahib and the 32-metre-high Nishan Sahib are visible from a great distance.

The marble *palki* stands out, framed in rich colours used in the interior of the *darbar* hall.

The place where the Tenth Guru rested did not have a Gurdwara for a while, till Motha Singh, a devout Sikh from a nearby village, identified the sacred spot and raised a platform to memorialise the visit. Details about Motha Singh are lost to history. However, local people continued to pray at Manji Sahib.

After Partition in 1947, it was administered by the Dharmarth Board of Patiala and East Punjab States Union (PEPSU). The merger of PEPSU into Punjab in 1956 led, a few years later, to the control of the historical shrine passing to the Shiromani Gurdwara Parbandhak Committee. Recently, the administration has been handed over to the Haryana Gurdwara Parbandhak Committee. Nada Sahib is considered one of the most significant historical Gurdwaras in Haryana.

Even before you approach the Gurdwara, you can see the Nishan Sahib atop the 105-foot (32 m) high flagpole, which is to one side of the courtyard, near the site of the old shrine, or Manji Sahib.[70]

The new building, built through *kar sewa* led by Baba Harbans Singh,[71] was inaugurated in 2006. It is made in the traditional Sikh architectural style. The Gurdwara has a two-storey domed structure with a large rectangular meeting hall adjacent to it. Devotees climb the steps past the Darshani Deori to arrive at the entrance. The 5,000 square-foot Darbar Hall has an arch, the inner portion of which is decorated in a contemporary manner informed by tradition. The inside has a rich blue colour with graphic representations of Sikh symbols and geometric designs. The mezzanine runs along the side, and it has been decorated with extensive mirror work that reflects the shafts of light that emanate from the series of chandeliers in front of the *parkash asthan*. Around the marble *palki* are areas where *katha* and *kirtan* are performed.

The sounds of Gurbani being recited are heard outside the Gurdwara since there are 21 rooms earmarked for *akhand path*.

70 *Mahankosh* has a reference to the Gurdwara it identifies as being in the then Pinjore police station area of Rajpura tehsil of Patiala State.

71 Baba Harbans Singh Ji Kar Sewa Wale (1923-2011) led voluntary teams who renovated/constructed many Gurdwaras. He is credited with the construction of the *sarovar* at Bangla Sahib, Lakhi Shah Banjara Hall at Rakab Ganj, and many Gurdwaras, including Majnu ka Tilla, Bala Sahib, Damdama Sahib, and Moti Bagh.

Khanda-chakkar is a prominent theme in the facade where the alabaster stands out against the cerulean sky.

A spacious brick courtyard separates these buildings from the complex comprising the *langar* hall, which has provision to serve hundreds of people at a time. While there is considerable daily attendance, the numbers go up to 50,000 on Sundays. Puranmashi, or the full moon night, holds special significance for devotees, and thus, it is common to see as many as a hundred thousand devotees on these occasions. The New Year's Day is rung in by many devotees by listening to *kirtan* at this Gurdwara.

The Gurpurbs attract many more devotees, and the birth anniversary of Guru Nanak Dev and Guru Gobind Singh record numbers in hundreds of thousands. A *nagar kirtan* through the nearby town of Panchkula is held on Guru Nanak's birth anniversary.

A short 10-kilometre drive from the modern city of Chandigarh, the Gurdwara attracts a large number of pilgrims from the city. It is also a destination for non-Sikh tourists, and provisions have been made to provide shelter to hundreds of people. There are over a hundred rooms and eight dormitories for the devotees. Most of the visitors drive into the Gurdwara, and there is provision for parking a very large number of vehicles—with a six-storeyed parking lot supplemented by another three-storeyed one and open parking.

This historic Gurdwara's nodal position ensures a large *sangat*. Over the years, it has been expanded to accommodate the vast crowds that gather here for various special occasions and the devotees who visit daily.

Gurdwara Sri Guru Singh Sabha

SECTOR 19, CHANDIGARH, INDIA

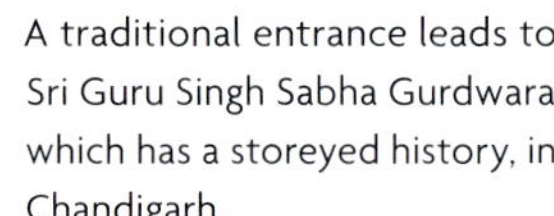

A traditional entrance leads to Sri Guru Singh Sabha Gurdwara, which has a storeyed history, in Chandigarh.

THE DISTINCTIVE architecture of Gurdwara Sri Guru Singh Sabha, Sector 19, Chandigarh, draws the eye towards one of the oldest Gurdwaras in the modern city, built by French architect Le Corbusier. The activities at the Gurdwara and its long association with the city make it a prominent landmark.

Sri Guru Singh Sabha wanted the architecture to reflect the new city that was being built as the Capital of Punjab, and in 1960 it asked Shivdatt Sharma, who was part of the team of architects assisting Le Corbusier and his cousin Pierre Jeanneret in Chandigarh, to design the building. After going through several hoops, the permission was granted.[72]

72 Karam Singh, President of Sri Guru Singh Sabha, Sector 19 (Nagla), wrote on 17 February 1960 to the Chief Town Planner of Chandigarh to request him to permit Sharma, who was working for the government, to design the Gurdwara. It would become Sharma's first private commission, albeit an honorary one.

ਗੁਰਦੁਆਰਾ ਸ੍ਰੀ ਗੁਰੂ ਸਿੰਘ ਸਭਾ ਸੈਕਟਰ 19-ਡੀ

White walls and marble *palki* stand out against the colourful *chandni* and soft furnishings.

As the architect records: "The design deviated from the replication of a traditional structure for a Gurdwara. Instead, I chose to evolve a structural solution, taking the sacred Sikh turban as a visual metaphor. Pierre Jeanneret expressed his satisfaction with this unique solution, an expression of symbolic architecture."[73]

The foundation stone laying ceremony of the Gurdwara saw Sant Isher Singh Rarewala, Jeanneret, Giani Gurdit Singh MLC, and members of the Gurdwara committee coming together to build this new place of prayer for the community. The original architecture had a large stainless steel *khanda* atop the Gurdwara. In later years, a traditional dome has been added to the structure, and some other changes have been made. The original plan also called for murals by artist Satish Gujral, which were never executed.[74]

The entryway to the Gurdwara from the road is conventional, with a three-arched *chhatri* in the middle and two single-arched ones on each side. Between them, you see the original arch of the Gurdwara, with a white dome that replaced the original steel *khanda* at some point. The dome is topped with a golden *kalas* and has a small *chhatri* atop it.

The *jora ghar* is right next to the entrance, and as you enter you see the *darbar* hall in the front, the *langar* hall to the right and Nishan Sahib to the left. The marble *palki* at the *parkash asthan* is executed in the traditional style, and there are a number of weapons kept in front of Guru Granth Sahib.

The Gurdwara has a storied history and has played a prominent role in organising *nagar kirtan* for various Gurpurbs. Its proximity to a bustling market and location in a central area has contributed to its popularity among the Sikh *sangat*.

73 S S Bhatti, in "Shivdatt Sharma: Life and Work", says: "Typical Sikh arch is the main feature adopted. Main arches start from the four corners of the square hall, measuring 80 feet by 80 feet. From their apex, the upper arch of the same form continues but with lesser span, thus decreasing the span and increasing the height. The top span covered with an almost flat slab with a gentle slope is in continuity with the entire form, thus terminating the building into an imaginary dome...."

74 Source: Ibid

The folds of the turban were a visual metaphor for the original design that was approved by architect Pierre Jeanneret.

The premises of the Gurdwara is large, and it has within it, besides the *langar* hall, facilities for travellers and provides space for the healing of the body through ayurvedic, homoeopathic, and conventional medicine. It also has a centre for physiotherapy and a modern diagnostic centre that offers a range of pathological and radiological tests, including X-ray, mammography, and DEXA.

The expansive compound of this Gurdwara in the city's heart also has Sri Guru Ram Das Preparatory School, which has classes I to V. The medium of instruction is English. The Gurdwara also supports and helps run Guru Nanak Khalsa Sr. Secondary School in Sector 30-B, Chandigarh, which was established on Baisakhi Day in 1965. Both these schools are open to boys and girls from all communities, providing financial assistance to those who need it.

Besides regular *kirtan*, special *kirtan darbars* are held every month. Gurpurbs and other important festivals are celebrated with great enthusiasm, and every year the Gurdwara organises *nagar kirtan* on the birth anniversary of Guru Nanak Dev.

Rooms are earmarked for *akhand path*, and effort is made to educate the younger generation by involving them in Punjabi and Gurmat classes. Those who show interest are also taught the *tabla*, the harmonium, how to perform *kirtan*, and the meaning of Gurbani. During summer vacations, camps are held for children.

As one of the earliest Gurdwaras in Chandigarh, Sri Guru Singh Sabha, Sector 19, has played a prominent role in community activities. The Gurdwara's modern architecture reflects the face of tradition—nourished by the sacred practices and activities that transcend time—in a city that was created anew as an expression of modern times and needs.

Gurdwara Bangla Sahib

NEW DELHI, INDIA

EVOTEES come to Gurdwara Bangla Sahib to be healed—the water from the *sarovar* is believed to have curative powers. Dulcet sounds of Gurbani being sung by the *ragi jathas* soothe the soul, and arguably the largest *langar* in India's Capital nourishes the body. The beautiful white building, with its golden domes and *chhatris* in the classical Sikh architectural style, stands out against the Lutyens' buildings of New Delhi and the modern ones around it.

Guru Harkrishan stayed in Delhi at the house of Raja Jai Singh, a high-ranking general of the Mughal Court and also the ruler of Amber, which later became the kingdom of Jaipur. Gurdwara Bangla Sahib marks the bungalow where Raja Jai Singh hosted the Eighth Guru in March 1664.

The four-storeyed Gurdwara, which retains some elements of the Rajasthani architecture of the original bungalow, is about a kilometre from Connaught Place, abutting the Gol Dak Khanna, or the circular post office, with Baba Kharak Singh Marg and Ashoka Marg marking its two sides.

The marble-clad Bangla Sahib stands out against the buildings of Lutyens' Delhi and the modern ones around it.

The *darbar* hall is richly embellished and *kirtan* is telecast daily.

Emperor Aurangzeb had summoned the Guru since his elder brother, Ram Rai, had disputed the Guru's succession. Before passing on, Guru Har Rai, their father, had nominated his successor on the principle of merit rather than the feudal concept of primogeniture, which was widely practised then. Ram Rai, the elder brother, was found lacking. When asked by Aurangzeb to explain a particular stanza in the *Adi Granth*, which the Emperor had been told was defamatory towards Islam, Ram Rai substituted a word and gave an explanation that satisfied the Emperor. When Guru Har Rai heard that Ram Rai had changed the words of the *Adi Granth* instead of defending the scripture and explaining it correctly, the Guru rebuked and disinherited him. Sensing the opportunity of creating a division among the Sikhs, Emperor Aurangzeb's court kept Ram Rai in Delhi and supported him in his bid for succession.

The capital of Mughal India was then in the grip of cholera and smallpox, and the scheduled meeting with the Emperor was postponed. The Guru devoted himself to serving the sick. His service drew in hordes of afflicted, and he used water from a well in Raja Jai Singh's bungalow to heal them. Many were healed, and the young Guru's fame spread. More people came, and he distributed food and healing herbs among them. Even as he provided succour to the countless, he contracted the smallpox infection himself.

The Guru kept himself in isolation at the bungalow for four days, and, on the fifth, he asked to be moved to the banks of the Yamuna river, where he passed away on 30 March 1664. Gurdwara Bala Sahib stands there. Raja Jai Singh dedicated the bungalow to Guru Har Krishan's memory, and several followers of the Guru continued to gather there to listen to Gurbani.

A successful attack on Delhi by an army led by Jassa Singh Ahluwalia, Baghel Singh Karorsinghia, Jassa Singh Ramgarhia, Rai Singh Bhangi and Gurdit Singh took the victorious Sikhs to the Red Fort on 11 March 1783. Mughal Emperor Shah Alam II offered them a *nazarana*[75] of Rs 3 lakh.

75 Tribute.

Devotees line up at the *chhabeel* for handfuls of blessed water in the *parkarma* of the Gurdwara.

Baghel Singh Karorsinghia negotiated for permission to raise Gurdwaras on Sikh historical sites. He identified historical sites and built Gurdwaras there.[76] He supervised the construction of this Gurdwara at the site in 1783. The building has been reconstructed many times since then. It was one of the two significant Sikh religious shrines that survived the redrawing of maps and represented tradition amid the change and modernity of Imperial Delhi,[77] as envisaged by the British architect Sir Edwin Lutyens. After Partition, which brought a large influx of displaced people from what became Pakistan to India, the number of Sikhs in India's Capital increased dramatically, leading to the Gurdwara being expanded.

One has to climb up a flight of stairs to reach the level of the main entrance of the four-storeyed building with its magnificent marble-lined *parkarma* and *sarovar* that was expanded in 1973.

The Gurdwara has a large high-ceilinged hall for the congregation, with a golden *palki* and extensive gold-leaf work on the pillars and the arches around the sanctum sanctorum. The ceiling has elaborate *nakashi* craftsmanship with deep red and blue designs decorated with gold. The hall and the floor are covered in white marble with *jaratkari* work that uses coloured stone inlays in botanical designs. Naturally, *kirtan* is a regular feature and is telecast every day.

The doorway is covered with silver sheets embossed with floral patterns, and the *darbar* hall has exquisitely carved pillars. The well, from which the Guru gave water to the afflicted, still provides water, which is sipped by the devotees from the *chhabeel* in the *parkarma*, just outside the main building.

76 Gurdwara Sis Ganj, where Guru Tegh Bahadur attained martyrdom, Gurdwara Rakab Ganj Sahib, where the Ninth Guru's body was cremated; Gurdwara Bangla Sahib, where Guru Harkrishan stayed; Gurdwara Bala Sahib, where the Eighth Guru was cremated, as were, later, Mata Sundri and Mata Sahib Kaur; Gurdwara Majnu ka Tilla named after a Sufi saint who met Guru Nanak; Gurdwara Moti Bagh, where Guru Gobind Singh camped; and Gurdwara Mata Sundri.

77 The other is Gurdwara Rakab Ganj near the Central Secretariat.

Langar at Bangla Sahib serves tens of thousands of people daily and is considered the largest in Delhi.

Widely seen as a refuge, Bangla Sahib is well known for its *langar*, considered the largest in Delhi. It serves over 30,000 people a day. On festivals and special occasions, the number doubles or even triples. The birth anniversary of Guru Harkrishan, along with the Gurpurbs of other Gurus, are commemorated with great zeal and devotion.

In keeping with the heritage of healing touch that Gurdwara Bangla Sahib is famous for, there is a Guru Harkrishan Polyclinic that provides outpatient facilities for those in need. It also has provisions for many medical tests, including MRI, CT-scan, and digital X-ray, a service provided at nominal rates to benefit both citizens of Delhi and visitors. Medicines prescribed are also available at minimal rates. As expected, the facility is quite popular with Sikhs and non-Sikhs alike.

A Central Sikh Library possesses rare books for readers. Baba Baghel Singh Sikh Heritage Multimedia Museum showcases the Sikh ethos with a rich collection of paintings of historical events associated with Gurus and their Sikhs. Underground parking makes life easier for visitors.

Placed as it is in the heart of New Delhi, Bangla Sahib Gurdwara has a special significance in the hearts of local devotees, many of whom pay obeisance each morning and evening.

Gurdwara Sis Ganj

DELHI, INDIA

URU TEGH Bahadur offered his life to defend the principle of freedom to practise one's religion—any religion. The shrine where the Ninth Guru's martyrdom took place is in what was and still is a bustling bazaar of Delhi, near the Red Fort that used to be the seat of imperial power during Mughal rule.

Guru Tegh Bahadur defended the principle of freedom to practise one's faith. Gurdwara Sis Ganj marks the place where he was martyred.

Let's go back to Anandpur Sahib in Punjab, where the Ninth Guru received a delegation of Kashmiri Pandits led by Kirpa Ram. They told the Guru that Nawab Iftikhar Khan, the Subedar[78] of Kashmir, was persecuting and pressuring them to convert from Hinduism to Islam.

The Guru asked the delegation to inform the Subedar that if he could persuade the Guru to convert, they would do so too. The matter escalated, and in time, Emperor Aurangzeb's officials summoned the Guru to Delhi. En route, at Bassi Pathana, he was detained, jailed for three months, and meted out the harshest treatment. The Mughal authorities then took him to Delhi, where he arrived on 4 November 1675.

The Guru's trusted followers, including Bhai Mati Das, Bhai Sati Das, and Dayal Das, accompanied him to Delhi. They were all put in chains, tortured, and asked to convert. The followers remained steadfast in their resolve even as they were tortured to death.

78 Governor.

Guru Granth Sahib is placed above the spot where the Ninth Guru was martyred.

In an effort to weaken his resolve, the Mughal jailers ensured that Guru Tegh Bahadur witnessed the gory fate of his beloved followers. As was their norm, his jailers asked the Guru to perform a miracle, convert, or be put to the sword. He refused to perform a miracle, saying it was wrong to intervene with God's Will. He also refused to convert, and was beheaded on 11 November 1675.

The sacrifice of Guru Tegh Bahadur is unparalleled since he gave his life not for his own faith but for the right of others to practise their faith.[79] In time, the Guru's sacrifice transformed the socio-religious perceptions of the people of the country. It laid the ground for his son, Guru Gobind Singh, to emancipate his followers.

Gurdwara Sis Ganj Sahib marks the spot where the beheading took place. Under the cover of a fortuitous dust storm, some Sikhs removed his body and head. The body was cremated where Gurdwara Rakab Ganj is, and Gurdwara Sis Ganj Sahib in Anandpur Sahib stands where Guru Gobind Singh cremated the head of his father, which was brought to him at significant personal risk by Bhai Jaita.

Two centuries later, under the terms agreed to after Sikh forces took over the Red Fort on 11 March 1783, Baghel Singh Karorsinghia received the permission to raise Gurdwaras on seven Sikh historical sites,[80] including Sis Ganj.

The place of the Guru's execution had an issue. A part of a mosque abutted the proposed site. With the Emperor's permission, Baghel Singh removed it and built the Gurdwara. He tackled resistance by residents with the Emperor's authority and attached a *jagir*[81] of Rs 4,000. The Sikh contingent was in Delhi for nine months. They constructed the historic Gurdwaras during this time. However, soon after they left Delhi, the situation was reversed, and the mosque came up where Gurdwara Sis Ganj had been built.

Around 1857, British colonial authorities permitted Maharaja Sarup Singh of Jind to construct a Gurdwara at the site. However, the matter was challenged in court, and finally, Raja Ranbir Singh of Jind took the issue to the Privy Council, which ruled in favour of the Sikhs. The Gurdwara was then built in 1861.

79 In *Bachitra Natak* (Resplendent Drama), regarded as an autobiographical note of Guru Gobind Singh, the 10th Guru describes his father's martyrdom: "He protected their *tilak* and *janeu*: In this age of darkness, he performed a grand deed; He made the supreme sacrifice for the sake of faith; He gave his head but uttered not a groan. The martyrdom he endured to uphold righteousness; He gave his head but displayed not his charisma." (*Encyclopaedia of Sikhism* Ed. Harbans Singh).

80 Besides Gurdwara Sis Ganj, they were Gurdwara Rakab Ganj Sahib, Gurdwara Bangla Sahib, Gurdwara Bala Sahib, Gurdwara Majnu ka Tilla, Gurdwara Moti Bagh, and Gurdwara Mata Sundri.

81 A land grant that entitled the Gurdwara to revenues.

A perpetual flame is lit in a golden lamp and a portrait of Guru Tegh Bahadur in the miniature style is kept where the Ninth Guru was martyred.

The present building was constructed in the 1930s. Rai Bahadur Narain Singh, one of the contractors who built New Delhi, contributed substantially. Subsequently, it was expanded in 1971 and 1983, by including the areas of extant *kotwali*, the place of the Guru's imprisonment. The word *kotwali* reminds us of the police lockup it was; however, it has been transformed.

A flight of stairs leads devotees from the main entrance of the Gurdwara to the first floor, where the sanctum sanctorum is located. It is above the spot where the execution took place. The marble flooring here is rich with inlay designs of traditional floral patterns.

A blue and white carpet covers the floor of the deep hall. The ceiling has distinctive modern mirror work, and massive chandeliers light up the room. Scalloped arches with white marble facing and golden edging stand out. Each has a quotation from Gurbani on the top panel, which stands out in golden relief on a blue background. The mezzanine, which goes around the main hall, has marble *jali* barriers. The gilding on the *palki* and the flowers that adorn the area around Guru Granth Sahib add a distinctive touch.

Devotees walk down narrow stairs to reach the spot where Guru Tegh Bahadur was martyred. A continuous flame is lit in a golden lamp. A glass enclosure protects the heavily embellished area. Guru Tegh Bahadur's portrait in miniature style is placed in front. Some traditional weapons like the *katar*, the *khanda* and *chakras* are also displayed here.

The well where the Guru had his bath can also be seen in the Gurdwara complex. Visitors line up to drink water, served from it by devotees.

The former *kotwali* has been integrated and the *langar* hall is located there. The Gurdwara also has provisions for storing luggage and providing accommodation to devotees. The management runs a museum, a reference library, and Guru Tegh Bahadur Khalsa Girls Senior Secondary School near the complex, along with an underground parking facility.

The place where the martyrdom of Guru Tegh Bahadur took place is of tremendous historical and emotional importance to the Sikhs, and Gurdwara Sis Ganj, located in the bustling Chandni Chowk area, sees huge attendance from both the local devotees and pilgrims who come from far to pay obeisance.

Gurdwara Rakab Ganj

NEW DELHI, INDIA

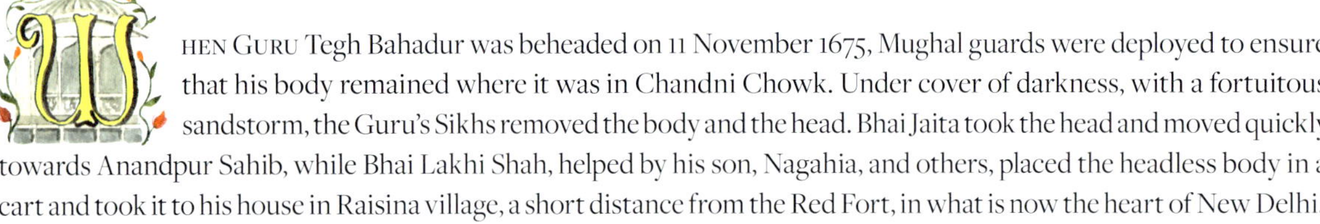

When Guru Tegh Bahadur was beheaded on 11 November 1675, Mughal guards were deployed to ensure that his body remained where it was in Chandni Chowk. Under cover of darkness, with a fortuitous sandstorm, the Guru's Sikhs removed the body and the head. Bhai Jaita took the head and moved quickly towards Anandpur Sahib, while Bhai Lakhi Shah, helped by his son, Nagahia, and others, placed the headless body in a cart and took it to his house in Raisina village, a short distance from the Red Fort, in what is now the heart of New Delhi.

Built where Guru Tegh Bahadur's body was cremated, Gurdwara Rakab Ganj is a towering tribute to the Guru who gave his life for the freedom of others to practise their faith.

Mindful that the Emperor's soldiers would not allow a conventional cremation to be performed, he reverentially kept the body in his home and set the house on fire that very night.[82] Bhai Jaita reached Anandpur Sahib, and Guru Gobind Singh cremated his father's head ceremoniously on 16 November 1675.

Gurdwara Rakab Ganj is located at the cremation spot that was originally Bhai Lakhi Shah's home. Guru Gobind Singh raised a simple memorial there when he visited Delhi at the invitation of Prince Muazzam, who later became Emperor Bahadur Shah I.

When Baghel Singh negotiated permission to build Gurdwaras at significant historical spots, he found that a mosque had been built on the exact spot where the Guru's ashes were buried. With the Emperor's permission, he dug up under the mosque that had come up there and showed the copper urn in which Bhai Lakhi Shah had originally placed the ashes. This allowed him to negotiate with the local population. Of course, he had Emperor Shah Alam II's *firman*,[83] which empowered

82 The area was called Rakab Ganj (also spelt Rikab Ganj), literally a colony of saddle-makers.
83 Imperial order.

ਸਤਿਨਾਮ ਵਾਹਿਗੁਰੂ

The golden *palki* is placed above the spot where the Ninth Guru's body was cremated.

him to build Gurdwaras in Delhi. Given the evidence and the situation, they agreed to vacate the holy ground. Gurdwara Rakab Ganj was built after that on the same spot.

At some point, local Muslims demolished the Sikh shrine and rebuilt a mosque there. After 1857, during the British Raj, the Sikhs took the matter to the court of law, which restored possession of the site to them, and they promptly rebuilt the Gurdwara.

New Delhi, Capital of Colonial India, placed the British Viceroy's mansion atop Raisina Hill. A new city was being laid out; they took the land of Raisina Hill.[84] While the imperial planners were mindful of the two historical Gurdwras—Bangla Sahib and Rakab Ganj Sahib—they demolished a portion of the boundary wall of the Gurdwara compound to make it conform to their masterplan. A prolonged agitation by the Sikhs, held in abeyance during World War I, ensured that the government rebuilt the demolished wall.

The partition of India resulted in an influx of Sikhs to Delhi from what became Pakistan. One of them was Harnam Singh Suri. In Rawalpindi, he had an automotive parts business and was a bank director. After 1947, he built his life anew in Delhi. When the *sangat* discussed funds for rebuilding Rakab Ganj Sahib, he offered his services and requested anonymity.

In time, the local committee decided that given the magnitude of his contribution, he would be recognised and no longer remain anonymous. Interestingly, Bhai Lakhi Shah, whose house was where Gurdwara Rakab Ganj was built, was a trader, as was Harnam Singh Suri, who was now rebuilding the Gurdwara.

The design of the Gurdwara is distinctive. The facade is uniform from all sides, and the Gurdwara building has domes in the typical Sikh ribbed architectural style, with an inverted lotus at the bottom.

The Gurdwara is built on a pedestal that is over 3 metres high. It covers the area where Guru Tegh Bahadur's body's cremation took place. As you go up a steep flight of stairs, you arrive on the ground floor with a very high ceiling and beautiful work done in shades of brown and beige. The carpet complements the top and gives a light touch to the interior, enhanced by the extensive use of white marble on the main floor, with panels that have colour-stone inlays in botanical designs. The doors are covered with embossed silver. Scalloped arches at the edge of the mezzanine at mid-height mark the first floor.

The circumambulation path around the *palki* has stairs going down to the place where the cremation took place. A raised platform on the marble floor marks the cremation spot. There is a glazed viewing area, and the ceiling and the sides are embellished with embossed gold plates. An old representation of Guru Tegh Bahadur painted in the traditional style and other artefacts have been kept there. Sacred relics preserved in the Gurdwara include two swords, a dagger, and two *katars*[85] Guru Gobind Singh gave to his wife, Mata Sahib Devan, before she departed from Nanded to reach Delhi in 1708.

The Gurdwara complex is enormous. It has various buildings, including Lakhi Shah Hall, used for large congregations, the office of the Delhi Sikh Gurdwara Management Committee, a large *langar* building, and residential accommodation for employees of the management committee. A new complex has provisions for dispensing *parshad* and storing devotees' shoes. An old well has also been restored. The Wall of Truth commemorates and gives the names of the victims of the anti-Sikh violence in Delhi in 1984. The International Institute of Sikh Studies, with a holographic auditorium, is another prominent institution within the complex. There is also accommodation for out-of-town pilgrims.

Gurdwara Rakab Ganj attracts a large congregation and serves as a focal point for the Sikhs of Delhi.

84 According to one account, the area around Raisina village was under the control of the Gurdwara management. The colonial government gave 100 acres of land near Hisar in compensation for the land they acquired.

85 Poniard, a push dagger.

Hemkunt Sahib Gurdwara

CHAMOLI, UTTARAKHAND, INDIA

Hemkunt Sahib is on the banks of a crystal-clear lake that reflects white snow-clad Himalayan mountain peaks, and is buried under snow in the winters.

NESTLED high in the Himalayas, 15,210 feet above sea level, is Hemkunt Sahib. Near it is a crystal-clear lake that reflects white snow-clad mountain peaks and the building of the historical Gurdwara, which is like none other. It is considered sacred because it has been identified as the place where Guru Gobind Singh is believed to have meditated in a previous birth.

The location of the Gurdwara, in Chamoli district of Uttarakhand, was decided by Pandit Tara Chand Narotam, a Nirmala Sikh scholar, who has written about it.[86] The Gurdwara was set up in 1934 by Bhai Sohan Singh of Tehri Garhwal, who had served as a Granthi in the Indian Army. Constructed with support from eminent individuals, including Bhai Vir Singh, the Gurdwara opened in the mid-1930s. It was looked after by Bhai Sohan Singh and Havaldar Modan Singh, who helped with the construction and continued to serve as the Granthi and caretaker, along with an associate.

86 *Sri Gur Tirath Sangrah (1883)* is his definitive volume about Sikh sacred spaces connected with the Gurus. The pioneering work lists the location and the name of the in-charge of the Gurdwaras.

ਸਤਿਨਾਮ
ਵਾਹਿਗੁਰੂ
OFFERING BOX

Pilgrims pay obeisance at the Gurdwara and are encouraged to make their way back to lower altitudes before the evening.

In 1960, Havaldar Modan Singh set up the Hemkunt Sahib Management Trust. The increasing number of visitors necessitated a bigger building, and the Gurdwara was built in its present form by architect Manmohan Singh Siali[87] with crucial inputs from Major-General Harkirat Singh, Engineer-in-Chief of the Indian Army. Inspired by Gurbani, they designed the roof "as a jewel that covered Guru Granth Sahib".

Construction started in July 1968. Building the Gurdwara was challenging due to the location, weather, and rugged terrain that had to be traversed. The last 15 km had to be negotiated on foot up a steep winding path. Various steel parts were built in such a way that they could be transported to the site. For the steel foundation, a mock-up was built at Gurdwara Rakab Ganj in Delhi. Different sections were numbered and then fabricated to ensure proper fitting. Moving some of these plates up the trail was a humongous task—it took a team of 30 men 10 days to take the five plates uphill. Prominent Sikh contractors contributed their best men for the task of building the Gurdwara, but it took time, and it was only by the mid-1970s that the roof was erected.[88]

The modern structure is informed by the traditional architecture of Harmandir Sahib and reflects the traditional lotus flower shape in a more flowing form than the stylised ones seen elsewhere. Appreciation of tradition can also be seen in the pentagonal base since the number five is rich with spiritual symbolism in Sikh heritage. The unique architecture and construction allow it to withstand the vagaries of extreme weather. In fact, the Gurdwara is buried under as much as 25 feet of snow in winter. It is only when the snow melts in May-June that the building emerges from under the white cover—unscathed and inspiring.

The inaccessibility, of course, adds to the allure of Hemkunt Sahib. Pilgrims drive up to Gobind Ghat and then face the 18 km trek from Gobind Ghat to Gobind Dham, or Ghangaria, as it was known earlier, up fairly steep mountain trails. A detour is sometimes taken through the Valley of Flowers, which has a bouquet of the best of the Himalayas in the season, with a vast variety of flowers, including blue poppies and lilies, carpeting the hillsides. Natural waterfalls are abundant, and you see the river Pushpwati gushing down the valley.

87 He joined the Punjab Capital Project, which planned Chandigarh in 1951, before going to the UK for post-graduation in urban design. At the instance of Maj-Gen Harkirat Singh, he joined the Military Engineering Service in 1964. Sardar Bahadur Karnail Singh's help in guiding and helping the project is also cited.

88 AstroLite was used for strength and insulation, and it has proved to be durable.

The Gurdwara is a steep 6 km climb from Gobind Ghat, and on the last leg you cross a glacier at one point. A staircase has also been cut out for the last kilometre, and many opt to take that. As you near the Gurdwara, you catch the sound of divine *kirtan* permeating the atmosphere. Most pilgrims also take a dip in the *sarovar*, some perform a *parkarma* of the *sarovar*, a difficult endeavour that entails crossing a part of a glacier, and partake of the *langar* before making their way back.

The journey is an assertion of the community's collective will to seek spiritual solace at one of the most picturesque Gurdwaras in the world.

Pilgrims experience the sublime as they look at Guru Granth Sahib, highlighted by natural light in the hall that shelters them from the elements. A blue *khanda-chakkar* banner forms the backdrop for the golden *palki*. The sounds of *kirtan* and *path* travel far in the hills, and the Hemkunt Sarovar reflects the Gurdwara, Nishan Sahib, and the high mountain peaks that form the backdrop. The programme is regularly telecast.

Langar is served, and throughout the arduous trek up to the Gurdwara, volunteers help the pilgrims. The Hemkunt Trust has also made Gurdwaras for pilgrims on the oft-taken route to Hemkunt Sahib. Thus, Gurdwaras have come up at Haridwar, Rishikesh, Srinagar, Joshimath, Gobind Ghat and Gobind Dham. The trust has continued in its task of providing good facilities for pilgrims and thus has remained active in developing infrastructure for them at these places as well as Hemkunt Sahib.

Hemkunt Sahib is snowbound, and thus remains inaccessible for nine months (October to June). Pilgrims make the most of the three months when it is accessible and throng this holy shrine in large numbers.

(left) The beautiful lake is surrounded by mountain peaks, as seen in this recreation of a survey plan drawing.

(right) Hemkunt Sahib Gurdwara as it was initially sketched.

Sri Guru Singh Sabha Dadar

MUMBAI, MAHARASHTRA, INDIA

THE HISTORY of Sikhs in Mumbai is intertwined with Sri Guru Singh Sabha, Dadar. Located in a multi-storeyed building, the Gurdwara was built on Dr Ambedkar[89] Road, where the famous Indian jurist and political leader had a printing press.

Sri Guru Singh Sabha, Dadar, has a significant place in the socio-religious activities of the Sikhs of Mumbai.

The management committee also manages the older Gurdwara near Victoria Terminus station on Dockyard Road, now called Shahid Bhagat Singh Road, which dates back to 1919. Besides being the hub of the small Sikh community in Bombay (now Mumbai), it also served as a staging area for Punjabis who sought to make their life abroad and waited to sail on the ships that would take them to their destinations.

Sri Guru Singh Sabha, Dadar, was formed in the 1920s, and it became a major organisation that sought to help Sikhs who came to Bombay. After Partition, there was an influx of refugees from what became Pakistan, and many of them arrived via the Frontier Mail that linked Peshawar to Bombay. Punjabi and Sindhi families got food and shelter in the city's Gurdwaras as they tried to build their lives anew. Sri Guru Singh Sabha, Dadar, played a significant role during that time.

89 Bhimrao Ramji Ambedkar (14 April 1891-6 December 1956) headed the committee that drafted the Indian Constitution and served as India's first Law and Justice Minister.

The second-floor *darbar* hall is spacious and well-appointed.

The Gurdwara building came up in the mid-1950s, and it is located in a commercial area. The ground floor has shops punctuated by a stairway that leads up, away from the hustle and bustle of the bazaar, towards the quiet of peace and spirituality. Even though the facade cannot escape the immediate neighbourhood, it still stands out because of the white colour, architecture, the massive dome atop the building, and the tall Nishan Sahib.

The Gurdwara has a significant place in the socio-religious activities of the Sikhs, and it has continued its tradition by providing a floor dedicated to serving the attendants of cancer patients undergoing treatment at the nearby Tata Memorial Hospital.

In 2012, it enlarged the area devoted to accommodating around 200 such patients. It also provides temporary accommodation for people from various parts of India seeking to make a life in the country's commercial capital.

A flight of stairs leads up from the commercial space on the ground floor to the first floor, with the management's offices and space allocated for patients. The main hall of the Gurdwara is on the second floor. It is 5,000 square feet, and the *maryada* of daily *path* and *kirtan* is observed here. The magnificent hall provides seating for 500-600 persons, and the *langar* caters to the devotees who visit the Gurdwara daily, as well as travellers and attendants/families of patients who live in the rooms within the premises. Weekends bring in larger crowds, while Gurpurbs attract thousands of Sikhs.

Although the number of Sikh families who live in the immediate vicinity has decreased, the Gurdwara continues to be popular with Sikhs of Mumbai. Among the events celebrated with great fervour are the birth anniversaries of Guru Nanak Dev, Guru Tegh Bahadur, Guru Gobind Singh, and festivals such as Baisakhi and Diwali.

Punjabis of Bombay's film industry have a strong connection with the Gurdwara. S. Mohinder,[90] who later became a famous music composer of Bollywood, used to perform *kirtan* at the Dadar Gurdwara.

The management also runs Guru Granth Vidyak Society School, and a homoeopathic dispensary is housed on the premises. The Gurdwara has been at the forefront of community outreach programmes. It has served people whenever need arose—recently in the aftermath of the terrorist attack at the nearby Taj Hotel in 2011 and during the Covid-19 pandemic. Sri Guru Singh Sabha, Dadar, thus, stands out for the *sewa* performed at the premises and by the various bodies it runs in Mumbai.

90 Bakshi Mohinder Singh Sarna (1925–2020).

Sri Guru Singh Sabha Ulsoor

BENGALURU, KARNATAKA, INDIA

THE PRESENCE of Sikh soldiers in the erstwhile Mysore state goes back to the time of Hyder Ali,[91] Tippu Sultan's father. However, Sikh families moved to Bangalore in the late 19th century, primarily due to military service and trade opportunities. During British Raj, some Sikhs came to Bangalore, and by the early 1940s, there were 20 families. They would gather in different houses on Sundays and pray together. A few years later, the Jolly family donated their motor garage to the *sangat*. Located on the banks of the Ulsoor Lake, this soon became the place where Sikhs met and prayed. The present magnificent building traces its roots to the Gurdwara that was inaugurated in the mid-1940s.[92]

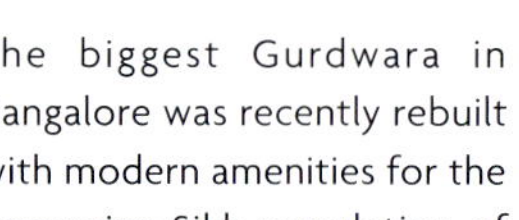

The biggest Gurdwara in Bangalore was recently rebuilt with modern amenities for the increasing Sikh population of India's IT capital.

More families came to Bangalore in 1947 after the massive displacement of Partition, and the numbers steadily increased. Apart from the land the family gave, more land was taken on lease from the civic body. The building is in a slightly hilly area, and since there were space constraints, a second floor was added in 1971.

As Bangalore became the IT capital, many North Indians moved to the city for work. The number of devotees at the Gurdwara kept increasing, especially on festival days. It is estimated that now there are around 23,000 Sikh families in Bangalore, among them many young men and women working in the IT sector.

91 Historian B.A. Saletore (1900–1963) established Hari Singh's presence from references in *Hydernamah*, a court biography of Hyder Ali, and other sources. Hari Singh, probably a local who converted to Sikhism, led a force of Sikhs supplemented by Rajput cavalry and mercenaries. References to other Sikh warriors, like Chattar Singh, Ranjit Singh and Surat Singh, have also been found.

92 The website notes that it was inaugurated by A G Russell in 1945. However, a plaque at the original site said: "This Gurdwara was opened by P M Jayarajan ESQ, ICS, Collector and District Magistrate CSM Station, Bangalore on 13th April 1946."

GURDWARA
SRI GURU SINGH SABHA

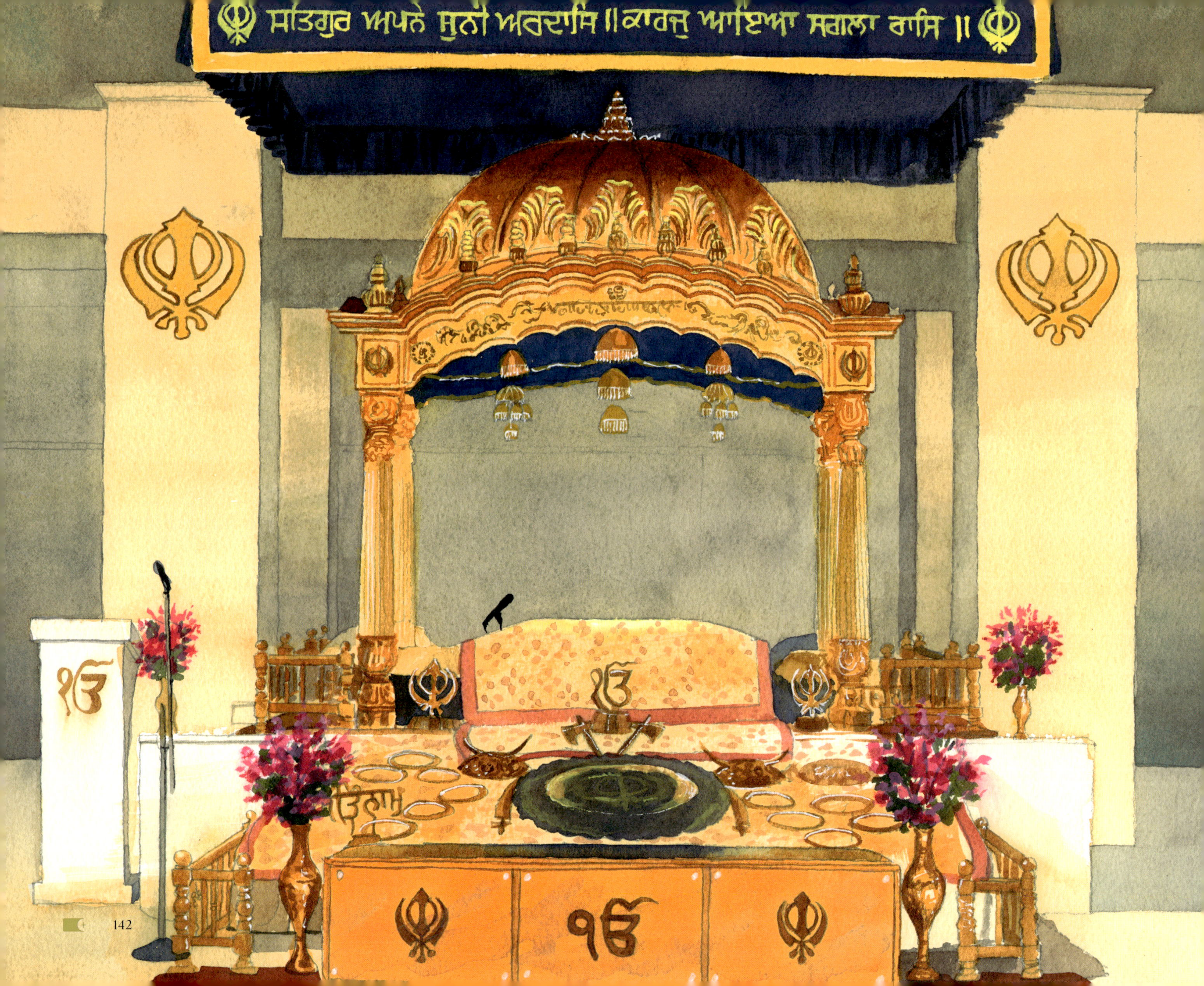

ਸਤਿਗੁਰ ਆਪਨੇ ਸੁਨੀ ਅਰਦਾਸਿ ॥ ਕਾਰਜੁ ਆਇਆ ਸਗਲਾ ਰਾਸਿ ॥

The *darbar* hall is spacious and the golden *palki* has the *khanda-chakkar* symbol in it.

The worldwide celebrations for the 550th birth anniversary of Guru Nanak became the trigger for a large-scale revamp, and in 2020, the old building was demolished. It was reopened on July 16, 2023, in a sparkling white edifice on Kensington Road, also known as Gurdwara Road. Designed by Arunjot Singh, the 8,000 square-foot building conforms to traditional architecture even as it provides modern amenities. It was built by Prestige Group.

The biggest Gurdwara in the city now has underground parking for 40 vehicles and a wedding hall and a catering hall in the basement. Large-capacity lifts can be used, as well as stairs. It is also accessible for the differently-abled and has a designated area, with easy access, for the elderly devotees. Glass windows, etched with the *khanda-chakkar* logo, are liberally used, as is white marble, giving the building a light feeling.

There is a large *langar* hall on the ground floor, which is necessary because on weekends the number of devotees is around 4,000, with Gurpurbs and other religious occasions seeing a spike of up to 25,000 visitors. There is also a large and modern kitchen besides offices on this floor.

The first floor has a spacious *darbar* hall, and the *parkash asthan* has the golden *palki* with the words "*Tu Mera Rakha Sabhni Thain*" and the *khanda-chakkar* in it. In front of the raised platform is a circular shield of wood with the *Ek Onkar* symbol embossed on it. There is space for a circular flower garland, which is often presented with fragrant white jasmine buds. The dome is decorated with elaborate geometric designs on a red base. A three-tiered chandelier, executed in wood with white inlay work, hangs below it.

The second floor has 10 rooms for devotees who wish to stay; another section is for the employees. Provision has been made for a library, which is under development, as is a clinic.

The Gurdwara also built Sri Guru Harkrishan High School, which was opened in 1997. It is from nursery to Class X, with around 550 students, mainly from the financially challenged sections of society. It has always been open to all, and now the students are overwhelmingly non-Sikh local children who make the most use of monetary assistance. They are given subsidised education and mid-day meals. Various organisations and individuals contribute towards this since the fee can't even cover the teachers' salaries.

Since it is considered the most important Gurdwara in Bangalore, a city with the largest population of Sikhs in Karnataka, outreach programmes and other initiatives are undertaken to engage with the wider community.

Nagar kirtan processions are held to mark the birth anniversary of Guru Nanak Dev and Guru Gobind Singh, in which thousands of local Sikhs participate. Gurmukhi and Gurmat classes for children have been held for the past 10 years on Sundays, and recently, *kirtan*, *gatka*, and turban-tying classes have also been introduced.

Gurdwara Baram Bala

HYDERABAD, TELANGANA, INDIA

HEN THE Sikh Army was sent to Hyderabad by Maharaja Ranjit Singh, it was bivouacked in what is now called Sikh Chawni, Maharaja Ranjit Singh Nagar, Attapur, Rajendranagar Road. This is where Gurdwara Baram Bala is located.

Let's go back to the year 1832 when Nasir-ud-Daula (Nizam IV), ruler of the Deccan region, requested Maharaja Ranjit Singh, ruler of Punjab, for Sikh Army assistance in maintaining law and order as well as revenue collection. Prime Minister Raja Chandu Lal of Hyderabad, recognising the renowned prowess of Maharaja Ranjit Singh's army, made the wise suggestion.

Maharaja Ranjit Singh, acceding to the Nizam's request, dispatched a contingent of 14 Risalas to Hyderabad Deccan,[93] with each Risaldar leading 100 soldiers. This formidable force, known as the Sikh Force , was stationed at Kishan Bagh, which came to be known as Sikh Chawni.[94] Land was allocated to accommodate the Sikh Force,[95] which established several Gurdwaras there, including Gurdwara Baram Bala, which became the main Gurdwara. The Sikh Force celebrated various festivals at this Gurdwara, making it the centre for religious congregations.

A contingent of Sikh forces sent by Maharaja Ranjit Singh established Gurdwara Baram Bala in 1832. A portion of the old building also stands. This Gurdwara building was inaugurated in 2018.

93 It was known as Hyderabad Deccan to differentiate it from Hyderabad Sindh.

94 The Lahore Darbar Royal Treasury paid the salaries of the Sikh Force until the demise of Maharaja Ranjit Singh in 1839. After that, the forces received their salaries from the Nizam's Treasury. The force was subsequently deployed in different districts of the Nizam Dominion.

95 Literally, Sikh Cantonment.

GURUDWARA SAHEB BARAMBALA
LANGAR HALL

ੴ
GURU KI GOLAK

The 10,000 square-foot *darbar* hall can seat 4,000 devotees simultaneously.

Gurdwara Baram Bala was pivotal in hosting religious gatherings, attracting Sikh *sangat*. The main congregation took place twice a year during Hola Mahalla and Dussehra celebrations. Now, functions are held more often.

The old Gurdwara was constructed in 1832 during the Asaf Jahi period.[96] Built using bricks and mortar, the Gurdwara served the community for many decades, even as the vagaries of nature took a toll. A lightning strike in the 1950s damaged some parts. The original time-worn building still stands but is no longer habitable.

The Sikh Force was disbanded in 1952 after the merger of Hyderabad State with India. However, the descendants of the Sikh Force chose to remain in Sikh Chawni. Around 1,200 Sikh families reside there, creating a unique community that has its own traditions.

In addition to the Gurdwara, educational institutions—Guru Nanak Pre-Primary School, Guru Nanak High School, and Guru Nanak Hockey Playground were established in 1990 to cater to the academic and athletic needs of the Sikh community. The Sikh Education Society, Hyderabad, manages the schools[97] and playgrounds.

In 2003, the construction of the present Gurdwara commenced and was completed by 2018. Gurdwara Baram Bala was inaugurated on 28 January 2018, on the 388th birth anniversary of Guru Har Rai. The grand event drew in the crème of Sikh religious leadership, including Giani Gurbachan Singh, Jathedar Sri Akal Takht Sahib; Giani Raghbir Singh, Jathedar Sri Kesgarh Sahib; Giani Harpreet Singh, Jathedar of Takht Sri Damdama Sahib; Giani Jyotinder Singh, Assistant Jathedar of Takht Sri Hazoor Sahib, Nanded; Baba Avtar Singh, Jathedar, Dal Baba Bidhi Singh, Sursinghwale; and Manjit Singh GK, President of the Delhi Sikh Gurdwara Management Committee.

96 The Asaf Jahi period represents the Muslim dynasty of Nizams who ruled the Hyderabad State. Other than Hazur Sahib, the Gurdwara was the first of its kind in southern India.

97 It was established in 1939.

Tokens issued to the soldiers of the Sikh Force of the Nizam of Hyderabad.

The Gurdwara is an architectural statement of the grandeur of the Sikhs of Hyderabad, and the facade reflects the Sikh architectural style, featuring five massive arches on each side, the traditional inverted lotus domes and *chhatris* that stand out against the sky. Architect Surender Singh, who lives in Hyderabad and has several Gurdwara projects to his credit, designed it.

The *darbar* hall on the first-floor spans 10,000 square feet, and 4,000 devotees can be seated simultaneously. The column-less hall of this size is the first of its kind in South India. It is surrounded by a 20-foot-wide *parkarma*. This circumambulatory path serves the spiritual purpose of the devotees while also enhancing the architectural beauty of the Gurdwara. The roof of the main hall is 22-foot high. Connected to the hall are the *sukhasan* room on the southwest side and the *akhand path* room on the south side, with a storeroom in between. The kitchen for preparing *karha-parshad* is in the south-east corner. There is also a Guru Granth Sahib Bhavan on the south and south-eastern side, which is well connected to a ramp used during the 'Agan Bhet Seva'.[98] The first floor is approachable by a ramp for the differently-abled.

The ground floor of the Gurdwara has a roof of 150 feet by 140 feet. This area serves as the *langar* hall, hosts multiple functions, and is designed to be versatile.

Gurdwara Baram Bala, situated in Sikh Chawni, holds great historical and religious significance. It has played a crucial role in the lives of the Sikh community in Hyderabad, attracting devotees from far and wide. With its unique architectural features and its connection to the Sikh Force and the vibrant Sikh community living in Sikh Chawni, this Gurdwara stands as testament to the rich cultural heritage and religious devotion of the Sikhs in Telangana.

98 Consigning to flames, with due reverence, of old and frayed editions of religious texts.

109
JAWAN
SIKH FORCE
109

HYDERABAD
DISTRICT POLICE
SIKH FORCE

Sri Guru Nanak Sat Sangh Sabha

CHENNAI, TAMIL NADU, INDIA

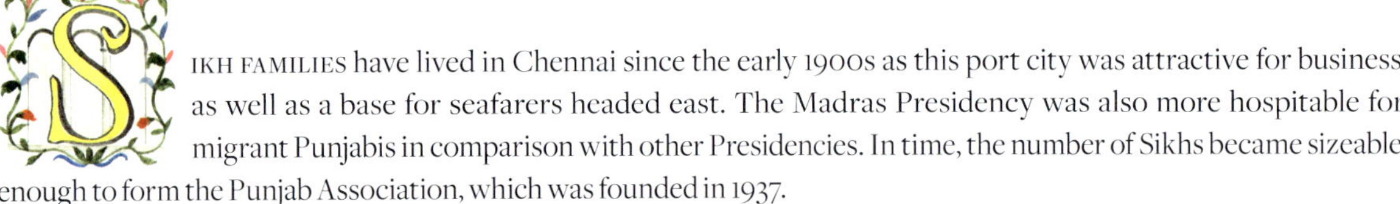

SIKH FAMILIES have lived in Chennai since the early 1900s as this port city was attractive for business as well as a base for seafarers headed east. The Madras Presidency was also more hospitable for migrant Punjabis in comparison with other Presidencies. In time, the number of Sikhs became sizeable enough to form the Punjab Association, which was founded in 1937.

The original building's limestone construction dates to the 1950s. Sikhs from far and wide had contributed to building it.

Lt-Col Gurdial Singh Gill[99] took up the leadership of planning and building the Gurdwara by starting the Sri Guru Nanak Sat Sangh Sabha in 1949. Construction of the Gurdwara building on G. N. Chetty Road began in 1952.

Hardyal Singh of Singapore led the ground-breaking ceremony on Baisakhi Day. "Oral history tells us that the *sangat* numbered nearly 2,500, and many of them travelled from Jalandhar, Ludhiana, Hoshiarpur, Moga, Delhi, and other towns like Jabalpur, Bokaro, Bombay, Hyderabad, Vijayawada, Bangalore, Coimbatore, and Calcutta to grace the occasion. Furthermore, native Tamils, Telugus, Sindhis, Gujaratis and Biharis were also present."[100]

99 Dr Gill (1893-1982), and his Scottish wife, Rena Lister Gill, were prominent figures of Madras. He was Director General of Prisons for the state and had a good rapport with Congress leaders C. Rajagopalachari and K Kamraj, who had been his wards during the freedom struggle.

100 *Historic Heritage of Sri Guru Nanak Sat Sangh Sabha Madras* by Ujagar Singh. *Punjab in the South*, April 2022.

The *darbar* hall is on the first floor, and devotees see a picture of Harmandir Sahib as they walk in to pay obeisance.

The society and the Gurdwara received significant support from Maharani Vidyawati Devi of Vizianagaram, who was also a North-Indian[101] living in the South. The local *sangat* contributed in various ways, and the government allotted the land.[102]

The original building is still the main Gurdwara, a double-storeyed structure built using lime. Maharaja Yadavindra Singh of Patiala designated T. N. Subramanian as architect-cum-engineer for the Gurdwara.[103] No wonder the building reflects a confluence of Sikh architectural flourishes and local norms. The *khanda-chakkar* at the centre of the facade has a twisted rope border molding that makes it look like a royal seal. The ground floor had rooms that were earlier used to provide shelter to Sikhs while they waited to secure a passage to Malaya or Singapore for work. They would often stay for months. It comes as no surprise that among the significant contributors towards funds for the Gurdwara were these early Sikhs from South-East Asia.

The *darbar* hall is on the first floor, accessible by climbing up a broad stairway that leads to it from the outside. A lift has been added in recent years on the side to enable easy access for those who need it. Light streams in from the large windows on the sides, and the walls are lined with doors that can be opened when needed. The golden *palki* dominates the room, and a picture of Harmandir Sahib forms the backdrop. The two-acre plot provided enough space to construct Sri Guru Tegh Bahadur Sahib Ji Hall. It has a *langar* on the ground floor and a hall for family functions on the first floor. The Sri Guru Nanak Multimedia Centre can accommodate 75 people and is used for Punjabi and *kirtan* classes, meetings, and interactive sessions. It also houses a library.

There are 28 rooms, many of which are used by patients, mostly non-Sikh, who visit Chennai for medical treatment. Quarters have been made to house staff members, and a guest house for visiting *ragi jathas*. The Gurdwara holds regular daily *diwans* and serves *langar* thrice a day. Hundreds of people comprise the *sangat* on weekends. Five to seven thousand people visit the Gurdwara on major festivals such as Baisakhi, and Gurpurbs of Guru Nanak Dev, Guru Gobind Singh, Guru Arjan Dev, and other Gurus.

The management of Sri Guru Nanak Sat Sangh Sabha Gurdwara also supports and administers Gurdwara Guru Nanak Dham, Rameswaram. Guru Nanak visited Rameswaram in 1511 and is believed to have stayed there for 19 days on his return journey from Sri Lanka. There was a small Gurdwara with a Charan Sthan and Bauli Sahib in Rameswaram. When Surjeet Singh Barnala was Governor of Tamil Nadu, a new Gurdwara was constructed.

Since there are no Sikh families there, the administrative control of this Gurdwara was assumed by the Sri Guru Nanak Sat Sangh Sabha in Chennai, which had primarily financed the new project. A Darshani Deori, which blends local and Sikh architecture, marks the entrance of the double-storeyed Gurdwara.

The 2.5-acre campus also has 24 rooms for pilgrims. It took the Sikhs hundreds of years to register a significant presence after Guru Nanak Dev visited Rameswaram and other places in the South.[104] Sri Guru Nanak Sat Sangh Sabha has played a stellar role in providing hospitality and necessary help to newcomers while becoming the community's centre of spiritual solace in Chennai.

101 She was a princess from Keonthal State. After the Gurkha War in 1815, the British sold a part of the state, including Chail, to the Maharaja of Patiala in 1815. Rest was restored to the hereditary rulers.

102 According to one account, in response to the request of the Sikhs via Lt Col Gill, the land was allotted by K. Kamaraj, who was then Chief Minister of Madras State.

103 Subramanian was then the Chief Engineer for Patiala Construction Company Private Limited, Patiala, a State Bank of Patiala subsidiary.

104 Rajinder Singh in *Sikhs and Tamil Nadu* points out that during the freedom struggle, many Sikhs arrested by the British in the northern parts of the country were sent to the South, and they spent their lifetimes in jails of the state in Salem and the Andaman Islands. Maharaja Ripudaman Singh of Nabha, who revolted against the British, was incarcerated in Kodaikanal till his death.

Gurdwara Bara Sikh Sangat

KOLKATA, WEST BENGAL, INDIA

HISTORICAL and spiritual landmark in Kolkata, Gurdwara Bara Sikh Sangat marks the visit of both Guru Nanak Dev and Guru Tegh Bahadur, the Ninth Guru. It is Kolkata's most important historic landmark and the hub of religious activity in the region.

Gurdwara Bara Sikh Sangat marks the visit of both Guru Nanak Dev and Guru Tegh Bahadur.

When Guru Nanak passed through the Sundarbans region, he stayed near the banks of the river Hooghly. The area was under the grip of an epidemic, and the Guru's presence in 1510 gave the suffering population a healing touch. He stayed there for 12 days and interacted with people, chanting the *shabad* "*Chanchal chit na pave pare*".[105] Raja Bhadar Mal, the local ruler, was impressed with the Guru's teachings and made a provision for his followers to gather even after the Guru left.

The *sangat* there was also blessed with the visit of Guru Tegh Bahadur in 1668 when the Ninth Guru was returning to Patna from Dhaka. The Guru composed the *shabad* "*Har ki jat nah koi jaane*"[106] there. Raja Hazuri Mal, whose estate extended to where the Guru stayed, was influenced by his teachings. Later, he maintained the *dharmsal*, where the Guru's followers would gather for spiritual meetings. After his death, the Raja's daughters continued with this *sewa*.[107]

Gurdwara Bara Sangat in Kolkata is a sacred place blessed by both Gurus. In the early days, the site of the Gurdwara was almost a forest and marshy area. It was part of the amalgamation of villages that eventually became Kolkata.

105 The restless mind does not find peace: Guru Granth Sahib, Page 1189

106 No one knows the state of Hari (although many have tried): Guru Granth Sahib, Page 537.

107 The popular and accepted account of both the Guru's visit can be traced back to the definitive *Twarikh Guru Khalsa* by Giani Gian Singh (1885), which is informed by the previous works of Kavi Santokh Singh and Bhai Ratan Singh Bhangu.

KHAZANA

The Gurdwara has eight floors. It is located on the busy Mahatma Gandhi Road in Kolkata.

Sikh presence in Kolkata had two territorial backgrounds: first were the Agrahari Sikhs of Bihari origin, and then came the Sikhs from Punjab. The latter's numbers were enhanced by retrenched World War I soldiers, often from mechanised divisions of the British Indian Army.[108]

The Gurdwara management went through some ups and downs in the 1920s and 1930s. Various groups controlled it, and it went into debt. Even some influential persons' intervention proved ineffective until Baba Ladha Singh Bedi, a local businessman, was appointed by the High Court to take over the Gurdwara Trust in February 1933,[109] a position he held till his death in 1939. The building was also renovated during this period.

Sikhs of Calcutta played a significant role in the Indian Freedom Movement.[110] The port of Calcutta was one of the most important for Sikh emigrants as they sought their fortune abroad. Often, they would need to stay in Gurdwaras till they could board a ship.

The Partition of India in 1947 created a fresh influx of Sikh migrants from East Pakistan (now Bangladesh) and West Pakistan. Many of them built their lives anew and moved out of the area where the Gurdwara is located. However, the Sunday gathering at the Gurdwara continued to attract large crowds. The old building became too small for the burgeoning community; it was demolished in 1959, and a new multi-storeyed building was raised. The present building can be traced back to the 1960s. It has been renovated and modernised many times since then.

The Gurdwara now has eight floors. It is a white building with golden domes at the top. It stands out on the busy Mahatma Gandhi Road, earlier called Harrison Road, in Kolkata.

The ground floor has an entrance at the centre and commercial establishments, including a bank, on both sides. An arched doorway, with a marble plaque bearing the words Gurdwara Bara Sikh Sangat,[111] frames the stairway.

As you go up the stairs, you see the first floor, which has a *darbar* hall. The magnificent space has massive chandeliers on the roof and the golden *palki* at the *parkash asthan*. It has a glassed-in mezzanine. The second floor has the offices of the management committee, and the third houses the *langar* hall, for which the kitchen is provided on the fourth floor. It also has accommodation for the Granthi Sahiban. A gallery for pilgrims is on the fifth floor, while the sixth and seventh have rooms for visiting devotees.

The Gurdwara also has a library, a nursery, and classrooms for students of Punjabi language and culture. *Langar* is served daily, and the weekends draw in more devotees. Major festivals that the Gurdwara celebrates include Guru Nanak Dev's birth anniversary, Guru Tegh Bahadur's Martyrdom Day, Guru Gobind Singh's birth anniversary, and Baisakhi.

The Gurdwara has played a leading role in providing food and medicines for those in need, reaching out to victims of natural disasters and calamities. It also conducts blood donation camps and health awareness programmes.

Gurdwara Bara Sikh Sangat is thus a historical and spiritual landmark in Kolkata that reflects the values and teachings of Sikhism. It is a place of prayer and service for the Sikhs and anyone who wishes to experience the grace and wisdom of Guru Granth Sahib. It is a place of peace and harmony that welcomes everyone with love and respect.

108 This background opened the transportation sector to them, and they were often seen driving buses and taxis.
109 He successfully negotiated the differences between the Agrahari Sikhs who stuck to Sanatani practices that were inimical to Punjabi Amirtdhari Sikhs. By April 1937, the Gurdwara had repaid all its debts, an issue that had landed it in legal problems.
110 While many Agrahari Sikhs were aligned with the British administration, most Punjabi Sikhs turned Calcutta into an important centre of anti-colonial struggles.
111 The words are inscribed in Punjabi, Hindi, English, and Bengali.

Gurdwara Janam Asthan

NANKANA SAHIB, PUNJAB, PAKISTAN

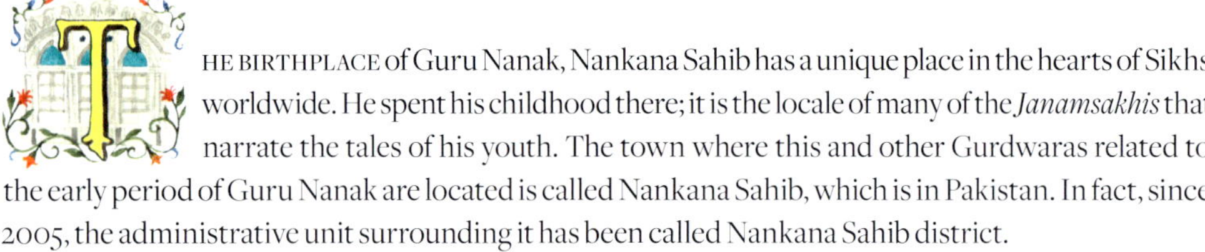

THE BIRTHPLACE of Guru Nanak, Nankana Sahib has a unique place in the hearts of Sikhs worldwide. He spent his childhood there; it is the locale of many of the *Janamsakhis* that narrate the tales of his youth. The town where this and other Gurdwaras related to the early period of Guru Nanak are located is called Nankana Sahib, which is in Pakistan. In fact, since 2005, the administrative unit surrounding it has been called Nankana Sahib district.

The ruins of Talwandi village hark back to antiquity when Rai Bhoi got this land as a *jagir*. He made this place his home and founded a new settlement called Rai Bhoi de Talwandi. Among the people who came to settle in the village were Shiv Ram Bedi and Banarsi, his wife. Shiv Ram became friends with the chieftain. In time, this close relationship continued between their sons, Rai Bular and Mehta Kalu, Guru Nanak's father, who was the village *patwari*, or revenue officer. In time, according to tradition, Rai Bular's family would give land and be a major contributor to the formation of the Gurdwara in Guru Nanak's memory.

Gurdwara Janam Asthan is the biggest and most famous in Nankana Sahib, although there are five other significant Sikh shrines in the city. It is unclear if it was originally built by the Guru's son Baba Lakhmi Chand, or grandson Baba Dharam Chand.

The birthplace of Guru Nanak is now in Pakistan. The historic Gurdwara Janam Asthan attracts many devotees from around the world.

The sanctum sanctorum is relatively small. Devotees pay obeisance and sit outside to listen to *kirtan*.

Guru Hargobind received a rousing welcome when the Sixth Guru visited the town in 1620-21. The subsequent 150 years are lost to history. During the time of rising Sikh power, the young Ranjit Singh made a pilgrimage to Nankana Sahib at age 12, and soon after, he succeeded his father as the head of the Sukerchakia Misl in 1792. He assigned a large *jagir* for the upkeep of the Gurdwara.[112] He would visit the Gurdwara many times, and in 1818 he built the building that exists now, and other historical Gurdwaras in the city.

Although there have been several renovations and improvements, the main building still reflects the essence of the shrine built by Maharaja Ranjit Singh. An imposing Darshani Deori is three storeys high with projected balconies, with the central one having three arches. The *deori* is painted white with embellishments highlighted in blue and gold. Marble is minimally used. At the top of the *deori* are small *chhatris*, and the domes with golden *kalash*, or finial projections. They flank the five-arched main *chhatri* at the centre, topped with a golden *kalash*.

The entrance is through a marble doorway with the words "*Gurdwara Janam Asthan Sri Guru Nanak Dev Ji*" inscribed in black in the Gurmukhi script. The Darshani Deori, like the main Janam Asthan building, dates to the time of Maharaja Ranjit Singh. In time, many additions were made. A panel marks where Diwan Tek Chand, ICS,[113] Commissioner of Gujranwala, laid the first marble stone in 1914.

Directly in front of the Darshani Deori is the main prayer hall of the Janam Asthan Gurdwara. Bhai Gurdas' quote is appropriately inscribed on the entrance: "*Satguru Nanak Pargatia Miti Dhund Jag Chanan Hoya*."[114]

The relatively small building[115] is where Guru Granth Sahib is installed under the same marble *palki* that has been there for centuries. The inner chamber is embellished with richly engraved marble panels decorated with botanical designs, and the central panel has the words "*Ek Onkar, Janam Asthan Guru Nanak Dev Ji*" engraved in bold letters.

112 The estate in the name of Gurdwara Janamasthan Sri Nankana Sahib was 17,765 acres as documented after the Sikh Gurdwara Act 1926.

113 Indian Civil Service.

114 Bhai Gurdas (d. 25 August 1636) was a scholar, chronicler of the Gurus and scribe. Guru Amar Das adopted him. The inscription means: "When Guru Nanak emerged, mist dispelled and (spiritual) light shone through on the world."

115 The SGPC had initiated an expansion project, allocating Rs 200,000 for a langar building and even laying the foundations for a larger facility a few months before the Partition of India that cut off the Gurdwara from the Sikhs, who overwhelmingly migrated to India.

Udasi *mahants*[116] managed most Gurdwaras. While the start was well-intentioned and positive, in time the *mahants*' descendants took over, and the original objectives were diluted, leading to administrative decay. Some individuals' decadence became particularly egregious, like that of Mahant Narain Das at Nankana Sahib. Matters came to a head on 20 February 1921, when his hired Pathan mercenaries fired at 150-200 protesting Sikhs, killing most of them. The snowballing agitation ignited a fervour for reforms in Gurdwaras[117] and the ousting of *mahants*. The Gurdwara was managed by a person from the SGPC even after Partition, and that arrangement lasted till 1965. Nowadays, the Pakistan Gurdwara Parbandhak Committee and local authorities administer the Gurdwara.

As you face the main hall, on the right is Gurdwara Shahid Ganj. This marks where the protesting Sikhs, martyred in 1921, were cremated. The Sikh *sangat* of Delhi gifted a large golden *palki*[118] in 2005, which is kept nearby in a glass enclosure, although it was originally designed for the main Gurdwara. Also seen nearby is the *beri* tree on which Lachman Singh, leader of the protesting Sikhs, was burnt alive after being tied with the tree by the Mahant's mercenaries. The tree is ringed by plaques that describe and depict the horrific act.

The large *sarovar* and the *langar* hall lie a short distance from the inner complex. The Gurdwara has become a centre for Pakistani Sikhs, largely Pashtun, who now run a school and teach their children secular education along with Gurmukhi and scriptures.

Nankana Sahib has, over the years, attracted many Sikhs from other parts of Pakistan, but the number is still only a few hundred families. The most important festival for the Gurdwara is the birth anniversary of Guru Nanak Dev, which draws in Sikhs from all over the world and is celebrated with much fanfare.

116 Religious heads of spiritual institutions, in this instance, Gurdwaras.
117 The agitation led to a series of actions that culminated in the enaction of the Sikh Gurdwaras Act of 1925 to manage historical Gurdwaras
118 Palanquin.

Darshani Deori is three storeys high with projected balconies. Marble is minimally used. At the top are small *chhatris*, and domes, each with its golden *kalash*, or finial projection.

Darbar Sahib Gurdwara

KARTARPUR, PUNJAB, PAKISTAN

HISTORY attracts devotees. At Kartarpur, however, history and geopolitics kept them away. After 1947, Darbar Sahib Gurdwara, Kartarpur, Pakistan, became 'far' for the vast majority of the followers of Guru Nanak in India. However, ever since the two governments created a corridor for Indian Sikhs to visit the Gurdwara in November 2019, it has become an example of how divides can be bridged.

"The Baba (Guru Nanak) came to Kartarpur, cast aside the ascetic robes he wore on his travels, and set up his base there to execute his mission," writes Bhai Gurdas.[119] In the dusk of his life, the Guru called for his parents, Bhai Mehta Kalu and Mata Tripta, his wife Mata Sulakhni and sons Lakhmi Das and Sri Chand, to join him as he settled down as a householder in this area, which now falls in Pakistan, just off the border between India and its neighbour.

Kartarpur thus marks a very significant stage in the life of the founder of Sikhism—the distillation, consolidation, and formalisation of his life's spiritual journey.

In this idyllic setting, he set up a settlement where residents devoted mornings and evenings to spiritual activities. Guru Nanak's followers made a beeline for his abode and would listen to the hymns sung by a *rabab*[120] player. In keeping with his teachings, the Guru expected them to engage in honest labour, necessary for worldly success, during the day. They were blessed by the presence of their Guru, who lived among them, practising what he preached. They led ordinary lives as lay people even as they evolved spiritually. The Guru demonstrated that spirituality did not need ascetic renunciation from the world, rather renunciation while performing worldly tasks and pursuits.

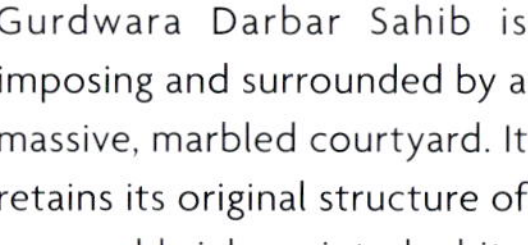

Gurdwara Darbar Sahib is imposing and surrounded by a massive, marbled courtyard. It retains its original structure of exposed bricks painted white. The window arches are plain.

119 A learned scribe and historian. (See footnote on page 161).
120 A stringed bow instrument.

ਸਤਿਨਾਮੁ
ਵਾਹਿਗੁਰੂ

Guru Granth Sahib is installed on the first floor, resplendent in the golden *palki* presented by the Delhi Sikh Gurdwara Management Committee in 2019.

Guru Nanak gave material shape to his teachings by gathering a community of his followers at Kartarpur for the last 18 years or so of his life. His disciples lived together and pursued their worldly duties while behaving ethically in their interactions with others and reciting Gurbani.

The community recited the verses of *Japji* and *Asa di Vaar* in the morning and *Sodhar* and *Aarti* in the evening. They would eat together at the *langar*. Everybody was seated on the ground in rows, irrespective of social status, and everyone contributed with *sewa*, the labour of love. Egalitarianism was thus practised.

The Guru's mother passed away in Kartarpur, as did his father. His sons grew up, and Kartarpur became a popular destination among those travelling while seeking the divine. Among them was Bhai Lehna, who became the Guru's follower. He compiled Guru Nanak's compositions. His devotion and capacity to learn were legendary. After six years, Guru Nanak put his Sikhs and sons to the test and found that the person most worthy of being his successor was Bhai Lehna, whom he anointed as Guru Angad Dev.

Much has changed in the five centuries since Guru Nanak settled down in Kartarpur, which was to become his final resting space. Different structures of the Gurdwara have developed over time. Teli Surat Singh Kamboh undertook a pilgrimage to Kartarpur in 1647, where he met the caretakers of Guru Nanak's *Samadhi* and *Mazar*.[121] Followers of Guru Nanak—Sikh, Hindu and Muslim—continued to venerate their master in their own manner. The damage caused by the floods of 1684 led to a permanent structure being erected by Budh Singh Doda.

Between 1765 and 1787, devotees carried out construction, aided by grants from diverse individuals, including Diwan Nanak Baksh, a minister to the Nawab of Hyderabad, and Raja Chandoo Lal. Let's also look at more recent history: a Hindu devotee, Lala Shyam Das, donated the money to help construct the present building of Darbar Sahib and the residential quarters in 1911-12.[122]

The changing course of the Ravi river and the threat of floods necessitated fortifications. More buildings were constructed in the 1920s with funds provided by Maharaja Bhupinder Singh of Patiala, whose name and contribution figure prominently on a marble plaque at the main entrance. Inside, another plaque proclaims that the foundation stone was laid by Sant Buddha Singh, head of Nirmal Ashram, Rishikesh, on 28 September 1929. Largely ignored since 1947, the Gurdwara received positive attention from the Pakistan government during the past few decades. The complex was renovated and vastly enlarged in 2019.

121 *Sikh Heritage Beyond Borders* by Dalvir Singh Pannu.
122 *Historical Sikh Shrines* by Major Gurmukh Singh.

There is a *mazar* outside the Gurdwara. Muslim devotees of the Guru pay their respects at this monument.

Gurdwara Darbar Sahib retains its original structure of exposed bricks painted white. The arches for windows are plainer and narrower than the more prevalent styles. The interior of the building, too, eschews embellishments. The entrance leads to Angitha Sahib, which marks the cremation spot of Guru Nanak Dev. It has a marble *palki*, covered with *rumalas* and flowers, on a platform. Beyond Angitha Sahib, to a side, are stairs that lead to the first floor where Guru Granth Sahib is installed. The chamber is relatively small, with arched spaces. Guru Granth Sahib is resplendent in the golden *palki* presented by the Delhi Sikh Gurdwara Management Committee in 2019. Through the windows, you see the vast courtyard that can accommodate thousands of pilgrims. The new complex has a *sarovar*, a *langar* hall, and various other buildings. Much effort has been made to provide facilities to international visitors.

What a change! The Partition of India in 1947 left the birthplace of Guru Nanak and many important Sikh Gurdwaras in Pakistan. An ignorant cartographer, selected ironically because of his lack of knowledge about the area, cut off this significant Sikh shrine from the Sikhs. Since it was in Pakistan, like most other Gurdwaras, it fell into a period of neglect. Darbar Sahib in Kartarpur was so close to the India-Pakistan border that people would see it using binoculars from Dera Baba Nanak on the Indian side.

Prime Ministers Atal Bihari Vajpayee and Nawaz Sharif had jointly declared in 1999 that the Kartarpur Corridor would allow visa-free travel for Indian pilgrims. It took 20 years to come to fruition, which was hardly surprising given the geopolitical issues involved. On 9 November 2019, a passage to Pakistan came alive for Indian pilgrims, who were welcomed by Prime Minister Imran Khan.[123] The Gurdwara was no longer 'tantalisingly near and yet so far'. Pilgrims from India could visit it now, and thousands have done so, including former Prime Minister Manmohan Singh and his wife Gursharan Kaur.

Most structures in Kartarpur Sahib are relatively modern, except for the well, which is believed to be 500 years old. The well has the old Persian wheel system intact, which uses a chain of earthen pots to draw up the water, although a tube well is now used for the purpose.

It is held that when Guru Nanak passed on, there was a dispute between his followers about whether he should be cremated following Hindu custom or buried as per Muslim norms. However, when the disciples raised the sheet covering his body, there were only flowers to be found, which were then divided up, and both sides performed the last rites in accordance with their own conventions.

Even as the Kartarpur Corridor remains susceptible to the vicissitudes of India-Pakistan relations, the renovation of the last resting place of the first Sikh Guru has put it back on the map for tourists and devotees alike. Visitors from India who come through the corridor must return by the evening. The Gurdwara, however, is open to others for staying the night.

The austere, white Darbar Sahib stands out against the blue sky, a beacon of hope that transcends the political divide and unites the people on both sides of the border.

123 The day fell on the 30th anniversary of the fall of the Berlin Wall, another man-made barrier that had divided people.

DEVAN ASTHAN

Gurdwara Sri Rori Sahib

EMINABAD, PUNJAB, PAKISTAN

ATURE'S fury, ravages of time, continued neglect and apathy of the local administrators—all contributed to a situation where, in July 2023, the beautiful brick building of Gurdwara Sri Rori Sahib collapsed.

(*Though much of what is described in this chapter is now sadly in the past, we have retained the present tense in its writing, and have chosen to celebrate this Gurdwara for what it once was. The painful realisation of a loss of tangible heritage makes this chapter particularly poignant.* Sangats *need Gurdwaras, just as Gurdwaras need* sangats.)

Distinctive architectural style and history mark Gurdwara Sri Rori Sahib, Eminabad, in Pakistan. The Darshani Deori stands out because of its brilliant brickwork and the fluidity that the architects show mastery over in a difficult medium.

Eminabad, or Saidpur as it was known then, was a major city east of Lahore. It had a nodal position on the trade route between Kabul and Lahore and was thus a flourishing town. Guru Nanak met Bhai Lalo and stayed with him during his first *Udasi*.[124] The incident often narrated is about how the local grandee, Malik Bhago, held a feast to which he invited all spiritual leaders. Learning about Guru Nanak, Malik Bhago extended the invitation to him too. However, the Guru preferred to stay at the home of Bhai Lalo, a poor

The imposing entrance to the Gurdwara was one of the finest examples of carved and moulded brickwork.

124 Long spiritual journey.

In recent years, religious services at the Gurdwara were resumed because of increasing interest among the visiting Sikh pilgrims.

carpenter who lived in the most ordinary manner. Malik Bhago was naturally upset at his invitation being ignored and demanded the Guru's presence. When the Guru arrived, he explained that he preferred to eat the humble fare of a person who earned his bread with honest hard labour, instead of a feast provided for by the sweat of the exploited.

The Guru visited Saidpur many times and was present in 1521 when Mughal Emperor Babur's troops ransacked the town and committed atrocities. The army captured him and many others, but he was soon released because of his evident divinity. Guru Nanak subsequently wrote a moving composition called 'Babur Bani', which decries the atrocities committed during Babur's invasion and enjoins the Lord to have mercy on His poor people.

There are several Gurdwaras in Eminabad, and Rori Sahib is the most prominent. Eminabad came under Sikh rule when Sardar Charhat Singh Sukerchakia occupied it during the 1760s. His grandson, Maharaja Ranjit Singh, is credited with building the Gurdwara's *pukka* structure and assigning a *jagir*, a land grant, for its upkeep.[125] This was the premier Gurdwara in the town. Its central building is a three-storey imposing structure of cut brickwork, which is topped with three *chhatri* like structures covered with a large central *gumbaz* (dome) with smaller *chhatris* (dome-shaped pavilions) on either side. A rectangular hall adjoins it on the left of the entry. A large *sarovar*, surrounded by low walls on two sides, is set askew to the right of the central entry tower. At the complex's rear is a room topped with an exceptionally exquisite ribbed white lotus dome with a circumambulatory *verandah*.

The imposing entrance to the Gurdwara was probably built after the Shiromani Gurdwara Parbandhak Committee took over the management on 28 February 1922. It showcases one of the finest examples of carved and moulded brickwork, baked to a fine shade of red, with Gurmukhi calligraphy standing out in a country where the script has all but vanished. The curvilinear embellishments stand tall, and the decision to leave the bricks exposed enhances their beauty.

125 Iqbal Qaisar in *Historical Sikh Shrines in Pakistan* says: "A large estate worth Rs 5,000 per annum and nine squares of agricultural land was endowed to the Gurdwara from the era of Maharaja Ranjit Singh."

A prominent Pakistani architectural historian, Kamil Khan Mumtaz, described the *deori* as "an architectural fantasy, showing an amazing dexterity with which brickwork has been used to produce plastic and almost sensuous quality. The production of these daring forms, which are based on traditional precedent, has extended the possibility of the use of bricks to a hitherto unknown limit." Such is the sweep and artistry of architectural embellishments that some writers drew parallels with the work of the Spanish architect Antoni Gaudi, a well-known exponent of Catalan Modernism. Here, however, the architecture faithfully retains its traditional underpinnings.

The curvilinear embellishments of gateways stood tall, and the exposed bricks had a unique beauty.

The words "Gurdwara Rori Sahib" stand out in relief, and just above the entrance is the quotation, "*Ret Aak Aahaar Kar Roraa Kee Gur Keea Vichhaiee.*"[126] from Bhai Gurdas' *Vaar* that describes how Guru Nanak obtained the grace of God and, after receiving Naam, wore the robes in the manner of the people he interacted with, embracing poverty also. The turrets and *chhatris* stand out, as do the multiple fluted arches, which are distinctive.

As you enter, you see the main building on the left. It dates to the early 19th century and is smaller than expected; when people gather in large numbers, they tend to sit outside to listen to the *kirtan*.

The Gurdwara complex was a victim of the hate-filled days that followed Partition, when it was damaged and a part burnt by zealots. The SGPC's administrative control ceased after 1947, and the Gurdwara became non-functional and came into a state of disrepair, parts of it crumbling, until the Pakistan government decided in 1993 to build a boundary to prevent encroachments. They also did some repair work.

The celebrations connected with Guru Nanak Dev's 550th birth anniversary in 2019 brought large groups to Gurdwara Rori Sahib. The government made the arrangements, and even filled the *sarovar* that had remained dry for an extended period.

Unfortunately, decades of lack of maintenance took its toll and in July 2023, after a storm, a major part of the Gurdwara came down. Only the back wall and a small portion of a side wall have survived while the dome, the central part, and the whole front have completely collapsed.[127] There is little possibility of this historic shrine of the Sikhs being restored.

126 "He fed himself with sand and milkweed plant; stones were his bedding."
127 As reported in Lahore's *Dawn* newspaper on 18 July 2023.

Gurdwara Nanak Shahi

DHAKA, BANGLADESH

Guru Nanak Dev stayed for an extended period in Dhaka in 1504 during his first *Udasi*, or spiritual journey. Gurdwara Nanak Shahi commemorates his visit, and it is near Dhaka University in Bangladesh. Tradition maintains that the Gurdwara was established during the time of Guru Hargobind by Bhai Natha, a missionary, with the support of local Sikhs. Guru Tegh Bahadur also stayed in Dhaka for an extended period.

The Gurdwara commemorates the visit of Guru Nanak, who stayed in Dhaka for an extended period in 1504, as did Guru Tegh Bahadur.

Details about the Gurdwara's subsequent history are hazy.[128] The Partition of India in 1947, which left Dhaka in then East Pakistan, proved inimical to the development of the Gurdwara in particular, and the Sikh minority in general. The situation deteoriated further during the riots of 1964 and the 1965 Indo-Pakistan war. There was just one Sikh, Bhai Swaran Singh, who looked after the Gurdwara with the help of his Muslim associate, Mohd-ul-Malik Haq. They were both killed when a mob attacked the Gurdwara in 1971, and the premises was walled up.

After the liberation of Bangladesh, Sikh troops, with the help of Capt. Bhag Singh[129] and officials of Takht Sri Harimandir Sahib, Patna, set out to restore the Gurdwaras they could find. The Gurdwara, also known as Ramna Shahi, was found, and Indian troops cleaned up the place and restored it. The Provisional Government's top members, including Bangladesh's acting President Syed Nazrul Islam, Prime Minister Tajuddin Ahmed, and other ministers, attended the special congregation to mark the restoration of *maryada*.

128 Certain documents show the historic building in its present form dates back to the 1830s, when the East India Company administered the region.

129 A World War II veteran, Capt Bhag Singh (1903-1992) who was awarded the MBE, he was the founding editor of the monthly *Sikh Review* (est. 1953), which he edited till ripe old age. After that Saran Singh, IAS (retd) and Partap Singh DIG (retd) took over.

ਗੁਰਦੁਆਰਾ ਨਾਨਕ ਸਾਹੀ
ਢਾਕਾ
গুরুদুয়ারা নানক শাহী
ঢাকা
GURDWARA NANAK SHAHI
DHAKA

Bangabandhu Sheikh Mujibur Rehman, who had been under arrest at the time of the liberation of Bangladesh, came to the Gurdwara at the invitation of Lt General Jagjit Singh Aurora in 1972. This resulted in much goodwill and became an occasion to carry out essential repairs.

Later, extensive renovations were done in 1988-1989 under the leadership of Harbans Singh,[130] with substantial contributions from the Sikh diaspora. A *parkarma* verandah was constructed on all four sides of the original building to protect it from the elements. A research centre and guest house were added in 2006-7.

Since there is a negligible Sikh population in Bangladesh, most of the *sangat* is of local non-Sikh believers and visitors. The impetus, efforts, and funds for most of the improvements for the Gurdwara have come from Sikhs outside the country.

The complex is approached through a large arched gateway with *chhatris* with small domes at the edge and a triple-domed *chhatri* at the centre. As you drive in, you see the building, topped by a large dome embellished with the *khanda-chakkar* symbols. They are all painted white, with the embellishments executed in light blue.

A new building has been constructed, featuring a *langar* hall on the ground floor and a congregation hall on the first floor. Guest rooms have been built adjacent to the congregation hall to accommodate visitors.

The newly built main congregation hall on the first floor is spacious, measuring approximately 30 feet by 30 feet. The raised marble platform[131] is made of white marble and has a marble *palki*—natural light streams in from triangular windows, with a chandelier helping when needed. The biggest gathering is on Fridays.

Various rooms have been added, including those used as guest rooms. Office space has been provided within the premises to serve as the administrative centre for the Gurdwara committee. The garden has a beautiful fountain since 2020, enhancing its aesthetics. While there have been several additions over the years, some features referred to in earlier accounts are missing, including a *sarovar* that was apparently filled up in the 1960s, and a well, which can't be seen now.

The vicissitudes of time resulted in a loss of relics, like historic *Hukamnamas*, and some of the original manuscripts, which were seen by the researcher G. B. Singh in 1945 and Capt. Bhag Singh in 1971. However, Gurdwara Nanak Shahi, Dhaka, still has two historical manuscripts of Guru Granth Sahib. Of these, the Damdami Bir is of historical significance. Another manuscript, called the Sunheri Bir,[132] is richly illuminated.[133]

Guru Tegh Bahadur also visited Dhaka and spent time there. Another Gurdwara in Dhaka, Gurdwara Sangat Tola, is associated with his visit. A pair of *kharavan* (wood sandals) that belonged to Guru Tegh Bahadur is placed in a glass case. These are said to have been handed down through generations. Mata Kanchan Devi[134] was the last custodian, and she gave the *kharavan* to the Gurdwara. The *firman*, or imperial directive issued by Shaista Khan, the Mughal Governor at the time, granting land to Guru Nanak's Home and exempting it from taxes in perpetuity, is also kept at the Gurdwara.

As Bangladesh has no Sikhs, *sewa* is performed by Sikhs from India, who serve for the duration of their visa and are then replaced by the next team. The *sangat* comprises Sikh officials serving in various international organisations, business houses, and local people, both Hindu and Muslim. The *diwan* is held on Fridays and is popular with people in the area and students at the adjacent University of Dhaka.

130 An IAS officer, he headed the International Jute Organisation in Dhaka at the time.

131 It is said that the platform was originally a black stone with the Guru's footprints on it, but it has been lost to time.

132 It is said to be the 10th recension of the original.

133 The Singapore-based Thukral family has financed the conservation efforts for both manuscripts, work on which has been done, in Dhaka, by a Delhi-based conservationist.

134 She was called Sikher Mata, or the mother of the Sikhs.

Guru Nanak Satsang Gurdwara

KUPONDOLE, LALITPUR, KATHMANDU, NEPAL

The Gurdwara was extensively renovated for Guru Nanak's 550th birth anniversary celebrations and has an impressive building.

SIKHS have lived in Nepal for ages, ever since Guru Nanak Dev visited the territory on his way towards Tibet during his Third *Udasi* (1514-1519). In the 19th century came the royal presence of Maharani Jind Kaur. The widow of Maharaja Ranjit Singh was given asylum in Nepal shortly after she arrived in Kathmandu on 29 April 1849. She lived there till 1860. After she left, Sikhs who served in her forces settled near Nepalganj, close to the Indo-Nepal border. Currently, a few serve in the Nepal police and armed police forces.

In modern times, Sikh migration to Nepal is traced back to 1957-58, when the first road of the Nepal Tribhuvan Highway was built from Raxaul (India) to Kathmandu (Nepal). After that, the transportation industry got a new face when Sikhs migrated to Nepal and entered the transport business. Manohar Singh, who joined the water works department in 1931 as an engineer, was among the prominent early immigrant Sikhs in Nepal. His son Hardyal Singh was an engineer with the road department. Dr D.D. Seth, a Punjabi woman, was the gynaecologist to the royal family of Nepal.[135]

135 The Royal Family honoured them with medals and other decorations for their exemplary services and they played a significant role in the acceptance of other Sikh immigrants in Nepal.

GURDWARA
GURU NANAK SATSANG

The *parkash asthan* has a beautiful *palki*, a blend of local and traditional elements.

The community had a significant presence by 1958.[136] With concerted efforts of the *sangat*, led by Ranbir Singh Choudary, Jagir Singh, Pritam Singh, and Man Mohan Singh Sethi, funds were collected to buy land and build Guru Nanak Satsang Gurdwara, Kupondole, Kathmandu. Given his expertise and devotion, Satyapal Sachdeva led the construction effort[137] and served as a Gurdwara office-bearer.

The double-storeyed Gurdwara, which opened at this location in 1999, is inspired by traditional Sikh architecture, with the *chhatris* and the traditional inverted lotus dome at the corner. The white Gurdwara building with arched windows stands out. The central facade has a cantilevered bay window on the first floor covered with dark glass. When you enter, you see the words "Gurdwara Guru Nanak Satsang" in English inscribed at the lower end of this window.

Stairs from the main entrance lead to the lobby and the *darbar* hall, lined with doors with fanlight windows allowing natural light to stream into the room. The *parkash asthan* has a beautiful *palki*, a blend of local and traditional elements.

The Gurdwara also has a *langar* hall where free meals are served to all visitors regardless of religion or background. *Langar* is served every Saturday. The main activities in the Gurdwara are on the weekend. A new guesthouse was built recently. It has 23 rooms with modern facilities. Rooms are also available for visitors.

The Gurdwara was extensively renovated for Guru Nanak's 550th birth anniversary celebrations in 2019. Certain parts were refurbished more recently too. It has become the most significant Gurdwara for the *sangat* of Kathmandu. To commemorate the 400th year of Guru Granth Sahib in 2004, Nepal Rashtra Bank minted a silver coin with a face value of Rs 250. Later, in 2019, three new coins were minted to mark the 550th birth anniversary of Guru Nanak. These coins are legal tender in Nepal.[138]

Besides regular prayers and *kirtan*, the Gurdwara also conducts weddings of Sikhs of Nepal. It is much recognised for its service in providing help during natural disasters and other times of need.

The Gurdwara also provides education to children of the Sikh community in Kathmandu, and actively participates in charitable activities such as supporting disadvantaged communities. Guru Nanak Satsang Gurdwara in Kupondole is the only Gurdwara sustained and governed by the community. Other Gurdwaras in Nepal are taken care of by the government's Guthi Sansthan.

136 With the initiative of Pritam Singh and a few other Sikhs in 1957, a Gurdwara was set up in a small, rented room in the heart of the city, a place known as New Road. In 1965, the Gurdwara was shifted to a place on the banks of Bagmati river called Akhada.

137 He was a prominent construction contractor who had many outstanding buildings to his credit. He was also at one time a member of Raj Parishad, the Upper House, representing the King's Party.

138 They have a face value of Rs 100, Rs 1,000 (silver coins) and Rs 2,500 (silver coins). The local Sikhs note the efforts of the then-Indian Ambassador Manjeev Puri.

(*left*) Antiquity is visible in the building of Prachin Udasi Guru Nanak Math, Balju, which traces its origin to Guru Nanak's visit to Kathmandu during his third *Udasi*.

(*right*) Guru Granth Sahib dominates the sanctum sanctorum, which has pictorial representations of Guru Nanak, Guru Gobind Singh, Baba Sri Chand, and others.

The Prachin Udasin Shri Guru Nanak Muth, near Balaju in Naya Bazaar, is the oldest, and traces its origin to Baba Sri Chand, Guru Nanak's elder son.[139] Maintained as a *dera* by Udasi followers of Baba Sri Chand, the Math has what is said to be the oldest hand-written manuscript of Guru Granth Sahib in Nepal. It follows its own customs, that are distinct from those practised in Gurdwaras. Headed by Mahanta Naiyam Muni Udasi,[140] it faces many challenges, including land encroachment.

Shri Raj Rajeshwori Udasin Nirmal Akhada and Guru Nanak Muth Udasin Bhasmeshwor are both located on the premises of the Pashupati Conservation Area, along with the Thapathali Udasin Muth, Gyaneshwor Udasin Muth and Shobha Bhagwati Udasin Muth in Shobhabhagwati.[141]

The small but vibrant Sikh community in Nepal connects with Gurbani and each other through the congregations and activities at Guru Nanak Satsang Gurdwara, the most important spiritual and cultural centre for the community.

139 He founded the Udasi sect.

140 He is the 31st Udasi of the Muth, appointed by the government of Nepal.

141 Article by Alisha Sijapati in *Kathmandu Post*.

Guru Nanak Darbar

DUBAI, UNITED ARAB EMIRATES

THE FIRST 'official' Gurdwara in the Gulf region, Guru Nanak Darbar, opened on 17 January 2012, fulfilling the spiritual and social need of the Sikhs.[142] It serves over 50,000 devotees living in the United Arab Emirates. The community was given the 12,400-square-foot plot by the government in Jebel Ali, Dubai, along Sheikh Zayed road connecting Dubai to the UAE capital Abu Dhabi. It has built the beautiful three-storeyed edifice at the T-junction of two broad roads.

Modern in the execution of traditions developed over centuries, Guru Nanak Darbar, Dubai, fulfils a long-standing spiritual need of the Sikhs in the UAE.

The historic project began in May 2008, and the foundation stone was laid in June 2010. The culmination of a long desire of the local Sikh *sangat* was a result of dedicated efforts of a team of local Sikhs.[143]

The basic design was conceptualised by Delhi-based Aakar Architects.[144] The project was concretised by the Dubai-based architectural firm Holford Associates, and the interiors were designed by the UK's Richard Adams, who had worked on Sri Guru Singh Sabha Gurdwara in Southall, London.[145]

The corner plot allowed for the provision of two entrances[146] to the Gurdwara, one from each road. Inside, a 54-metre *parkarma* is covered with traditional grill work. A water body flowing along the road frontage echoes the traditional *sarovars* in Gurdwaras of Punjab, including Harmandir Sahib. A shimmering effect created by light reflecting from the water and falling on the building adds to its sublime feel.

142 Till then, the Sikhs had prayed in private homes or temporary accommodations. It took 27 years of effort to get permission to establish the Gurdwara.
143 Dr. Surender Singh Kandhari, a local business person, has been widely credited for his leadership in this project.
144 The architect owner couple, Gurpreet Singh and Sanchita Singh, worked on it.
145 The 100,000-square-foot building cost around US $20 million.
146 One is used for ingress and the other for egress, thereby regulating the flow of traffic.

ਜੋ ਮਾਗਹਿ ਠਾਕੁਰ ਅਪੁਨੇ ਤੇ ਸੋਈ ਸੋਈ
ਤੇ ਜੋ ਬੋਲੈ ਈਹਾ ਊਹਾ ਸਚੁ ਹੋਵੈ ॥

The pillar-less *darbar* hall on the first floor is embellished with 24-carat gold work on the walls and ceilings. It is complemented by intricate paintings and murals depicting scenes from Sikh history.

On entering the Gurdwara, the building's grandeur and attention to detail have an immediate impact. There is a grand staircase to cater to large numbers, with the area magnified by tall windows letting in natural light through stained glass. For senior citizens and the people with health conditions or impairments, elevators have been provided. The ground floor has the reception desk, Gurdwara office, and the *jora ghar*. The dining hall, kitchen, pantry, and storerooms are also located there, as are the public conveniences.

A pillar-less *darbar* hall on the first floor is embellished with 24-carat gold work on the walls and ceilings. It is complemented by intricate paintings and murals depicting scenes from Sikh history, lit up by the traditional fluted arches and stained-glass windows during the day.

At the *parkash asthan*, Guru Granth Sahib is placed on a raised marble platform with a gold-plated *palki*. Beautiful stained-glass windows form the backdrop. Kirtan is performed daily for the thousand or so devotees that come. Fridays, which are public holidays, bring in much larger gatherings, and naturally, on Gurpurbs and other religious occasions, the number is in the tens of thousands.

The main hall has a 7.2-metre-high ceiling, crowned by a dome measuring 18 metres. Created to impress, Italian Murano glass chandeliers add to its charm. The *sangat* sits on the soft lavender carpet that covers the floor. Near the main hall, two rooms have been allocated for holding *akhand path* privately by devotees.

A multi-purpose hall serving up to 3,000 persons is often used for wedding ceremonies. The Gurdwara management has a keen interest in inculcating religious and ethical values in the younger generation. Children are taught Punjabi and *kirtan* on Saturdays. Adults learn correct pronunciation in Gurbani Santhiya classes.

Adequate parking has been provided in three levels of underground facilities that accommodate 140 cars. Guru Nanak Darbar is a big establishment with 35 full-time staff and dozens of volunteers who help when needed.The *langar* hall accommodates about 900 persons at a time; on Fridays, the total number of meals served can cross 10,000, and on Gurpurbs and Baisakhi day, it can well be over 40,000. The kitchen that serves the *langar* is state-of-the-art—besides a dough kneader, it has a chapati-maker that bakes 1,800 rotis an hour. The *langar* is also popular with the locals and is often used for community outreach.

The Gurdwara has taken several initiatives to promote interfaith understanding by hosting events. Jebel Ali Village's 'worship village' has seven churches besides Guru Nanak Darbar and a new Hindu temple. The Gurdwara has hosted office-bearers and priests of other religions at get-togethers that seek to foster greater understanding and communal harmony. It also hosts interfaith *iftars*. Celebrating Baisakhi in 2017, it organised a breakfast diversity event that attracted people from over a hundred nationalities, many dressed in traditional clothes. The Gurdwara earned a Guinness World Award for the event.

Devotees celebrate festivals with great enthusiasm, when extraordinary arrangements are made for the events, erecting special *langar* tents when needed. Eminent *kirtanias* and Sikh scholars are flown in for such events, and then there is the festive look provided by special lighting that highlights the unique architectural features of the Gurdwara.

Modern in the execution of traditions developed over centuries, Guru Nanak Darbar, Dubai, is a shrine that brings solace to Sikhs even as it spreads the message of universal brotherhood that is at the core of the Sikh religion by engaging with other faiths.

Khalsa Diwan Society

MANILA, PHILIPPINES

HE FIRST place where Indian expatriates living in the Philippines prayed together was the Khalsa Diwan Society in the Capital. It is the primary spiritual destination for the Sikh and Sindhi communities. Sikh presence in the Philippines dates back to 1762. They were part of a British expeditionary force of European and Indian soldiers that conquered Manila in the then-Spanish colony of the Philippines. However, that presence was short-lived.

Sikhs have been in the Philippines for a long time, and the Khalsa Diwan Society, Manila, dates to the 1930s.

Sindhi traders established themselves in the Philippines soon after the annexation of Sindh by the British in 1843. Some Punjabis also followed after Maharaja Ranjit Singh's Empire fell in 1849.

In 1902, the British colonial authorities recruited Punjabis from Sangatpur village to build British fortifications and military cantonments[147] in the Philippines. Other Punjabis who followed were "reserve soldiers of the Indian army who served with the Malay Police or Hong Kong Police."[148]

The Gurdwara dates to 1930. The seven subscribers who formed the original Khalsa Diwan Society were: Chanan Singh, Ram Singh, Harnam Singh, Partap Singh, Talok Singh, Inder Singh, and Santa Singh.

147 *Encyclopedia of Indian Diaspora* by Brij Lal, Oxford.
148 Sir Henry Johnson, quoted by Brij Lal.

KHALSA DIWAN
INDIAN SIKH TEMPLE

ਵਾਹਿਗੁਰੂ

Guru Granth Sahib is installed in the *darbar* hall, with a nice carpet, on the first floor.

"On March 6, 1930, a 650-square-metre plot was purchased in Paco District, along Isaac Peral Road, at the cost of £ 13,000. The foundation of the building was laid on January 5, 1932, and the building was completed in record time on April 30, 1932,"[149] says Ajit Singh Raye.[150] The Nishan Sahib was unfurled on 23 July 1933. When the Gurdwara was started, the Punjabi community was tiny, numbering around 100. The numerically and financially stronger Sindhi community (then numbering 400) also contributed to the Gurdwara and was part of the regular congregations for many years. Even now, they make a beeline for the Khalsa Diwan Gurdwara during the celebrations that mark the birth anniversary of Guru Nanak Dev.

The Philippines was a colony of the United States of America till 1946, and the economy was dominated by American companies, which employed many of the local Sikhs. It was also a take-off point for those who emigrated to the US. Netaji Subas Chandra Bose visited Manila in early 1940. In meetings held at the Gurdwara, he raised funds for the Indian freedom struggle. It was following Indian Independence that there was a slow and steady influx of Indian immigrants in the Philippines, which further picked up in the 1990s.

The building of the Gurdwara is functional, rather than ornamental. The main door under the dome dominates the front. As you enter, you see a sign that simply reads "Khalsa Diwan, Indian Sikh Temple". It has lasted a long time and has needed only a few additions since it was built. Some expansion took place in 1992, with a particular focus on the frontage. Minor renovations and additions have been undertaken from time to time.

Guru Granth Sahib is installed in the prayer hall on the first floor. The hall floor is covered with a nice carpet, and the pillars do not have many architectural embellishments. *Langar* hall is in the basement.

Regular prayers are held every day. Sundays attract more devotees, and the number goes up fivefold to around 500. *Puranmashi* is marked with prayers and draws in a good crowd. The Gurdwara also provides refuge to Sikhs in need.

The festivals of Baisakhi, Diwali, and Lohri are observed with special fervour. Guru Nanak Dev's birth anniversary is an occasion for which the Gurdwara organises a *nagar kirtan* and attracts over 2,000 devotees during the day.

The *sangat* has undertaken fund-raising efforts to help people during various natural calamities and provide food, clothing, and other necessities to affected communities. Given its importance among Indian expatriates, the Gurdwara is a destination for all Indian ambassadors. In 2019, Indian President Ram Nath Kovind visited the Gurdwara.

A vast majority of the *sangat*, nearly 99 per cent, is from the Doaba and Malwa belts of Punjab. Ever since they started migrating to the Philippines, Sikhs have found a niche in micro-financing, and are colloquially known as "5-6 Bumbay".[151] In the process, they have weathered various challenges as they seek to make their livelihood. A sizeable number are also shopkeepers. Sikhs and the Sindhi community in Manila form the mainstay of the Gurdwara.

149 'Indian Community in the Philippines' in *Rising India and Indian Communities*.
150 Former Professor and Dean of the Asian Center, University of the Philippines.
151 An informal lending system that charges 20 per cent per month. Thus, if a borrower borrows five pesos, he has to pay six pesos next month.

Central Sikh Temple

SINGAPORE CITY, SINGAPORE

MODERN Gurdwara building, which is also the biggest in Singapore and the oldest such institution, the Central Sikh Temple at Towner Road stands out for many reasons, including its architectural excellence and service to the community.

Sikhs in Singapore date back to 1881 when they formed a contingent of the British Straits Settlements Police Force. The original Sikh immigrants had a small Gurdwara within the police barracks. In time, merchants and others migrated, needing a bigger space. Wassiamull, a Sindhi merchant, headed the committee that raised the funds with which they purchased a large bungalow in 1912. It housed the Gurdwara initially, till community needs triggered a reconstruction in 1921 and resulted in a two-storeyed building. The congregation hall was on the first floor, and the ground floor served other requirements for the welfare and education of the community.

The land being acquired by the government necessitated the move to the new location. The new building is built on a plot of land around 14,000 square feet at 2 Towner Road, at the junction with Serangoon Road. It was inaugurated on Guru Nanak Dev's birth anniversary by then-Singapore President Wee Kim Wee on 16 November 1986. Based on the traditional Gurdwara design, the entrance canopy won the Singapore Institute of Architects Architectural Design Award.

The Central Sikh Temple, Singapore, was founded in 1912. It is now in this award-winning architectural edifice, which has many facilities for devotees and visitors.

CENTRAL SIKH TEMPLE

A white *palki* in a modern design stands out against the red carpet in an acoustically designed *darbar* hall.

The Central Sikh Temple is also known as the Wada Gurdwara and is governed by a board appointed under the Central Sikh Gurdwara Board Act, enacted by the Singapore Parliament. The 25 elected members work within the framework of the rules of the Act. The board also manages another major shrine, the Silat Road Gurdwara. That was also upgraded recently. These are the only two Gurdwaras recognised by the Singapore Government as public temples, differentiated from societies.

The entrance of the Central Sikh Temple is topped by a 42.6-foot (13 metre)-high dome, one of the biggest in Asia. The dome's exterior has white mosaic tiles, which, together with the design, evoke the traditional Gurdwara structures. *Chhatris*, bigger ones at the corners and smaller ones between them, and *jharoka*-like windows add to the classic look. Overall, the exterior uses Sardinian pink granite.

The Central Sikh Temple has the largest *darbar* hall in Singapore, with a water body in front of it. The hall is column-free, air-conditioned, fully carpeted, and is located under the dome, whose interior is white, with grey and gold mosaic. A red carpet leads you to a distinctive *palki* in pristine white. It is a modern design heavily inspired by tradition. In the canopy, the *khanda-chakkar* symbol at the centre is flanked by the words *Sat Nam* and *Wahe Guru*. Traditional motifs seen in Gurdwaras in Punjab heavily influence the intricate design. The sides curve down, which gives a feeling that the top is floating on the three-tiered base.

Particular attention has been paid to acoustics by installing one of the best sound systems, which can relay the *raagi jathas' kirtan* flawlessly. The second floor has enough space for about 500 people to sit.

Droplets of water from fountains reflect light in the inner courtyard, which has a shallow pool with blue mosaic tiles and a golden *khanda-chakkar* symbol. A modern interpretation of a covered *parkarma* edged with arches surrounds it.

The *langar* hall and kitchen are on the first floor, and a sub-basement car park has slots for 50 cars. Next to the building is the seven-storey tower, an annexe, where the community facilities are located. These include a small dormitory, rooms for visitors, residences for priests, a classroom for religious studies, a library and museum dedicated to articles and books related to Sikhism, as well as administrative offices.

Gurpurbs and other significant events for the Sikhs are celebrated with zeal.

The Gurdwara is popular with Singaporeans. It is the favoured venue for the *Anand Karaj* ceremonies of most Sikhs in Singapore. Attendance for such ceremonies is large, and the *darbar* hall is often packed. After the *Anand Karaj* ceremony, the *sangat* partakes of *langar* and then participates in the *doli* ceremony.

A few hundred Sikhs attend the Gurdwara on weekdays, shooting up to two thousand or more on weekends—naturally, special programmes and Gurpurbs see *sangat* in the thousands.

Provision for Punjabi education and *Gurmat sangeet*, together with lectures/classes on Sikh principles, all provide the necessary services to the *sangat*. During the Covid-19 lockdowns, the Central Sikh Temple was the only Sikh place of worship allowed to open, with a strictly controlled attendance, underlining its status as the Wadda Gurdwara.

ੴ
ਸਤਿਨਾ
ਵਾਹਿਗੁਰੂ

Khalsa Diwan Sikh Temple

HONG KONG, SPECIAL ADMINISTRATIVE REGION, CHINA

A NEW Gurdwara building with a history of over a century, the Khalsa Diwan Sikh Temple, Hong Kong SAR, dates to 1901 (officially inaugurated in 1902), when it was built by Sikhs that came with the British. It was rebuilt in the late 1930s[152] but was damaged in the bombing by Japanese planes in World War II. The *sangat* built it again and later extended it in the 1980s. Damage caused by adjoining construction and the increasing number of Sikhs in the congregation triggered the need to demolish and build anew. A five-year renovation project followed. Located in Wan Chai district of Hong Kong, at the junction of Queen's Road East and Stubbs Road, the new 76,000 sq ft Gurdwara opened on 8 November 2022.

The new three-storeyed Gurdwara has a white glass-reinforced concrete exterior, and it stands out because of its unique architecture and century-old heritage.

Sikhs have worked and lived in Hong Kong SAR since the 1840s, brought along by the British Imperial authorities from India. A small Sikh contingent in the British police and army in Hong Kong carved out its own place, and later the numbers were augmented by the China Field Force. The Gurdwara was the first temple for the 700-strong Sikh community. The British government had allotted the land for it, and the *Hongkong Telegraph* of 12 May 1902 described the opening in some detail:

152 The *China Mail* of 14 September 1933 says: "Demolition work has begun on the old Sikh Temple in Gap Road, in preparation for the erection of a new temple which is to be twice the size of the old one.... Since 1902 the temple buildings have been considerably enlarged and improved, and a crematorium was added in 1917." By this time, the Gurdwara was known as Khalsa Diwan.

ੴ
ੴ
ਸਤਿਨਾਮੁ ਵਾਹਿਗੁਰੂ

A raised marble platform with rich inlay work forms the base on which Guru Granth Sahib is ceremonially placed. It rests under a golden canopy with a *chandni* inside it.

"Every credit is due to members of the Sikh and Hindu community of Hongkong for the generous manner in which they have subscribed to the funds for a new temple... yesterday morning, the temple—Sri Guru Singh Sabha, Hongkong—was fittingly inaugurated. A large gathering attended the ceremony and, after meeting at the Central Police Station, marched through Wanchai to the Gap behind Morrison Hill, where the new temple has been erected."[153] Hongkong was spelt as one word until 1923, when it officially became two.

Historically speaking, the Hong Kong Gurdwara played a significant role in the Ghadar Movement (most active between 1913 and 1917) to liberate India from British rule. Some of the important leaders of the movement had arrived in the West on ships via Hong Kong. In 1914, the Gurdwara was host to the Sikhs who boarded the Japanese ship *Komagata Maru* for a journey that became historical because they were not allowed into Canada, where they sought to make new lives.

An estimated 15,000 Sikhs live in Hong Kong. The local community of Sikhs and Sindhi devotees raised HK$230 million for the new Gurdwara and is proud that it has no loans, as donations have taken care of the entire cost. The need for the new Gurdwara arose because of the cracks in the old building that were probably caused by construction and excavation in an adjoining plot. The old building was declared unsafe.

The tall new three-storeyed building has a white glass-reinforced concrete exterior, which stands out because of its unique architecture. The scalloped arches with *jali* work bring in the traditional architectural elements, as do the golden domes that top the building. Many features, including the marble inlay centrepiece of the lobby, have been imported from India.

The ground floor has a library with over 2,000 books, computers, and digital facilities to provide a haven for learning about the heritage of the Sikhs. There are various halls for big functions/congregations, meeting rooms and offices. There is even a bathroom especially to bathe the dead to serve the community. A kindergarten Khalsa School run on the premises is an English-medium school. Activities that keep students engaged include regular Punjabi classes, tutorials, *gatka*, and *kirtan* training. A children's summer camp is a big draw.

153 *Hongkong Telegraph* adds: "Afterwards, a general meeting was held at which there were present Subadar Ikbal Singh, R.A., president of the committee; Jemadar Lal Singh, H.K. Police, vice-president; Lala Sham Das, representing the Hindus on the committee; Seth Wasia Mall, representing the merchants and Sirdar Kehr Singh, representing the watch-men; Bhai Raga Singh, priest; Subadar-Major Sirdar Khan, H.K.R. (who assisted in getting the band); Subadar Teja Singh, former president of the committee, who came from Singapore to take part in the ceremony; Subadar-Major Sri Garjadhar Pershed, 5th Hyderabad Regt.; Subadar Langh, 22nd Bombay Inf. A number of Europeans were also present, including Mr B. Brotherton Harker, the architect."

Naturally, *langar* is a major part of the new Gurdwara, with a spacious hall and a modern kitchen equipped with various automated gadgets.

On the second floor is the spacious main hall that has a blue carpet with a floral pattern. A fixed golden canopy is placed over Guru Granth Sahib instead of the more common four-pillar *palki*. The wall opposite the entrance has a panel with golden engraving and mirror work that forms the backdrop to the Manji Sahib, which is placed on a raised marble platform with rich inlay work in traditional floral designs. Light streams in through windows, and from recessed lighting and the chandeliers.

New arrivals in the city can find refuge for up to two weeks at the Gurdwara in this prime location while they find their feet. Around 300-400 people visit the Gurdwara daily, with the number going up to 2,000 on Sundays; Gurpurbs attract over 5,000.

Sports are encouraged, and the Gurdwara has a proud record of sponsoring the annual Guru Nanak Hockey Tournament for over 50 years. Hong Kong's Hockey Association League teams compete in the tournament.

The Gurdwara also attracts non-Sikh Hong Kong residents who want to know more about the Sikh religion and culture. The management has made special provisions to welcome them, take them to the *langar*, and share information about the Sikh religion with them.

Khalsa Diwan Sikh Temple is the first and only Gurdwara of the Sikhs in Hong Kong, where they have a century of presence. Hong Kong was colonised by the British till it was returned to China in 1997. The Gurdwara serves the estimated 15,000 Sikhs who live in what is now the Special Administrative Region (SAR) of the People's Republic of China. It was fittingly inaugurated in its latest version on the occasion of the birth anniversary of Guru Nanak Dev, which is the biggest festival for the Sikh and Sindhi communities in Hong Kong.

The old Gurdwara building was built by early Sikh settlers in the early 1900s.

Gurdwara Guru Singh Sabha

BANGKOK, THAILAND

THE HISTORY of the Sri Guru Singh Sabha, Bangkok, dates to 1911, and it is located at 565 Chakkraphet Road. It is conveniently close to the shopping district that has Indian commercial establishments and is near the famous Old Siam Complex.

Sikh presence in Thailand goes back to 1902 as indicated by the fact that the Thai government donated a plot of land to the community in 2002 to mark the centenary of Sikh presence in Thailand.[154] The early migrants were from Gujranwala, Sheikhupura and Sialkot districts of pre-Partition Punjab. They found a niche in commerce as sales assistants and peddlers. With their hard work and acumen, over time, they prospered.

Land for the complex was purchased in 1932, and a three-and-a-half-storey building was constructed in less than six months. During World War II, many Sikhs sought shelter in the Gurdwara. Once two bombs fell on the building, though they failed to detonate and no one was injured. However, the structure suffered significant damage and had to be evacuated. It was soon repaired.

The new six-storeyed Gurdwara building has a total constructed area of 1,440 square metres and is widely recognised as one of the most prominent Gurdwaras in Southeast Asia.

154 According to some accounts, Sikhs came to the kingdom of Siam, as Thailand was known, earlier.

Traditional *gumbads* atop the Sri Guru Singh Sabha Bangkok building are visible from a long distance. It stands at a complex that was purchased in 1932.

An increasing number of Sikhs in Thailand triggered a need for a larger building. In 1979, the *sangat* resolved to build a new Gurdwara at the same spot. The project was carried out over two years. When the new six-storeyed (five floors plus a mezzanine floor) Gurdwara building was inaugurated by Panj Piaras, it was widely recognised as one of the most prominent Gurdwaras in South-East Asia, with a total constructed area of 1,440 square metres.

The Gurdwara has three entrances: a three-metre-wide walk through a lane from Chakkraphet Road; an entry from the door facing Italian lane on Chakkraphet Road; and an access via Jindamanee lane.

The ground floor has rooms dedicated to the priest and preachers. The Nanak Mission Sukhshala clinic has served needy patients for over five decades, giving free treatment to all. It is run and sponsored by the Sri Guru Singh Sabha. Audio CDs, religious books, *rumalas*, etc., are sold in another room, and there is a *jora ghar*. A dining hall also serves the religious preachers and pilgrims from abroad staying temporarily at the Gurdwara. The Sri Guru Singh Sabha Committee office is also located in the building, with a small meeting room on the mezzanine floor above it.

The stairwell leading to the *parkash asthan* has 84 steps.[155] Five elevators whisk away the visitors to various floors. There is another lift that leads to the big hall on the second floor that is often used as the *langar* hall. However, it also serves for hosting dinners during weddings or even as a lecture hall. The mezzanine partially covers the area, and the large multipurpose hall is used for meetings and other religious activities. It is considered the third floor.

155 They symbolise the 8.4 million births and deaths before reincarnation.

The *parkash* asthan is in the middle of the Gurdwara with a beautiful golden *palki* on a raised marble platform with golden embellishments.

The *darbar* hall on the fourth floor is about 15x37 metres, with wall-to-wall carpeting. The *parkash asthan* is in the middle of the Gurdwara with a beautiful golden *palki* on a raised marble platform with golden embellishments. Guru Granth Sahib is placed under a golden dome. Beautiful chandeliers illuminate the area, supplemented by the natural light that filters in from two sides through arched windows. The stage for the *ragis* is to the right, and two massive AV screens display the *shabad* as it is rendered.

Religious ceremonies begin daily at 4.30 a.m. with the *parkash* of Guru Granth Sahib and last till around 6.30 p.m. *Langar* is open to all and serves around 450-550 people on weekdays. Many needy local people, including those of Burmese origin, and visitors all sit together to eat.

A Thai Sikh School is on the fifth floor, providing education for children up to kindergarten. While half of the top floor is used as *sukhashan asthan*, the other half is used for various activities by Thai Sikh students.

There are 13 Sri Guru Singh Sabhas in as many cities across Thailand, affiliated with the Sri Guru Singh Sabha, Bangkok. The body also runs two schools.

Sikhs in Thailand are predominantly businessmen, most of who have made their mark in the textile trade. Estimated at around 50,000 strong in Bangkok, they have good relations with the King, the royal family, and the Thai government.

Old-timers proudly recall that when Giani Arjan Singh, Head Granthi of the Gurdwara, passed away in 1993 after 42 years of service, he was honoured with a Royal Salute at his cremation. Many Sikhs have made a name in providing philanthropic services individually, and the Gurdwara has provided medical aid, food, and other assistance to people not only within the premises, but also outside as and when needed.

Sri Guru Nanak Darbar Tatt Khalsa Diwan

KUALA LUMPUR, MALAYSIA

Sri Guru Nanak Darbar Tatt Khalsa Diwan Gurdwara, Selangor, Kuala Lumpur, celebrated its centenary in 2018.

ONE OF Malaysia's oldest and largest Gurdwaras, Sri Guru Nanak Darbar Tatt Khalsa Diwan Gurdwara, Selangor, Kuala Lumpur, celebrated the centenary of its establishment in 2018. The history of the Sikhs in the country goes back to the beginning of the 20th century. A fair number of Sikhs, most of them from the Malwa region in Punjab, lived in the Setapak and Ampang areas in Kuala Lumpur by 1910. The setting was pastoral, as were the occupations, including dairy farming and handling bullock carts.

They built a new Gurdwara in 1918 on a 1.7-acre plot.[156] Subsequently, the community raised a Punjabi School (1924-1998) that had 800 students at its peak. It was the first primary school to be recognised by the government, where education in Gurbani and Punjabi was imparted. Job-oriented technical and electrical courses were also run.

156 The community records the assistance of Captain Graham, Chief Police Officer of Selangor, in obtaining the present site.

GURU NANAK DARBAR TATT KHALSA DIWAN SELANGOR
ਗੁਰੂ ਨਾਨਕ ਦਰਬਾਰ
ਤੱਤ ਖਾਲਸਾ ਦੀਵਾਨ ਸਲੈਂਗੋਰ

A golden *palki* is placed under a golden canopy in the large *darbar* hall of the Gurdwara.

The number of students at the school fell considerably, and in 1994 the old building was demolished, and the construction of a new building started, which was completed in two years. A six-storey complex called Wisma Tatt Khalsa[157] was built towards the back of the building where the Gurdwara is located. Inaugurated on Baisakhi Day in April 1996 in conjunction with the Tercentenary Celebrations of the creation of the Khalsa worldwide, the multi-purpose building served as the Gurdwara while the purpose-built Gurdwara was under construction.

Wisma Tatt Khalsa stands facing Jalan Raja Bot.[158] The ground floor is given out on rent to defray expenses. The second floor houses Sri Dasmesh Private International School (now used by the Sri Guru Nanak Academy, providing free Gurbani classes for beginners and advanced learners). On the first floor is a large air-conditioned multi-purpose hall that can accommodate 800 persons. The community uses this to hold celebrations such as birthdays, anniversaries, engagements, and wedding receptions. *Malaya Samachar Press*, the only Punjabi newspaper in Malaysia, is housed on the second floor, as is the office of the Tatt Khalsa Diwan and a reference library. The third and fourth floors have accommodation for residents and visiting *ragis* and *kirtan jathas*. It is also a halfway home for the Indian diaspora awaiting documentation from the Indian High Commission in Malaysia or immigration clearance before returning to India.

Work on Sri Guru Nanak Darbar Tatt Khalsa Diwan, Selangor, the new Gurdwara, started with the ground-breaking ceremony on 14 April 1999, with Giani Bachittar Singh[159] laying the foundation stone. Binarancang Chartered Architects and Town Planners, Kuala Lumpur, worked on recreating the architecture of the period of Guru Arjun Dev, and it is striking in its non-contemporary period looks, even as it melds with the local architecture. A soft opening of the new Guru Nanak Darbar was held on 10 April 2002. Pritam Kaur[160] officiated this ceremony.

The 8,000-square-metre Gurdwara building has four towers that mark each corner. Each tower has a dome, as does the main building, where the central dome reflects the Sikh architectural norms best exemplified by Harmandir Sahib. It is covered with a golden mosaic and is topped with a pinnacle, or the *kalash*, with a delicate *chhatri* at the top.

157 Tatt Khalsa Complex.
158 Raja Bot Road.
159 Giani Bachittar Singh, originally of Bhai ka Bhagta village, served Tatt Khalsa Diwan Gurdwara for 30 years till his retirement in 1991. He was then designated Head Granthi and stayed in the Gurdwara, guiding others, till he passed on in 2021.
160 Ranjit Singh Kaleke, her late husband, had played a significant role in the Gurdwara management.

The oldest manuscript of Guru Granth Sahib in the Gurdwara is installed in a distinct location.

Around 100 vehicles can be parked in the basement. A massive painting of the Harmandir Sahib complex, including Akal Takht, dominates the entrance of the ground floor. Near it is the entrance to the large *langar* hall and the kitchen.

The *darbar* hall is on the first floor and can accommodate around 1,500 people. It has 10 bay windows, and valances of bright fabrics are used extensively. Nishan Sahibs are placed along the walls at regular distances. The *parkash asthan* is marked by a marble platform surrounded by a low brass railing. The eye is drawn towards the arresting, elaborately carved golden *palki*. A lovely dome brings in light.

Tatt Khalsa Diwan, Selangor, was prominent in publishing literature on Sikhism and also promoting the religion. From producing pamphlets to publishing the *Khalsa Malaya Darpan*, a Punjabi newspaper, it served the community by keeping the Gurmukhi script and literature alive in the inter-war years. It organised the first *granthi* training course and Sikh Sammelan in 1955 and invited Professor Taran Singh[161] to speak to the participants. *Malaya Samachar*, a tabloid in Punjabi, has been published from there since 1984.

While *path* and *kirtan* are performed daily at the Gurdwara, the gathering on Sunday is more extensive than on weekdays. On Thursdays, a *naujawan satsang* is held in the evening, and an *istri satsang* programme in the afternoon.

With a commitment to tradition and an eye on the future, Guru Nanak Darbar Tatt Khalsa Gurdwara and its management committee continue to serve the community through various religious, social, and educational endeavours.

During Covid-19 pandemic, the Gurdwara provided free meals and provisions to those in need. It is the biggest Gurdwara in South-East Asia.

161 Prof Taran Singh (1922-1981) was a scholar and teacher of Sikh studies.

ਤੂੰ ਮੇਰਾ ਰਾਖਾ ਸਭਨੀ ਥਾਈ

Europe

Sikhs have lived in the UK since the dawn of the British Empire. Maharaja Duleep Singh is considered the first major Sikh resident in Britain; in time, other Sikh Maharajas, their aides, students, and occasional visitors formed the seed community in the UK. The first Gurdwara was established in 1908.

The movement from India was relatively free until the passage of the British Nationality Act in 1948. Later, Sikhs arrived in large numbers in the 1960s as workers and professionals, with many bringing their families along.

Continental Europe, too, had a Sikh presence, again with royal families and their aides being the earliest. Maharaja Duleep Singh died in Paris in 1893. Sikh soldiers of the 15th Sikh Regiment arrived in Marseille, France, in September 1914; Sikh soldiers fought in France and Belgium in World War I.

Most returned to India after the war, except for those who had laid down their lives fighting. In World War II, Sikhs fought in Italy and Greece with great distinction. Many a War Memorial marks the sacrifice of these soldiers.

Migration in significant numbers to the UK happened in the post-World War II period when the British needed workers. British Commonwealth subjects from Tanzania, Uganda, and other East African countries also took refuge in the UK in the 1960s after the political atmosphere in Africa became hostile towards them. Given its historical ties, the UK has the second-largest population of Sikhs outside India and the largest in Europe.

Countries in Continental Europe had a token Sikh presence after the end of World War II, but most were transient visitors. Some students settled down after their studies, but their numbers were relatively small. Sikhs who had to leave Africa and, later, Afghanistan, also found a home in European nations and settled there. A more significant number of migrants were seen in the 1970s and 1980s.

Gurdwaras were established wherever they settled, and today there are vibrant Sikh communities in most Continental European countries, with a significant presence in Italy, Spain, Germany, France, the Netherlands, Belgium, Austria, and Switzerland.

NORWAY
UNITED KINGDOM
FRANCE
SWITZERLAND
ITALY
Europe

The Central Gurdwara

LONDON, UNITED KINGDOM

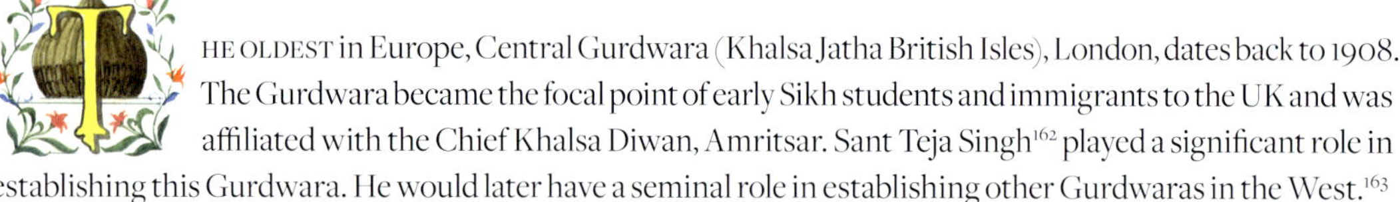

THE OLDEST in Europe, Central Gurdwara (Khalsa Jatha British Isles), London, dates back to 1908. The Gurdwara became the focal point of early Sikh students and immigrants to the UK and was affiliated with the Chief Khalsa Diwan, Amritsar. Sant Teja Singh[162] played a significant role in establishing this Gurdwara. He would later have a seminal role in establishing other Gurdwaras in the West.[163]

The oldest Gurdwara in Europe, Khalsa Jatha British Isles, London, dates to 1908. It was recently renovated.

Maharaja Bhupinder Singh of Patiala helped financially in getting a house in 1911 in Putney, South London, that served as the Gurdwara premises for two years. The building in Putney was named the Maharaja Bhupinder Singh Dharamsala, and it served as Gurdwara as well as a refuge for needy immigrants. Two years later, Sant Teja Singh identified a new place, 79 Sinclair Road, Shepherd Bush, London, and again, with the Maharaja's help, acquired it on a long lease.

162 Sant Teja Singh (1877–1965) was one of the five students sent by Sant Attar Singh of Mastuana Sahib to study in the UK and to provide religious guidance to the growing number of Sikhs who had moved there in the mid-19th century. He was the first turbaned Sikh to be allowed to enrol at the University of Cambridge.

163 These include Khalsa Diwan Society Abbotsford, BC, Canada, and Gurdwara Sahib Stockton, CA, USA.

ਧੰਨੁ ਸੁ ਤੇਰਾ ਥਾਨ ਹੈ ਸਚੁ ਤੇਰਾ ਪੈਸਕਾਰਿਆ ॥
ੴ
ੴ

The recently renovated *darbar* hall is aesthetically appointed. It has a white *palki*, illuminated by a large chandelier.

Among those in the Gurdwara's *sangat* at the time were Maharaja Bhupinder Singh, Bhai Kahn Singh Nabha, Princess Sophia Duleep Singh, and Hardit Singh Malik[164] and his brother Teja Singh Malik. The *dharamsala* became a home away from home for Sikhs travelling to far-off places like the USA and Canada; it welcomed Sikh students and, several times, provided a base for revolutionaries on their way to India to participate in various agitations.

By the 1930s, many women had joined the congregation and taken up duties at the Gurdwara. From 1932, Asa Singh Grewal, formerly of the British Indian Army, served the Gurdwara full time till his death in 1968. The Gurdwara led Sikh activities that took place in the city at the time. These included outreach programmes wherein the Gurdwara hosted events, including tea, at various fora and presented the Sikh point of view. A particular part of the *sangat* comprised non-Sikh English people.

For 63 years, it stood as the main rallying point for the community in London and attracted many people who stayed there, including the revolutionary Udham Singh. It became a forum that raised funds for community causes in the UK and social causes in Punjab. When the lease to the three-storeyed building expired, new premises were needed. Thus came the move to purchase Norland Castle, a building on Queensdale Road, London,[165] where the Gurdwara now stands.

The building comprised a *langar* hall and kitchen at the basement level, the main *divan* hall on the ground floor, and a first-floor gallery. Since then, various managements have done renovations and additions, including buying nearby buildings to provide more accommodation and services. The Gurdwara has hosted many top Sikh leaders who visited London. The collection of tape-recorded *kirtan* by the Gurdwara is worthy of special mention.

Soon after it came into existence, Khalsa Jatha started sending volunteers to arriving ships to guide newcomers to the Gurdwara, where they found food and lodging. Keeping up its tradition of hospitality, it continues to provide temporary accommodation to students and visitors.

164 He was President of Khalsa Jatha. He studied at Oxford, was a pilot in the Royal Air Force, and was Indian Ambassador to France.
165 The Gurdwara moved there in 1969 after extensive work and rebuilding.

The old building in Putney was used for the Gurdwara since 1911 for many years. The building was called Maharaja Bhupinder Singh Dharamsala.

Around 2016, there was a need to renew the building since it had fallen into a state of disrepair. An initiative led by British businessman Peter Virdee raised funds and undertook an extensive refurbishment that touched virtually every part of the Gurdwara.

This renovation initiative involved many volunteers, and because of their efforts, the Gurdwara shines. The massive chandelier in the *darbar* hall illuminates a beautiful room with white walls and a white *palki*; no wonder the Gurdwara has been a venue for both making and screening films.

Since its inception, the Central Gurdwara has been at the forefront of providing help whenever and wherever needed. To cite two examples, it became a rallying point for the community when a massive fire broke out on 14 June 2017 in a nearby apartment block. It was prompt in providing help to the affected, even as the building was being refurbished. During the Covid-19 pandemic, in May 2021, the Gurdwara and the Virdee Foundation distributed hundreds of clinical grade oxygen concentrators to facilities treating patients in Punjab, India.

Community outreach programmes have been integral to the interaction of the Sikhs with Londoners, and these continue till date, including guided visits for schoolchildren. The *langar* is popular with local people and students. The Gurdwara holds regular classes in *kirtan* and *gatka*. It faces parking issues, although it is near a subway station.

The oldest Gurdwara in Europe has a history that makes it part of the heritage of the Sikhs in the UK.

Sri Guru Singh Sabha

SOUTHALL, LONDON, UNITED KINGDOM

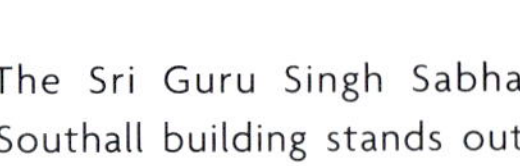

The Sri Guru Singh Sabha Southall building stands out with an imposing golden dome and white domelets.

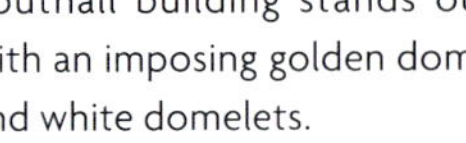

LEADING Gurdwara in the UK, Sri Guru Singh Sabha, Guru Nanak Road, earlier known as Havelock Road, in Southall, was inaugurated by then HRH Prince of Wales Prince Charles (now King Charles III) on 30 March 2003, although the history of the Gurdwara dates back to the 1950s.

Sikhs started settling in Southall in the 1940s.[166] Initially, individuals' homes were used as Gurdwaras, but the population growth demanded a large building. Sikhs got together and formed the Sri Guru Singh Sabha, Southall, in 1964, which led to the opening of the first Gurdwara, which also became the headquarters of the Sabha. East-African Sikhs migrated to Britain in large numbers in the mid-1960s.[167]

The selected site in Southall Green was originally a dairy, which was transformed with volunteer work into a house of worship within weeks. Maharaja Yadavindra Singh of Patiala visited the newly purchased site in 1965, and he exhorted the *sangat* to "let the Gurdwara's Nishan Sahib (flag) be visible from London's Heathrow Airport." The Nishan Sahib near the entrance of the Gurdwara is, indeed, its prominent feature.

166 The Khalsa Jatha: British Isles Gurdwara, established in 1911, was the only Gurdwara in London till then. The "Shepherds Bush" Gurdwara, also known as Bhupinder Dharmsala, served as a temporary refuge and was an essential part of the lives of the Sikhs in Britain.

167 They held British passports and therefore were entitled to settle in Britain, the Commonwealth Immigrants Act (1962) notwithstanding.

A golden *palki* stands atop a raised carved marble platform at the *parkash asthan*.

On 27 January 1967, marking the 300th birth anniversary of Guru Gobind Singh, the Gurdwara was inaugurated by Sant Syed Prithipal Singh of Patiala.[168] The first *granthis* at the Gurdwara were Bhai Mal Singh, Giani Khem Singh, and Giani Gurdeep Singh. In the coming decades, it would attract many scholars, *ragis*, and *katha vachaks* from India and around the world. The social life of many Sikhs in London revolved around the Gurdwara and the *sangat* there.

The new Havelock Gurdwara was designed by Architects Co-Partnerships Ltd and commissioned in 1998. The building work on the £17m project, which has won acclaim for its architecture, started on Baisakhi Day in 1999 and took three years to complete. While construction was going on, the *sangat* met at the refurbished Park Avenue Gurdwara.

The building covers a total area of 6,000 square metres. The *darbar* hall is on the first floor and can seat up to 2,000 people at a time, and the gallery can accommodate more for meditation or listening to Gurbani. There is also a community centre, an extensive library, and a teaching room. The multi-use hall is also utilised when the numbers are too large, for example, during Gurpurbs, weddings, and other ceremonial occasions. It can accommodate up to 800 people. At the *langar* hall, over 20,000 meals are served on Gurpurbs and other significant gatherings.

While the imposing golden dome and white domelets make it stand out from afar, the beautifully lit interior of the *darbar* hall, with natural light streaming in, makes for a fascinating interior. Various architectural elements, such as ribbed arches, highlight the visual appeal of the ceiling, and the hall itself leads to the *parkash asthan*, where the golden *palki* stands atop a raised carved marble platform. A large stained-glass window forms the backdrop. It has the *khanda-chakkar* motifs and those with geometrical and botanical patterns. Stained glass has been extensively used throughout the building, channelling light and highlighting various areas.

168 The only son of Pir Muzafar Hussain of Mirpur, Kashmir, he converted to Sikhism in Lahore in 1935, as did his family. He died in 1969 while visiting Kanpur.

A large stained-glass window forms an arresting backdrop.

The *langar* hall, too, is attractively appointed. *Langar* is served daily from 7 am to 9 pm, attracting both Sikhs and non-Sikhs. The kitchen is modern, with gadgets that are expected in this day and age.

The road in front of the Gurdwara was renamed Guru Nanak Road in 2021 before Guru Nanak's 551st birth anniversary was celebrated. Thus, Havelock Road between King Street and Merrick Road reflects the name of the founder of the Sikh religion instead of Major-General Sir Henry Havelock, a British general.[169] There is parking facility in the basement for about 100 cars, and space for more across the street.

The Gurdwara organises a Sikh studies course, Punjabi classes for adults, and school visits where schoolchildren are introduced to Sikh cultural practices. It is a licence holder of the Duke of Edinburgh scheme, in which many children have participated. A programme focused on women is called Kaur Connect. A community clinic provides legal, medical, and well-being advice and essential treatment. The football club is often the focus of the youth. The Gurdwara also supports *gatka*, wrestling, netball, MMA, and boxing.

A *nagar kirtan* procession was held for the first time in 1967 when it attracted 7,000 participants. The Gurdwara has been at the forefront of organising these processions every year. The organisation ensured that turbans and other Sikh practices were allowed at work and social places from the 1970s.

The organisation runs the Khalsa VA Primary School. It is a voluntary aided school for boys and girls aged 3 to 11. Located at Norwood Hall, Tentelow Lane, Southall, it opened on 1 September 2009 and moved to its new purpose-built building a year later. It has become one of the better schools in the borough and provides a much-needed education to Sikh students in a safe environment.

Sri Guru Singh Sabha in Southall with its Gurdwaras at two nearby locations—Havelock Road and Park Avenue—a school, and some other properties, is Europe's largest organisation and has provided spiritual and cultural guidance to immigrant Sikhs for generations.

169 He played a significant role in the Anglo-Sikh wars and later in the British Imperial response to the Indian Revolt in 1857.

Gurdwara Singh Sabha Culte Sikh France

BOBIGNY, PARIS, FRANCE

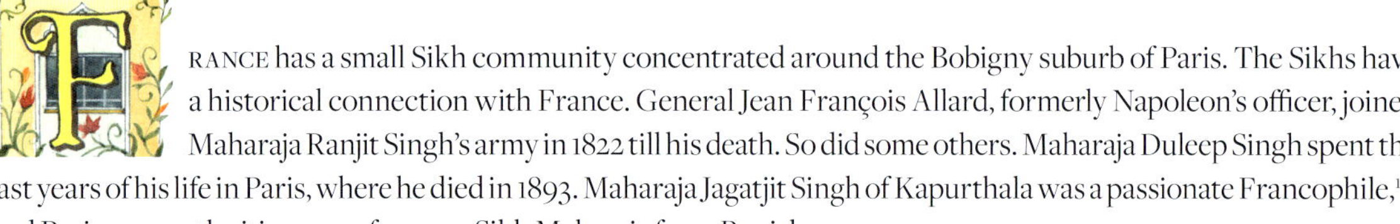

France has a small Sikh community concentrated around the Bobigny suburb of Paris. The Sikhs have a historical connection with France. General Jean François Allard, formerly Napoleon's officer, joined Maharaja Ranjit Singh's army in 1822 till his death. So did some others. Maharaja Duleep Singh spent the last years of his life in Paris, where he died in 1893. Maharaja Jagatjit Singh of Kapurthala was a passionate Francophile,[170] and Paris was on the itinerary of many a Sikh Maharaja from Punjab.

The first brick of Gurdwara Singh Sabha Culte Sikh France was laid by Jathedar Joginder Singh Vedanti, then Jathedar of Akal Takht, in 2004.

The Sikhs came to France in significant numbers as troops that fought for the Allies in World War I.[171] They were welcomed as liberators, and some decided to make France their home. The first Indian Ambassador to France was the decorated World War I hero and pilot Hardit Singh Malik.[172] Another significant influx was in the 1980s, more so after 1984.

Sikh immigrants would meet at various places, in a room of a church, in the apartment of a Sikh which had space, and, later, at a yoga studio. The need for a Gurdwara was acute. In the mid-1990s, the *sangat* purchased a building on Rue de la Ferme

170 The Maharaja (1872-1949) spoke French and Spanish fluently. The French language, culture and aesthetics captivated him, and the Palace of Versailles inspired his palace in Kapurthala.

171 Some 20 per cent of the Indian troops (138,000 as per the UK Parliament motion record) that fought in Belgium and France in World War I were Sikh. The monument erected at Neuve-Chapelle recognises those who laid down their lives in battles that decimated many Sikh regiments.

172 He served as Ambassador from 1949 to 1954 and was awarded Grand Officer of the Legion of Honour by the French Government. He wore his turban while flying for the Royal Flying Corps and later for the RAF in World War I. A helmet that fitted over his turban was also specially designed for him.

GURDWARA SINGH SABHA
FRANCE
CULTE SIKH

ਸਤਿਗੁਰ ਨਾਨਕ ਪ੍ਰਗਟਿਆ ਮਿਟੀ ਧੁੰਧੁ ਜਗਿ ਚਾਨਣੁ ਹੋਆ ॥
Gurdwara Singh Sabha France Culte Sikh
16-20 Rue De La Ferme,
Fax: +33 148 32 5469

The interior of the *darbar* hall has been done up in the classic vein, with the *parkash asthan* at the far end of the hall.

for the Gurdwara, where they held regular *diwans*. In time, two adjoining ones were also purchased. When they had three buildings, they decided to build a larger Gurdwara by combining the plots of these buildings.

The first brick of Gurdwara Singh Sabha Culte Sikh France was laid by Jathedar Joginder Singh Vedanti, then Jathedar of Akal Takht, in 2004, in the presence of 3,000 Sikhs gathered from various towns of France and other parts of the world.

The new two-storeyed Gurdwara with a basement and underground parking took shape with the efforts of the *sangat*. Kartar Singh and David Bonga's architectural expertise was engaged, and they incorporated Sikh symbolism in the design. The architects executed the three domes atop the Gurdwara building to symbolise the three cardinal principles of the Sikh way of life—*naam japna*, *kirt karna* and *wand chhakna*.[173] They have also built three *deoris*. The large double-storeyed entrance with scalloped arches gives access to the religious area of the Gurdwara (the *darbar* and *langar* halls); the second, smaller one provides access to the underground car park; and the third access to the library and the administrative area of the Gurdwara, which opened to the *sangat* in 2011, on Baisakhi Day, in the presence of an estimated 8,000 persons.

Seeing the scalloped arches and domes framing a building in Paris is an arresting sight, and there are plans afoot to make more architectural changes that will bring in more traditional elements seen in Gurdwaras of Punjab. This is likely to be a complex process that will require approval by local municipal authorities.

The interior of the *darbar* hall has been done up in the classic vein, with the *parkash asthan* at the far end of the hall—natural light streams through a row of large windows near the roof. Although there are Sikh households around the Gurdwara, and they attend the daily *darbar*s, Sundays are when the larger gathering of around 3,000 persons takes place. The Gurdwara has provisions to house visiting *ragi jathas* and some visitors. *Langar* is served daily.

The rigid interpretation of the laws on laïcité (the French principle of separation between the State and religious institutions) had some unhappy consequences when, in 2004, visible symbols of religious identity were banned in public schools in France. This included turbans and Muslim headscarves. The law was zealously enforced. Sikhs had to remove turbans to renew passports and documents such as driving licences and identity cards. Although irritants remain, the government has, in recent years, asserted that "practical solutions have been found to reconcile their religious practice with the principles of the French Republic."[174]

Sikhs in France are small in number, but they are a visible minority and have made themselves more so since the 2004 laws. The Baisakhi *nagar kirtan* organised by the Gurdwara is a significant event in the cultural calendar of Paris. In 2017, "The Baisakhi of the Sikhs in Bobigny" was declared an "Intangible Cultural Heritage" by the French Government's Ministry of Culture. The annual feature attracts thousands of participants. Police figures put their number at 10,000 in 2023.

The Gurdwara facilitates a two-week Gurmat camp every summer and winter. There are Sunday Punjabi and Gurmat classes for children (3 to 15 years). Kirtan classes are also held every Sunday, and a *kirtan darbar* is held on Wednesday night. Saturday is when French is taught to the *sangat*.

The Gurdwara maintains a library where all are welcome. Like other Gurdwaras, it has an open-door policy. Since 2014, it has collaborated with the Seine-Saint-Denis Tourist Office and other departments to organise trips for non-Sikhs to inform them about the Sikhs and their culture.

173 Simply speaking, they are: Meditating and remembering God's name, working and earning through honest labour and dealings, and sharing with others.

174 The quote is from a statement from the French Embassy in India. "Outside the premises of public schools, wearing the Sikh turban is very much allowed in public space, contrary to the allegations of certain radical organisations. Only the *burkha* is banned in public places, for obvious security reasons," it says.

Gurdwara Singh Sabha

NOVELLARA, REGGIO EMILIA, ROMAGNA, ITALY

ITALIANS played a prominent role in the court of Maharaja Ranjit Singh, and over 5,000 Sikhs lost their lives in Italy in World War I. Maharaja Yadavindra Singh became Indian Ambassador to Italy in 1965. However, immigration to this tip of Europe in significant numbers is a recent phenomenon. In the middle of the Padana Valley, in the Reggio Emilia province, is Gurdwara Singh Sabha, the largest in Italy. Novellara is a little township of about 14,000 inhabitants. The area is mainly pastoral, and the Sikh immigrants have made a name in the region's dairy farming industry, famous worldwide for its Parmigiano Reggiano cheese.

Unlike some urban centres, the local authorities have been welcoming towards the immigrants who have come in increasing numbers since the 1980s. The former President of the European Union, Romano Prodi, was present at the inauguration of the Gurdwara in 2000. It marked the culmination of a long struggle to establish the community and create a common area where everyone could pray. The Gurdwara is a popular venue for weddings and other ceremonies, and it invites *parcharaks* and *ragi jathas* to perform on a regular basis.

The main building is two storeys and has a modern kitchen and a big *langar* hall on the ground floor, and the *darbar* hall is on the first floor. It was inaugurated in 2000.

GURDWARA SINGH SABHA NOVELLARA
TEMPIO SIKH
SATNAM
ਸਤਿਨਾਮੁ
WAHEGURU

ਸਤਿਨਾਮੁ
ਵਾਹਿਗੁਰੂ
ASS. GURDWA
SINGH SABH

The 1,250-square-metre *darbar* hall has the *palki*, with the words *Satnam Waheguru* written prominently in black on a white background, along with graphics representing the *khanda* and the bowl of *Amrit*.

The Gurdwara is located on the outskirts of the city. The community bought 17 acres of land and built the two-storeyed Gurdwara based on a plan by an Australian architect. You enter the premises through a vine-covered arch, and as you look up, you see the tall Nishan Sahib on the side and the main building with the five-arched entrance that reflects the traditional design. Several *khanda-chakkar* emblems in steel are seen on the roof, shining against the sky.

The main building is two storeys and has a modern kitchen and a big *langar* hall on the ground floor, and the *darbar* hall is on the first floor. The 1,250 square metre *darbar* hall can accommodate at least 1,500 people at a time. The *palki* has the words *Satnam Waheguru* prominently in black on a white background, along with graphics representing the *khanda* and the bowl of *Amrit*.

Another building has recently been built, again with a kitchen and a hall on the ground floor and a large hall on the first floor. This is used for community events like weddings and *bhog*s, and also for such occasions when the number of people exceeds the capacity of the main hall.

The Baisakhi parade, organised by the Gurdwara, is a high-visibility event that draws in a crowd of thousands from various parts of Italy and other countries in Europe. The parade starts from the Gurdwara and goes through the historic centre of Novellara. A glass enclosure for the *palki* and Guru Granth Sahib, a large motorcade, thousands of participants, *gatka* demonstrations, and the inevitable food for all mark the occasion, which attracts a large number of local people, and also local, regional and national political leaders.

Immigrants benefit from the services provided by the municipality of Novellara, aimed at facilitating their integration with the local people.[175] In this part of Italy, Sikhs are often seen as ideal immigrants—filling the gap left by retiring local dairy workers—hard-working and family-oriented.

The Gurdwara holds *diwans* every day, and *langar* is also served daily. The Gurdwara has some rooms for short-term stay of devotees. Resident staff members perform the daily duties, but as with all other Gurdwaras, the volunteers shoulder most of the responsibility.

The evening *diwan* draws in around 200 persons, while the *sangat* goes up to 2,000 on Sundays and as much as 5,000 on Gurpurbs and other important occasions.

Of course, the Baisakhi parade, organised by what is considered the largest and the oldest purpose-built Gurdwara in Europe, draws in a huge crowd, one that exceeded 20,000 in 2023.

Italy has the largest number of Sikh immigrants in the European Union. With land, climate and pastoral lifestyle, this area brings back recollections of Punjab to those who have sought to make their lives anew. The Gurdwara is at the centre of their social and spiritual life.

As immigration patterns changed and family reunification allowed more and more women to join the menfolk who had immigrated earlier, the community now reflects a more wholesome picture. Sunday classes are held for children to learn *kirtan*, *gatka*, and the Punjabi language. During vacations, special effort is devoted to teaching children about their cultural and religious background.

175 They include learning the local language and getting acquainted with civic services and instructions on how to get the "Permesso di Soggiorno per Soggiornanti di Lungo Periodo", the permit to stay for a long time.

Shri Guru Nanak Niwas

LIER, DRAMMEN, NORWAY

Gurdwara Shri Guru Nanak Niwas in Lier, on the outskirts of Drammen, was founded in 1991.

THE STRONG desire among expatriate Sikhs in Norway to keep their heritage alive compelled them to open the first Gurdwara in Oslo in 1983, where 150-200 Sikhs would congregate on weekends.[176] Drammen is around 40 km from Oslo. As the number of Sikhs living in Drammen grew, they wanted their own Gurdwara.

Gurdwara Shri Guru Nanak Niwas in Lier, on the outskirts of Drammen, was founded in 1991. The main Gurdwaras in Norway are thus relatively near each other in Oslo and Drammen. They coordinate with each other so that major festivals are celebrated on different days by these Gurdwaras to enable the *sangat* to attend both events.

Initially located in a small house, the Drammen Gurdwara was enlarged when the community bought an adjoining plot. Before the new Gurdwara building came up, the Sikhs had to deal with hurdles that came in various forms, including municipal challenges and raising funds. However, today Shri Guru Nanak Niwas Gurdwara is identified as a significant institution for a community that numbers far fewer[177] than the number of Sikhs in many other countries in Europe.

176 *Sikhs in Europe: Migration, Identities and Representations* by Kristina Myrvold. Routledge.
177 In 2023, the government registered fewer than 5,000 Sikhs.

SRI GURU NANAK NIWAS
GURDWARA

ਵਿਣੁ ਬੋਲਿਆ ਸਭੁ ਕਿਛੁ ਜਾਣਦਾ ਕਿਸੁ ਆਗੈ ਕੀਚੈ ਅਰਦਾਸਿ ॥
ਸ੍ਰੀ ਅੰਮ੍ਰਿਤਸਰ ਸਾਹਿਬ
ੴ

The *darbar* hall is well appointed, and a framed impression of Harmandir Sahib forms the backdrop for the *palki*.

The new Gurdwara was inaugurated on 11 April 2011. The imposing building cost an estimated 3 million euros, and it serves more than a thousand Sikhs who live in the vicinity. The distinctive Nishan Sahib and domes serve as visual identifiers that also make the building stand out. The Gurdwara has four entrances that signify that it is open to all.

The *sangat* engaged a local Norwegian building contractor to construct it. He brought in an architect, and the plans were reviewed and finalised by the *sangat*. The building is approved for up to 500 visitors and has large and spacious halls. The *diwan* hall is the largest, and there is a well-appointed room for *sukhasan*. Like in many urban Gurdwaras in India, there is a large screen on which devotees can read the transcription of *kirtan*, as it is sung, in Gurmukhi, its transliteration in English, and an English translation. *Langar* can be served in two halls, and a full-fledged kitchen is used to prepare the food.

The Gurdwara also has a conference facility, which can be used for interfaith dialogue and student visits. There are also classrooms, offices, washrooms, etc. The Gurdwara has parking facilities, but Sunday gatherings and special events stretch them. The green area around the building is used for children's outdoor activities during Sikh camps.

Local rules do not allow for the overnight stay of anyone in the main building. Therefore, a separate accommodation is earmarked for the ragi *jatha* to live in. There are daily *diwans* in the morning and evening.

The Gurdwara draws in an estimated 50 Sikhs on weekdays, and there is light *langar* of tea, milk, and snacks for them and other visitors. Traditional *langar* is served on Sundays when the number of devotees ranges from 200 to 500. The numbers swell during seasonal visits of *kathavachaks* and even more so for special *diwans* on Gurpurbs when more than 500 devotees are to be seen. The Gurdwara is also a popular place to celebrate life events such as birthdays and weddings, or other important occasions such as *bhog* for the recently departed.

Turbandagen, or Turban Day, is organised on Baisakhi Day in Oslo. Non-Sikh Norwegians are introduced to turbans and invited to wear them.

Children's education, Gurmat sangeet training and Gurbani recitation are among the religious activities carried out at the Gurdwara: voluntary *sewadars* and the *ragi jathas* pitch in to help the younger generations. *Gatka* training is sometimes conducted by visiting experts.

Community outreach is emphasised, and visits of non-Sikh Norwegians are organised. The Gurdwara participates in the annual Baisakhi parade in Oslo. Various banners in Norwegian inform the public about the Sikh religion and people, who are few in number even as they are a visible minority.

Introducing the Sikh heritage to the younger generations has been a significant motivator in encouraging Punjabi classes, and this endeavour by the Gurmat Naujovan Sabha began in 2005. By 2010, the body was named Unge Sikher, and it has become the primary body for younger Sikhs to meet each other and learn more about their religion.

Turbandagen, or "Turban Day", has also been organised on Baisakhi Day since 2010 in Oslo. At this event, non-Sikh Norwegians are introduced to turbans and invited to wear them. This vibrant symbol of Sikh identity has found a positive response and has attracted many people.

A major issue that affected Sikhs of Norway was the Norwegian government's requirement, since 2014, that the new passport and national identity card show visible ears in the photo, like in France. The rule naturally created problems since, typically, the turban covers the ears. It took six years, but on 1 October 2020, the government announced the change in regulations in favour of the Sikhs.

In a country where they encounter a language and culture very different from what they are used to in Punjab, the immigrants find the Gurdwara a refuge. In this Punjabi oasis, they can speak in their mother tongue and find comfort in the religious practices of their forefathers.

SPIKERSUPPA
13 APRIL 2019 KL 12

Gurdwara Sahib Switzerland

LANGENTHAL, BERN, SWITZERLAND

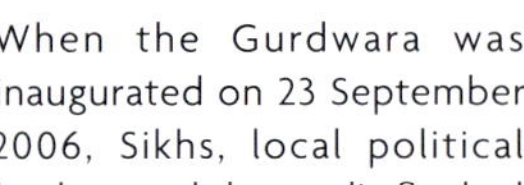

When the Gurdwara was inaugurated on 23 September 2006, Sikhs, local political leaders, and the media flocked to it.

HE TRADITIONAL architecture of the Gurdwara in Langenthal, Switzerland, makes it distinctive. The tall Nishan Sahib and the white building with *gumbads* and *chhatris* give a touch of 'home' to the *sangat*, and it benefits from being around an hour's drive from Zurich, Bern, and Basel—towns with a significant Sikh population. The local Sikhs selected the location because it was central to the various areas where Sikh families lived.

Langenthal, located in an agricultural zone, is also known for its porcelain ware factories, some of which are near the Gurdwara building. The white building with golden tips in the sky stands out in the industrial area outside the city. Traditional designs from Punjab inspired the architect Bernhard Bieri. While the building was being constructed, artisans were brought in from India to help with the project, which started with 730 square metres of land being donated by Dharam Singh and Karam Kaur in 1996. The couple, who owned a business, had migrated from Bhanguani village, near Hoshairpur, India, to Switzerland, and their son Ranjit Singh Mafuta played a significant role in the building's construction.

The local Mayor, Hans-Jürg Käiser,[178] was very sympathetic to the project and helped the community, but it still took years to receive the required permissions. The Gurdwara has a 16-metre-high dome, the first Gurdwara in Europe with traditional Sikh architecture and the look and feel of Gurdwaras in the Indian subcontinent.

178 He would later hold other important federal positions and head the Swiss army.

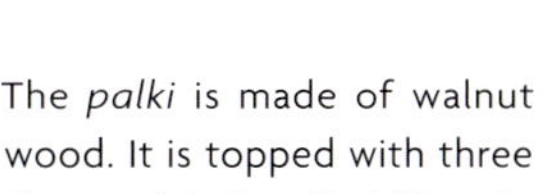

The *palki* is made of walnut wood. It is topped with three domes. A bejewelled *khanda-chakkar* adorns the *palki*.

Given the small number of Sikhs in Switzerland, the challenges of integration into a society where they are visibly different took time. The local administration's cooperation, and the local *sangat*'s determination to have their Gurdwara finally bore fruit.[179]

The foundation stone was laid on 11 January 2001. Prominent people at the ceremony included Singh Sahib Prof. Darshan Singh, Giani Pritam Singh, Mayor Hans Jürg Käiser, and Bhai Harjinder Singh. Construction started in right earnest on 25 October 2002. Even as the work progressed, there were many hiccups, both financial and issues related to local administration, that had to be overcome. However, the community persevered, built bridges with local businesses involved in the construction, and garnered support from the residents.

When the Gurdwara was inaugurated on 23 September 2006, Sikhs flocked to it, as did the local political leaders and the media. The wide coverage that it attracted proved to be a boon for the local Sikhs, and it raised their profile in a country where they are few.

The magnificence of the building of the Langenthal Gurdwara is for all to see. However, it is not the oldest in Switzerland. The Daniken Gurdwara came up in 2002 near the Gogsen nuclear plant. There are other Gurdwaras, too, many of them in rented buildings.

The main hall of Langenthal Gurdwara is on the first floor, where the *parkash asthan* of Guru Granth Sahib is. It is an expansive room, with natural light streaming in from the sides. It is 15 x 11 metres and easily accommodates the *sangat* for functions that attract a larger audience.

The red carpeted floor contrasts with the white walls, and as you enter, you see a *palki* made of walnut wood, topped with three domes, the more prominent in the middle and the smaller ones on the side. The *palki* was created in Punjab and is richly carved, with Gurbani inscriptions on all sides. A bejewelled *khanda-chakkar* adorns the *palki*. Large steel *khanda-chakkar* and *Ek Onkar* symbols are placed before Guru Granth Sahib.

179 The Swiss people voted against constructing a minaret near a new mosque during the same period.

The Gurdwara has precious manuscripts, including a *Jap Sahib Gutka* signed by Bhai Daya Singh.

The *Sach Khand*, where Guru Granth Sahib is reverentially placed at night, is on the second floor. It is under the dome, and the walls and ceiling are lined with richly carved panels of Himalayan deodar wood. Beautiful *chinar* leaves dominate the motifs and point to the origin of the panels—Kashmir.

The *Sach Khand* also houses precious treasures of the Gurdwara. There is the *Jap Sahib Gutka*, signed by Bhai Daya Singh.[180] It mentions the names of two of Guru Gobind Singh's sons.[181] Karam Kaur got it from a Muslim family in Pakistan, and even though she offered a substantial sum for it, the family eventually gifted it to her. The Gurdwara also possesses another manuscript from the same period.

The Gurdwara annually holds two big and two smaller Gurmat camps for children. Sunday classes attract around 40 students where Gurmat and Punjabi are taught.

Stress is laid on maintaining and improving community relations. *Nagar kirtan*s have been organised, and the Gurdwara is a popular venue for various visitors, especially school and university students. Annual interfaith conferences have been held in the Gurdwara. The main attendance is on Sundays. For the convenience of working Sikhs and others, all Gurpurbs are celebrated on the corresponding weekends. Every year, two or three weddings are performed, and the Gurdwara is an attractive venue for Sikhs from other countries such as Russia, Romania, and France.

There are not many Sikhs in Switzerland, estimated at 600 in 2023. However, they experience a sense of pride when they look up at the tall Nishan Sahib and their distinctive Gurdwara stands out for its architecture and devotion.

180 The first of the five *Piaras* initiated into the Khalsa fold by Guru Gobind Singh on Baisakhi Day at Anandpur Sahib.

181 The relic was "piously" repaired at the University of Bern and dated to the Mughal period.

North America

Sikh immigration in North America can be traced to the early 1900s, with Canada and the USA receiving a few thousand immigrants.

In Canada, by 1912, they had established Gurdwaras in British Columbia—in Golden, Vancouver and Abbotsford. The first Gurdwara in the USA was in Stockton, California. The same year, a scholarship for six Indian students to the University of Berkeley was established by Sikhs prominently involved with the Stockton Gurdwara. Rising xenophobia, however, created impediments for the immigrants for many years until, eventually, immigration became easier because of changing needs and the political atmosphere.

Today, Canada has the largest population of Sikhs outside India, and the USA has the third largest. Sikhs in Canada have a prominent political presence, and several of them have been Cabinet ministers. In the USA, they have made their mark professionally as scientists, engineers, doctors, and academics, rather than politically.

Sikhs worked on the transcontinental railroad link in Panama. They also worked on the Panama Canal from 1890 to 1914. After the canal was built, many found employment in various American ventures in the area, while others set up small businesses. A small and vibrant community with its Gurdwara is extant in Panama. Sikh migration to Argentina and Chile is old, but the numbers are small.

CANADA
UNITED STATES
PANAMA
North America

Gur Sikh Temple

ABBOTSFORD, BRITISH COLUMBIA, CANADA

NATIONAL monument of Canada, Gur Sikh Temple in Abbotsford, British Columbia, is a testament to the pride, vision, strength, and resilience of the Sikh pioneers who braved prejudice and hardship to build what has become the oldest existing Sikh place of prayer in Canada.

Sikhs first moved to Canada around 1902, and about 50 Sikh pioneers toiled at Abbotsford Lumber Company, owned by the Trethewey brothers. They collected donated lumber to make their place of worship over three years. They would climb up a hill to the one-acre plot at the top bought by Sunder Singh Thandi and Arjan Singh under the aegis of the Khalsa Diwan Society. Other Sikh farmers and loggers in the area also pitched in.

The Gurdwara opened in 1911 and was officially inaugurated in 1912 in the presence of Sant Teja Singh, who had studied at Columbia University, New York, and Harvard University, Boston. He played a prominent leadership role for Sikh pioneers in the UK, Canada and the USA. Sikhs and non-Sikhs from many parts of Canada attended a grand ceremony.

Gur Sikh Temple is a national monument of Canada. It is a testament to the pride, vision, strength, and resilience of the Sikh pioneers who built what is the oldest existing Sikh place of prayer in Canada.

GUR SIKH TEMPLE
FOUNDED IN 1911
GUR SIKH TEMPLE
FOUNDED 1911

ੴ
ਸਤਿਨਾਮੁ
ਵਾਹਿਗੁਰੂ

The *parkash* of Guru Granth Sahib is on the first floor, whereas the ground floor is devoted to a museum.

Reflecting the architecture of the time and place, it was a simple rectangular building with a wood frame construction clad in wood siding with a gabled roof. An upper *verandah* runs on three sides. While the exterior styling melded with that of typical Canadian frontier town buildings of the time, the interior was a functional Gurdwara, with a kitchen and a *langar* hall on the ground floor and a prayer hall, with the *parkash* of Guru Granth Sahib on the first floor.

The sign displayed at the entrance proclaimed: "No person under the influence of liquor or using tobacco will be allowed in temple". However, it was open to all others and gave significant assistance, including board and lodging, to new immigrants. It provided invaluable support for Indians, primarily Sikhs, who were on the Japanese ship Komagata Maru, with 376 hopeful immigrants who were not allowed to disembark in Canada in 1914.

Overwhelmingly, the pioneers were men, more so since wives and children of immigrants from India were not allowed into Canada until 1918. It was only three years later that the arrival of the first wives of Sikh immigrants was recorded.

The Sikhs fashioned a 70-foot tree trunk into a flagpole for the Nishan Sahib by the end of that year. The Khalsa Diwan Society, Abbotsford, became the spiritual and community hub for new immigrants. It led the community as it faced various challenges, including seeking to restore its right to vote, something that took 40 years, till 1947.

The initial decades were tough, but the kinship of these immigrants helped them face the challenges and discrimination that inevitably came their way.

The original building was expanded at the rear in 1932 by extending the prayer hall. Further expansion took place in the late 1960s.

Sucha Singh Thandi donated land to build another Gurdwara to accommodate the community's growing needs. He was a nephew of the man who had bought the lot for the original site. Sunder Singh Thandi's wife, Mohinder Kaur, played a significant role in the Khalsa Diwan Society, which built the new, larger building that was completed in 1983 and is called the Khalsa Diwan Society. It manages the Sikh Temple.

Gur Sikh Temple was designated a National Historic Site by Canadian Prime Minister Jean Chretien on 31 July 2002. Realising the historical importance of the heritage building, a project to renovate it on the original frame began in 2002 and concluded in 2007.

In 2011, the ground floor became the first Sikh Canadian Heritage Museum, which preserves early Sikh heritage history and accounts of individuals who constituted the community. The government of British Columbia declared it a Provincial Historical Site in 2017.

A tableau of statues in the front yard depicts the famous episode of Bhai Kanhaiya, a celebrated Sikh of Guru Gobind Singh, who served water to all wounded, even those of the enemy. When his compatriots called him out, he said he saw only the faces of those in need, not their allegiances. It beautifully sums up the ethos of *sewa*, for which Sikhs are known and for which Gurdwaras become pivotal. Also seen are the statues of Sikh soldiers in red regalia strategically placed in the garden.

Abbotsford has indeed provided a unique confluence of history and continuing heritage by preserving the site of spiritual solace of the early immigrants in Canada. A modern and much more spacious Khalsa Diwan Society Gurdwara across the road now caters to the needs of the growing number of Sikh families in the region. The old and the new indeed come together in Abbotsford.

Khalsa Diwan Society

VANCOUVER, BRITISH COLUMBIA, CANADA

NE OF the oldest Gurdwaras in Canada is not so old. The present building in South Vancouver is the second one. The Khalsa Diwan Society came into being on 22 July 1906 and was registered on 13 March 1909. The first Gurdwara was built in 1908 at 1866 West 2nd Avenue in the Kitsilano neighbourhood. It served the few thousand Sikhs living in British Columbia then. The Sikhs engaged the architect William Henry Archer to design a wood frame Gurdwara that echoed the style of the surrounding buildings. However, it stood out with the Nishan Sahib at the centre of the roof and a mosaic of Guru Nanak on the gable.

As a community centre, it had a secular role and hosted people of all denominations from India. Besides religious gatherings, it was the hub of cultural and social activities of the community. It was also where the Ghadar Movement took ground, as did resistance to discriminatory immigration policies in Canada then and the demand for the right to vote.

A plaque installed in 2016 at the original site reads: "Built in 1908 by the Khalsa Diwan Society, the Second Avenue Gurdwara was the first Sikh Temple in North America. It was the centre for spiritual, political, social, and economic life for Indians of all faiths. It was at the forefront of social justice campaigns for immigration reform and regaining the right to vote in 1947. The nearby blocks were home to many in the community and close to the False Creek sawmills where they worked. Sold in 1970, after many years of fundraising to build the Ross Street Temple, the 2nd Avenue Gurdwara lives on in the stories of the community pioneers."

Khalsa Diwan Society Gurdwara was built to be "modern enough to fit in with the surrounding area and appeal to young Sikhs while keeping traditional aspects for elders."

KHALSA DIWAN SOCIETY
VANCOUVER

The golden *palki*, resting on a white marble platform, dominates the *darbar* hall, reflecting light from an enormous chandelier.

To fulfil the growing community's needs, the society bought 2.75 acres of city land in 1968 and built a new Gurdwara. Arthur Charles Erickson, a legendary Canadian architect, and his partner Geoffrey Massey created a unique building with an "inverted lotus" dome that, while being modern, reflected the centuries-old tradition of the faith. Indeed, his brief had been to design a Gurdwara "modern enough to fit in with the surrounding area and appeal to young Sikhs while keeping traditional aspects for elders."

The modernistic two-storey concrete building has a square floor plan with three progressively smaller cubes rotated at an angle of 45 degrees placed above. At the top is the dome fashioned out of stainless-steel bands echoing the shape and design of traditional Gurdwara domes. Circular skylights puncture the smaller cubes, visible from the main hall of the Gurdwara.

The gateway to the Gurdwara complex echoes the dome, with two stainless steel bands joining in the shape of arch-like palms stylistically joined in the traditional Indian greeting gesture. A tall Nishan Sahib dominates the skyline.

The Gurdwara was completed in 1970 and opened on Baisakhi Day to accolades from the community and architectural circles. It is generally called Ross Street Gurdwara, after one of the streets that it intersects. The street leading to the Gurdwara is now called Khalsa Diwan Road.

A steel and glass pavilion frames the entrance to the main hall. Inside the hall, light streams from the skylights, adding a playful touch to the cubistic boundaries of the architecture. The enormous circular chandelier dominates the aesthetic of the hall, immediately drawing the eye towards the *parkash asthan*.

While the hall has a patterned soft blue and gold carpet, in the centre runs a golden carpet that leads to a golden *palki*, resting on a white marble platform, in which Guru Granth Sahib is installed. An interior passage around the upper floor of the main hall allows the devotees to circumambulate Guru Granth Sahib without exposing themselves to the elements. This passage has balconies on the east, west and north sides, from where the congregation and the *palki* are visible. Light gold-touched parapets reflect a warm hue.

A representation of the old building of the Gurdwara.

Part of the past is preserved in the form of the mosaic of Guru Nanak from the old site that has been reinstalled. The Gurdwara building has a *langar* hall, a kitchen, some accommodation for the staff, and an area for administrative work.

In time, a community centre, planned initially, was added to the compound. The Guru Nanak Resource Centre features a library, Komagata Maru Museum, Senior Centre, Community Support Services, and a bridal room. The community celebrates Gurpurbs and other significant events on the Sikh calendar with great fervour. Weddings and *bhogs* are significant events for individuals and are held there.

Visits of distinguished Indians, including Rabindranath Tagore and India's first Prime Minister Jawaharlal Nehru, to the old building affirmed its importance. The same tradition continued as Indian Prime Minister Narendra Modi and then Canadian Prime Minister Stephen Harper came to the new building in 2015. The management had spent over two million dollars making various improvements to the Gurdwara.

A year later, on 26 August 2016, the main Gurdwara building was severely damaged in a fire. The Gurdwara continued to hold regular services and ceremonies using an adjacent building and a tent. After extensive renovation and restoration, it was reopened on 18 November 2018. Political issues have become divisive occasionally, but the common spirit that binds the Sikhs to their Gurdwara has tided over most differences. The support it provided to immigrants for over a century has forged strong bonds in the community.

The activities at the Gurdwara, including the teaching of Gurmukhi and Gurbani, keep the bond with the younger generations alive, and thus fulfil the mandate given to the architect who designed a new building while keeping alive the traditions and architectural grammar of one of the oldest Gurdwaras in Canada.

SIKH TEMPLE

Ontario Khalsa Darbar

MISSISSAUGA, ONTARIO, CANADA

What was originally a small farmhouse is now the Ontario Khalsa Darbar, which is considered the largest Gurdwara in Canada.

HAT IS now the largest Gurdwara in Canada started small with a farmhouse, built on less than two acres of land, which was bought in 1973.[182] The Gurdwara is located at the intersection of Dixie Road and Derry Road in Mississauga, and it is now in a 40-acre area, owned and run by Ontario Khalsa Darbar Inc.

The first Gurdwara in the region was opened in Ontario in a small house at 269 Pape Avenue in Toronto.[183] Before this Gurdwara, Sikhs used to gather on the weekends alternately at the homes of relatives and friends to conduct *path*, *kirtan* and *ardas*.

In Mississauga, the community started holding weekly *diwans* in a rented gym hall of Malton Public School on Sundays. By 1973, there were around 25-30 families around the area of Mississauga and Brampton municipalities, and although the funds were tight, they pitched in to buy the land with a small building on it from a farmer named Vincent Marino for $1,06,000.[184] The area was zoned as "agricultural," and had to be changed to "institutional" for it to function and grow as a Gurdwara, which took considerable time and effort, more so since Dixie Road had to be widened.[185]

182 The governing constitution was registered with the Province of Ontario, Canada, on 5 October 1976.
183 Not only was the Gurdwara 50 km from Mississauga (Malton), but parking was also an issue since only street parking was available.
184 Monthly payments of $800 were made to Marino, and the funds came mainly from the trustees—Mohinder Singh (Galt, Ontario), Avtar Singh Bhogal (Brampton), Rawal Singh (Fiji Wale), Surjeet Singh Kohli, and Jai Singh Minhas. After the Ontario Khalsa Darbar was incorporated on 15 October 1976, the trust was dissolved, and the property was transferred in the name of the Corporation on 15 December 1976.
185 Dalip Singh, a retired Indian Army officer, played a significant role in sorting out these issues.

ਓਨਟਾਰੀਓ ਖਾਲਸਾ ਦਰਬਾਰ
ONTARIO KHALSA DARBAR

ਧੰਨੁ ਧੰਨੁ ਧੰਨੁ ਜਨੁ ਆਇਆ ॥ ਜਿਸੁ ਪ੍ਰਸਾਦਿ ਸਭੁ ਜਗਤੁ ਤਰਾਇਆ ॥

When the *parkash* of Guru Granth Sahib took place for the first time on 23 September 1978 in the living room of the farmhouse on Dixie Road, the *sangat* could have hardly imagined that one day it would be this beautiful *darbar* hall.

The *parkash* of Guru Granth Sahib for the first time at the site took place on 23 September 1978, in the living room at the farmhouse on Dixie Road. The community was small, and financial constraints necessitated intervention from better-off individuals.[186] The situation improved with time. Designed by Dharam Malik, a Harvard-educated Canadian architect, a temporary building was constructed on the left of the original farmhouse.

The foundation of a 25,000 sq ft building was laid on 10 April 1982 and inaugurated on 25 June 1989. The Gurdwara building, designed by Hardial Dhir Architects, provided the base for further expansion as needs of the community grew. More land was purchased in adjoining areas.[187] Two years later, the foundation for building an extension was laid. This added approximately another 1,10,000 sq. ft to the built-up area. The 135-foot-high Nishan Sahib was erected in 1998.

The main hall is approached by going up a flight of steps. It houses a silver *palki* and a raised stage on the left for the *ragi jathas* to perform *kirtan*. The hall has been constructed in such a manner that it is usually partitioned into many prayer halls, but on festivals and Gurpurbs, it is opened out to accommodate the large number of devotees. Directly behind the *palki*, there is a partition for Hall No. 2, and again a partition for Hall No. 3 and No. 4 (a large prayer hall is on the third floor, directly above the gymnasium hall).

The large *langar* hall is in the basement. A huge modern kitchen is situated in a corner. The offices and washrooms are along the west side on the first, second and third floors. There are rooms for *ragi jathas* along the east and west sides. On the third floor in the southwest corner is a beautiful *sach khand* room. A new elevator was installed recently to take people from the ground floor to the second and third floors.

The Gurdwara has a massive car park on the west side, which can accommodate around 5,000 vehicles. On the other side, there is a large area with grass, which has grounds for games such as soccer and basketball. For indoor games, there is the huge gymnasium hall.

186 On average, the donations were about $30-$35 each week, whereas the rent for the hall was $100, and the mortgage was $800.
187 In 1993, 25 acres for $2.5 million; in 1995, 11.5 acres for $2.3 million; and later 0.5 acres for $0.5 million were purchased. That adds up to 39 acres purchased for a total cost of $ 5.5 million.

Kiratpur Park has been established to provide for the ashes of the deceased to be immersed in flowing water in a solemn setting for performing the last rites.

The Etobicoke Creek, with year-round running water, is next to the sports ground, and this is where Kiratpur Park has been established to provide for the ashes of the deceased to be submersed in flowing water. The park provides a solemn setting for performing the rites.

Keeping the youth in mind, the Gurdwara supports activities such as the soccer league, field hockey, basketball, *kabaddi*, *gatka*, karate, and gymnastics.

A multimedia museum provides information about Sikh heritage, while community activities include blood donation clinics and police training for young aspirants. The Newcomer Information Centre helps students and recent immigrants to Canada. A youth camp is organised in the summer for young Sikhs, and there are seminars to alert them about societal dangers like drug abuse. Religious activities such as Gurmat *parchar* and *katha* are held regularly, and Amrit Sanchar twice a year.

Classes are held for teaching Punjabi, *kirtan*, harmonium, and the *tabla*, as well as subjects such as science, English, and maths to help young students.

Every year *nagar kirtan* is organised in Toronto in collaboration with all Gurdwaras in the Greater Toronto Area and neighbouring cities and towns under the banner of the Ontario Sikh Council, in which about 30,000 Sikhs participate.

Vincent Marino would never have imagined in 1973 that his simple farmhouse would one day be a gleaming white building and form the nucleus of an institution that would transform the area around it and become a hub of Sikh activities in the Greater Toronto region.

Sikh Temple

STOCKTON, CALIFORNIA, UNITED STATES OF AMERICA

The first Gurdwara in the USA is now a historic landmark and has a storied past. It established educational scholarships, was the cradle of the Ghadar Party, and much more.

HE FIRST Gurdwara in the USA came up in Stockton, California. Established by the Pacific Coast Khalsa Diwan Society in 1912, it quickly became the religious, social, and cultural hub of Punjabis in particular, and Indian immigrants in general, who were largely on the West Coast.

The official plaque reads: "Sikh Temple, 1915 and 1929: The First Sikhs came to California from India's Punjab Region in 1899. The Pacific Coast Khalsa Diwan was formed in 1911 near Stockton. The first Sikh Temple ever built in the US was completed on this site on 21 November 1915, and it is now the library. The second temple of Byzantine Revival style was dedicated on 7 January 1930. This Gurdwara is the oldest centre of Sikh worship and culture in the country. —Stockton Historic Landmark No. 50 Designated by Stockton City Council 2004."

Jawala Singh[188] and Wasakha Singh[189] are considered co-founders, and they served as the Granthis of the Gurdwara. After many trials and tribulations, they arrived in America and bought a 500-acre farm a few years later. Small congregations were held for fellow immigrants at this farm in San Joaquin Valley, a few miles from Stockton, before the Gurdwara came up.[190]

---

188 Jawala Singh (1866-1938) left Thathian village in 1905 and reached San Francisco in 1908. In 1913, he became Vice-President of the Ghadar Party. On party direction, he led a group of revolutionaries arrested on arrival at Calcutta on 29 October 1914. He was sentenced to life imprisonment. After release in 1933, he devoted himself to issues of farmers.

189 Wasakha Singh (1877-1957) of Dadehar village in Amritsar district, was a Granthi in the British Indian Army before he resigned and went to San Francisco. He was on the executive committee of the Ghadar Party. He, too, went to India and was detained in Madras on 7 January 1915. He was imprisoned many times and even sent to the notorious Andaman Islands prison. Released in 1920 due to poor health, he remained an activist who led a *jatha* in the Guru ka Bagh Morcha. In 1934, he became Jathedar of Akal Takht.

190 "Before World War II/India's Independence, the temple served Sikhs, Muslims, Hindus, and the Catholic wives and American-born children of the Punjabi pioneers," says UC Davis in its Pioneering Punjabis Digital Archive.

SIKH TEMPLE

ਜੋ ਮਾਗਹਿ ਠਾਕੁਰ ਅਪੁਨੇ ਤੇ ਸੋਈ ਸੋਈ ਦੇਵੈ ॥
ੴ
ਗਦਰੀ ਬਾਬਿਆਂ ਦਾ ਇਤਿਹਾਸਿਕ ਅਸਥਾਨ
ਗੁਰਦੁਆਰਾ ਸਾਹਿਬ ਸਟਾਕਟਨ
ਕੈਲੀਫੋਰਨੀਆ

In the *darbar* hall, the first *pauri* of *Japji Sahib* is inscribed in Gurmukhi, along with its English translation. *Kirtan darbars* are regularly held.

From these meetings came the idea of forming the society, which, with Sant Teja Singh as its president, purchased the land in Stockton in 1912 and built the Gurdwara by 1915, further expanding it in 1929. At that time, the number of Sikhs in the region was small, and most were engaged in agricultural activities. The Gurdwara became their spiritual and social hub.

Showing remarkable prescience and realising the value of education, in 1912, the Pacific Coast Khalsa Diwan Society established the Guru Govind (sic) Singh Sahib Educational Scholarships for five Indian students to join the University of Berkeley. They were open to "all properly qualified Indian ladies and gentlemen, without distinction of race, caste or creed."[191]

Daleep Singh Saund, the only Sikh recipient, would serve the Gurdwara as a Granthi and also Secretary. Later, he taught, became a California judge, and the first Asian to be a member of the House of Representatives in the USA.

The Ghadar movement arose from the Gurdwara, which stands in the same place as the original one. Jawala Singh became vice-president, and it received significant financial support from him personally and from the *sangat*.[192] The Holtville farm of Jawala Singh and Wasakha Singh became a training ground for young revolutionaries. They eventually donated it to the Gadhar Party.

Ghadar newspaper, in Punjabi, was printed at the Stockton Gurdwara, and even now, the printing machine[193] has been kept in the old building, which is called Ghadri Babbe Memorial Hall. A picture gallery showcases the visual history of the Gurdwara and the Ghadar movement, which are intertwined. In the early pictures, we see the rich diversity of the diaspora, with people of various socio-economic levels gathering. Men wore traditional kurta-pyjamas or three-piece suits; ladies wore the conventional salwar-kameez, sarees or skirts. The engagement of the local population with the community is also evident. There is a picture of Sarojini Naidu at the Gurdwara from 1929,[194] a photo commemorating the donation of $26,000 to the Indian Consulate in San Francisco after the 1962 war,[195] and a gallery of portraits of prominent Sikhs. Valuables, including offerings, were probably kept in a safe[196] in the old building.

191 The words "both sexes" are in bold in the original notice. The first batch comprised a Christian, a Sikh, a Muslim and three Hindu students. They received the cost of transportation from India and expenses in the USA. They were housed in 'Guru Nanak Dev Vidyarthi Ashram' at 1731 Allston Way, Berkeley, a house bought for this purpose by the Pacific Coast Khalsa Diwan Society.

192 The Guru Govind Singh Sahib Educational Scholarships, primarily funded by Jawala Singh and his friends, were discontinued because of the increasing financial pressure on the society, which needed funds for the Ghadar Movement and to build the Gurdwara.

193 The platen machine is by Chandler and Price Co, Cleveland, OH, USA and is the "New Style" introduced in 1910.

194 A poet, freedom fighter and a close associate of Mahatma Gandhi, Sarojini Naidu (1879–1949) was the second woman president of the Indian National Congress.

195 The hourly wage at that time was $1, which was a considerable sum.

196 The customised safe by Waltz Safe & Lock Co. of San Francisco, CA, has the words Sikh Temple inscribed.

Ghadar newspaper, in Punjabi, was printed at the Gurdwara, and the printing machine has been kept in the old building, called Ghadri Babbe Memorial Hall.

The new building is the centre of religious activities, with regular *kirtan* and service. It was built in 1929 and has been extensively renovated and expanded. Inscribed atop it are the words "Sikh Temple" in English and "Gurdwara Sahib" in Gurmukhi. The spacious main hall is well-lit, and a plaque behind Guru Granth Sahib declares that this is the historical place associated with the Ghadri Babas. The first *pauri* of *Japji Sahib* is inscribed in Gurmukhi, with the English translation on the other side. Kirtan *darbar*s are a regular feature there.

The Gurdwara has run the Sunday Khalsa School for over two decades. Children learn the Punjabi language, Gurbani, and history. It regularly sponsors sports events, including powerlifting, running, and other cultural activities. Gurbani memorisation contests are also held. The annual Baisakhi Day parade is a big draw for the people.

The Gurdwara, with its iconic brick building, stands tall today. Its history, the foresight of its founders, the perseverance of those who followed them, and the involvement of the Gurdwara management beyond the traditional activities of Gurdwaras, all have shaped its distinct identity and ethos. When Sikh Temple, Stockton, was first inaugurated, the founders had to deal with local protesters. Today it is a celebrated symbol of the diverse population of San Joaquin county.

CLEVELAND OHIO U.S.A.

Sikh Gurdwara

SAN JOSE, CALIFORNIA, UNITED STATES OF AMERICA

GOLD-TOPPED white domes that stand out from the earth tones of the main building make a subtle and definitive statement against the cerulean sky as one looks at the Gurdwara atop a hill of the Mount Diablo range in San Jose, California. With panoramic views and architecture that reflects tradition, Sikh Gurdwara San Jose is considered the biggest in North America. Located in Evergreen district, the Gurdwara serves the Sikh community of the Bay Area and the state of California at large.

With panoramic views and architecture that reflects tradition, Sikh Gurdwara San Jose is considered the biggest in North America.

The architectural tradition of Gurdwaras in the Indian subcontinent informs the building, even as it makes a distinct statement with its fountains that maximise the impact of panoramic views. Los Angeles-based Malkiat Singh Sidhu, an alumnus of Bombay's Sir J.J. School of Architecture, was the lead architect of the Gurdwara. Another architect from Los Angeles, Pralad Singh Grewal, also contributed to the design.

The 500-vehicle parking gives a good indication of its popularity as well as planning. Indeed, parking was an issue that made the Gurdwara management committee look for alternatives and move from the original site on White Road, San Jose, where the Gurdwara dated back to 1984. More space was also needed for the growing community. They bought a plot at Quimby Road in 1990, and more land was added to it later. However, this 40-acre apricot orchard near East San Jose Foothills, with zoning permission for a place of worship, was where the Gurdwara

SIKH GURDWARA - SAN JOSE

ਸਤਿਨਾਮੁ ਕਰਤਾ ਪੁਰਖੁ
ਨਿਰਭਉ ਨਿਰਵੈਰੁ ਅਕਾਲ ਮੂਰਤਿ
ਅਜੂਨੀ ਸੈਭੰ ਗੁਰ ਪ੍ਰਸਾਦਿ ॥

The *Ek Onkar* symbol and the *Mul Mantra* written in gold on black form the backdrop to the *palki*, and the *darbar* hall has space for 2,500 devotees.

was meant to be. In 1996, the land was bought, and by the following year, five religious leaders of various faiths took part in the ground-breaking ceremony.

When it started in 2004, the Gurdwara comprised the main, north, and south halls. Soon, the Gurdwara started attracting Silicon Valley Sikhs in large numbers. The second phase of the construction, which involved raising the Main Diwan Hall and other buildings, was completed in 2011. The principal speaker at the inauguration ceremony on Baisakhi Day was the then-Governor of California, Jerry Brown. An estimated 20,000 devotees were at the Gurdwara that day.

With its clerestory windows shaped in the traditional scalloped arches, both light and tradition get the architectural nod. Four pillars, linked by traditional arches, have heavy swag curtains framing the sanctum sanctorum wherein Guru Granth Sahib rests.

The Main Diwan Hall has a capacity of 2,500 persons,[197] and there is often good attendance on weekdays. Sundays attract devotees in much bigger numbers.

The *Ek Onkar* symbol and the *Mul Mantra* written in gold on a black background form the backdrop. The entire wall has arches, each inscribed with couplets from Gurbani. The theme of the arches is echoed within, even where there are no windows. The ceiling has embossed acoustic tiles, which ensures good sound fidelity. Audio-visual equipment and screens make the stage visible for the very large crowds on days when the Gurdwara is very busy.

The *langar* hall with a large capacity has been given special attention. Seen on the wall are paintings that showcase Sikh heritage. Installed in December 2018 while celebrating the 550th birth anniversary of Guru Nanak, these paintings by Jarnail Singh (1956-2025) cover themes including the importance of *langar*, historical events and Sikh warriors. One painting depicts the episode of the young Nanak's father asking him to buy goods to trade. Instead, moved by the plight of a band of hungry ascetics, Nanak spent the money on buying food for them. This is traditionally considered the first instance of *langar*. Another painting shows Mata Khivi, wife of Guru Angad Dev, serving *langar* to the devotees. Yet another painting depicts Emperor Akbar partaking of *langar* with ordinary people.

197 The Fire Department safety notice of 2,585 persons is prominently displayed.

Gold-topped white domes that stand out against the earth tones of the main building as one looks at the Gurdwara atop a hill of the Mount Diablo range in San Jose, California. A series of fountains enhances the look.

Given its large size, there is a requirement for a sizeable number of volunteers, who have been provided with a kitchen with a large cold room and various other modern amenities, including commercial dishwashing equipment. Some of the produce served in the *langar* is grown in the Gurdwara's 40-acre complex. The *langar* is very popular with the wider community of Indian expats in Silicon Valley, with people often bringing in their non-Indian origin friends.

The Gurdwara has a Sunday School, which has 750 students. It has been active since its inception in providing students with the requisite skills to understand and learn Gurbani and the Punjabi language. Classrooms are named after historical figures. Even though there are 13 classrooms at present, there is a need for more, and an additional storey is planned atop the original complex to provide for greater classroom space. Provision has also been made for housing the staff within the complex.

The stunning premises of the Gurdwara makes a striking venue for weddings. At times five marriages have been solemnised in a single day in special halls reserved for the purpose. The Gurdwara runs a free medical clinic, which is recognised by the medical authorities in the city.

Landscaping deserves special mention. A series of disabled-accessible fountains, and a big waterfall that comes down a steep landscaped hill at the main entry, add to the uniqueness of the place. The Gurdwara is also equipped with a massive solar energy system.[198] The facilities run on solar electricity, and there are also EV charging stations.

The location, architecture, and the range of services the San Jose Gurdwara provides make it stand out, even as it expands to accommodate the needs of an increasing *sangat*.

198 It was the biggest solar system in the city (at 434 kilowatt) when it was installed in 2010.

Gurdwara Sikh Cultural Society

NEW YORK, UNITED STATES OF AMERICA

THE OLDEST Gurdwara in the north-east United States has a new building, more prominent than ever. The Sikh Cultural Society was registered in 1965, and it initially served 20-odd families in the area.[199] As time went by, the numbers increased, and by April 1972, the society bought an old Methodist Church in Richmond Hill, Queens, for $65,000, which it paid in cash.[200] With its architecture intact, the building became a hub for community activities.

The four-storeyed building has elements inspired by important Sikh shrines in India and Pakistan. The 40-foot-high dome is a landmark.

Raja Mrigendra Singh of Patiala[201] served as the first Head Granthi of the Gurdwara from May 1974 for two years. Giani Gurdeep Singh[202] succeeded him in 1976, and he performed *sewa* until his death in February 2002.[203] Illustrious individuals followed him.

Most visitors from India would make a beeline to the Gurdwara. Among the prominent names are: then Prime Minister Indira Gandhi;[204] her detractors Prof Rajni Kothari and Ram Jethmalani; and many American political leaders such as Senators, members of Congress, New York State Governor and Mayors of New York City. The Sikh Cultural Society has played a leading role in shaping the opinion of the Sikh community regarding various issues facing the public in the USA, as also devoted attention to how Americans perceive the Sikhs and their issues. It sponsored a Sikh studies programme at Columbia University, NY, which ran from 1988 to 1999.

199 Sikhs of New York first got together to celebrate the birth anniversary of Guru Nanak in 1954. A decade later, they started meeting on weekends at private houses by rotation. The Sikh Cultural Society was formed after that. Notable leaders of the time included Sajjan, S. Sarna, Dhanwant Singh, Dr Harbans Singh, Kirat Singh Sethi, and Prof. Gurcharan Singh.

200 Sham Sani of Florida contributed $25,000 at that time and $33,000 later, and S. Sajjan Singh Sarna contributed $16,500.

201 Raja Dr Mrigendra Singh (1929-2014) was Maharaja Bhupendra Singh's son and brother of Maharaja Yadavindra Singh. He studied and taught the Nirmala tradition of scholarship and was an accomplished musician.

202 He had served as Head Granthi of Gurdwara Sis Ganj, Delhi, Singh Sabha in Kenya, and Singh Sabha in Southall, U.K.

203 He was 78 at the time and was widely respected.

204 Indira Gandhi visited on 1 August 1982. After 1984, the Sikh Cultural Society led the protests against Operation Bluestar and the 1984 anti-Sikh pogrom.

Gurdwara Sikh Cultural Society is one of the most important centres for Sikhs in America. It is at the forefront of public events in the area, including the annual Sikh Day Parade, held in Manhattan around Baisakhi Day every April since 1988. Sikh organisations from the tri-state region of New York, New Jersey, and Connecticut participate in the extravaganza, attracting thousands of people to Madison Square Park, where the parade culminates. The first parade had a float of Harmandir Sahib, and now many floats showcase Sikh ethos. Refreshments in various forms—fruit, sandwiches, etc.— are offered to bystanders, especially at Madison Square Park. Over the years, many local politicians, including the Mayor of New York City, have joined the parade celebrating the Sikh way of life.

A fire on March 8, 2002, destroyed the Gurdwara and took a life. For two years thereafter the congregations were held in temporary accommodations. Panj Piaras broke the ground for the 65,000-square-foot new building on Baisakhi Day in 2004. Chicago-based architect Amarjit Singh Sidhu designed the four-storeyed building.[205] He incorporated several elements in the exterior and the interior that are inspired by important Sikh shrines in India and Pakistan.[206] The 40-foot-high dome, with its special design, is a landmark of the Gurdwara.

The entrance on the 97th Avenue echoes the design of Darbar Sahib's Darshani Deori. As you enter, you see a common area with the usual conveniences, including the *jora ghar*. With its 14-foot ceiling, the *darbar* hall opens further as you walk towards the *parkash asthan*, where light streaming in from the top gives you a feeling of space.

The basement has a multi-purpose hall, the *langar* hall and the kitchen, which are in constant use since the *langar* is served on all days of the week.

The second floor has the *sukhashan asthan* for Guru Granth Sahib and five unique rooms where *akhand path* is held. They have been designed to make a common area available for larger gatherings when necessary. This is also the floor that houses the administrative offices of various officials and the library.

The third floor provides the living space for the Head Granthi and other *sewadars*, both permanent and visiting. The fourth floor has classrooms for students, both for special classes and after-school studies. Classes are held for young Sikhs on weekends to keep them connected with their roots. The environmentally conscious design uses triple-paned windows to increase insulation and reduce energy consumption.

The new Gurdwara building was used partially as it was being built. It has been in regular use since 2013, and local political leaders have also recognised its significance. In 2020, on the eve of the 551st birth anniversary of Guru Nanak, a street leading to it was named Gurdwara Street. The signboards for this street (No. 117 on 97 Avenue) were also installed on paths leading to this street. In April 2023, the intersection of the 118th Street between the 101st and 95th Avenues was renamed Guru Nanak Way.

Even as housing is provided for visitors and traditional activities are carried on, there is an outreach to the local non-Sikh community, including meet-and-greet events for political leaders and awareness campaigns, more so after the 9/11 attacks. American students, guided by their teachers, periodically visit the Gurdwara to learn more about the Sikhs.[207]

The Gurdwara organised blood donation camps and was a significant base for dispensing free groceries, food, and medical inoculations during the Covid-19 pandemic. The New York State Senate has declared April as Sikh Awareness Month.

205 An IIT graduate, he served as Assistant Architect in Le Corbusier's team in Chandigarh before migrating to the USA. He has designed several Gurdwaras.

206 Harpreet Singh Toor, then president of the Sikh Cultural Society who closely interacted with the architect, detailed how the dome was inspired by the "oldest Gurdwara in Pakistan," and the entrance echoed the Darshani Deori of Harmandir Sahib, Amritsar.

207 The Gurdwara is listed in the popular guide: "111 Places in Queens That You Must Not Miss".

Guru Gobind Singh Foundation

ROCKVILLE, MARYLAND, UNITED STATES OF AMERICA

N EXPANSE of white surrounded by verdant gardens, the Guru Gobind Singh Foundation in Rockville, Maryland, USA, showcases a modern Gurdwara rooted in heritage. Three stylised arches break the white facade, the central one being the main entrance of the Gurdwara at 13814 Travilah Road, Rockville. It is a 16-mile drive from the White House, Washington D.C.

Naturally, you notice the tall Nishan Sahib as you drive in, and as you enter the building, you see a large chandelier. The foyer leads to the main hall with a maroon wall-to-wall carpet. It has a seating capacity of over 250 persons. Niranjan Singh Sammi, an architect, designed the Gurdwara, assisted in various fields by Surinder Singh, Bhupinder Singh Sohi, Anoop Singh Babra, Hargurpreet Singh, and Chattar Singh Saini, all of whom provided services gratis.

When it was inaugurated in October 2005, the local *sangat*, which numbered around 300 at the time, as well as county elected officials and the people involved with the design and construction, were all present.

Langar is served in the lower hall. It has a commercial-style kitchen, which became prominent during the Covid-19 pandemic when it was used extensively for the Gurdwara outreach programmes. It provided cooked food to those in need, packed in individual boxes for easy disbursal. Office space is in the mezzanine.

The Gurdwara was inaugurated in October 2005, with the 300-strong local *sangat* and guests, including elected county officials, in presence.

The *parkash asthan* has a beautiful *chandni,* and natural light streams into the main hall through picture windows on both sides.

Natural light streams into the main hall through picture windows on both sides, providing a view of the beautifully landscaped surroundings. The facility has access to 175 parking spaces. Two rooms are located near the main entrance.

The management is especially proud of the design of the Guru Granth Sahib *parkash asthan* and how it stands out. It is inspired by Harmandir Sahib, Amritsar, and there is a beautiful *chandni* over the *asthan*. Regular *diwans* are held on Friday evenings, and on Sundays, mornings and at noon.Community events like weddings, anniversaries, and birthday celebrations are conducted as needed, mainly from Monday to Saturday, as are funeral prayers.

The Gurdwara is a venue for regular interfaith events, which seek to bring out significant interaction and understanding between members of various faiths. The *sangat* has played a prominent role in interfaith activities in the Washington area.

Sunday Gurmat school and week-long summer Gurmat camps have been held regularly by the Guru Gobind Singh Foundation for the past 25 years. Special attention is paid to children's activities, and classes are held to train these young Sikhs in *gatka*. An annual health fair takes care of the physical well-being of the *sangat*.

The foundation was established in 1985 and started its interfaith activities in 1987. It has taken particular interest in increasing awareness about the Sikh identity in various schools and other institutions. It invites students and teachers to visit the Gurdwara and learn more about the Sikhs.

Naturally, Baisakhi and Gurpurbs attract the largest number of people, and a *nagar kirtan* is also a regular feature on these occasions. On average, 300 people attend the congregation every Sunday, with the number going up to 500-plus during Gurpurbs, Baisakhi and New Year celebrations.

The Gurdwara management has a Gurmat Sangeet Academy, which teaches the *rabab*, *tabla*, and other musical instruments. A 'Kids Diwan' is held on the last Friday of each month.

An annual Gurbani recitation competition for children, in cooperation with the National Sikh Center, evokes keen interest, and the winners get prizes. There is a free medical clinic that is open to all on Sundays.

The Guru Gobind Singh Foundation serves not just Sikhs but the entire community. It goes beyond dealing with Sikh issues to broader community matters, holding vigils when tragedies occur in other religious communities, meetings to control gun violence, emergency evacuation training, active shooter training, etc.

The Secretary, Dr Rajwant Singh, has been involved in interfaith activities for decades. He also leads the EcoSikh initiative for combating climate change, which has presence in India and other countries too.

Divinity students in particular, and school and college students in general, are regularly hosted to create awareness among them regarding Sikh and Gurdwara traditions.

Gurdwara Guru Nanak Sahib

PANAMA CITY, PANAMA

SIKH ARRIVAL in Panama dates to the late 19th century. They were engaged first in construction work for a transcontinental railroad link, and later at the Panama Canal from 1890 to 1914. The work involved manual labour, and the struggle included battling yellow fever and other diseases. The contractors favoured Sikhs because of their reputation for hardiness and work ethic.

After the canal's inauguration, the American Fruit Company became a significant employer of Sikhs. A section became door-to-door salespeople, while others started driving *chivas*, which were basic colourful public transport vehicles, in which people, goods, and livestock shared space.[208]

In time, many Sikhs returned to Punjab, while others moved to Canada and other Western countries, including the UK. However, various projects and facilities in the Panama Canal Zone provided employment opportunities for Sikhs. With the increasing use of the canal for maritime traffic and the presence of US interests, including military bases, the country's economy centred around the canal's banks. In 1941, the Canal Zone became the headquarters for the US Southern Command. The US has always been the primary user of the canal, providing various economic opportunities.

The two-storeyed Gurdwara was inaugurated in 1986, and it is the hub of the Sikh community which first came to Panama in the late 19th century.

208 The word 'chiva' in Spanish means a goat and refers to the bumpy ride passengers in these vehicles get. They are still prevalent in rural South America.

GURDWARA GURU NANAK SAHIB

The *parkash asthan* on a marble platform captures attention in the minimalistic *darbar* hall.

The work profile of Sikhs changed, and those engaged in various jobs in the Canal Zone started small businesses, became landowners, etc. But they did not have a formal place to pray together during this period and used various houses in rotation for the weekly congregation.

Gurdwara Guru Nanak Sahib, Panama, was built through the efforts of the local community[209] and it was inaugurated in 1986. A local architect designed the Gurdwara, and he was guided on the required aesthetics by the management.

There were over a thousand Sikhs then, and most of them worked directly or indirectly for the Canal Zone. Many were transiting through Panama on their way to the USA and Canada. As opportunities dwindled in Panama, several Sikh families moved to greener pastures, primarily in the North American continent. The number of Sikhs in the country has dwindled now.

Located at Iglesia, 5 Quebrada De Piedra, Panama City, the two-storeyed Gurdwara, with each floor measuring 600 square metres, stands out with its tradition-inspired architecture and five domes on the roof—the central dome and four *chhatris*.

As you enter, you see the *langar* hall, where volunteers serve a large number of devotees and visitors. A new kitchen has been built adjacent to the Gurdwara, in a lot which is also used as a recreational area.

The first floor has *darbar* hall in the centre with the *sach khand* to one side. The beautiful hand-carved door depicts Guru Gobind Singh with the words *Sat Nam* on one panel and Guru Nanak Dev with the word *Waheguru* on the other. The richly carved doors were made by a Panamanian craftsman who worked on the design given to him. The *parkash asthan* is on a marble platform, while the main hall is minimalistic.

Guru Gobind Singh Car Park has space for around 100 vehicles. Another lot adjoining the Gurdwara has slides and swings for children. The new 70-foot-high Nishan Sahib was erected on Guru Nanak Dev Gurpurb in 2023.

209 The names of Rattan Singh, who had a financial company, and Parkash Singh are often cited.

The beautiful hand-carved door depicts Guru Gobind Singh, with the words *Sat Nam*, on one panel, and Guru Nanak Dev, with *Waheguru* written, on the other.

The Gurdwara opens in the morning and evening for prayers on weekdays and Saturdays. On Sundays, it is open from 8 am to 3 pm, which is when most people visit. *Sangrand*, the first day of each month of the Indian calendar, is commemorated with a special programme. Around 70 people attend the congregation on Sundays, but the gathering is larger when Gurpurbs and other auspicious days are celebrated. A regular granthi is on the rolls, with one worker to assist him. Young volunteers from the Sikh community come whenever needed to perform *sewa* at the Gurdwara.

Punjabi and Sindhi devotees also visit the Gurdwara, especially on *Sangrand* and Gurpurbs of Guru Nanak Dev and Guru Gobind Singh. Baisakhi is celebrated with special enthusiasm.

Owing to the long Sikh presence in Panama, some Sikhs there are fourth-generation, with many speaking Spanish, English, and Punjabi. The number of Sikhs in the community may be small, but they have impacted the region for over 125 years. Today, they own finance companies, farms where they grow bananas and other crops, departmental stores, and other businesses. Many hold jobs in businesses, while others are in the civil service. The Gurdwara is a major bastion of the Sikhs in this part of the world.

South America, a continent that borders Panama has, overall, the least number of Sikhs. However, there is a significant historical community in Argentina, and Sikh presence has been recorded in Mexico, Uruguay, Peru, Chile, Surinam, Venezuela, and Costa Rica.[210]

Gurdwara Guru Nanak Sahib, Panama City, is a reminder of the community's contribution to the country and its main economic engine, the Panama Canal.

210 *Sikhs in Latin America: Travels among the Sikh Diaspora* by Swarn Singh Kahlon

Africa

Sikhs first arrived in the African continent in the 1890s. They were part of the British contingent in the Boer War in South Africa (1899 – 1902). The British East African colonies were linked by railway lines built and operated by a large number of skilled Sikh immigrants from India. Sikh locomotive drivers were highly regarded in Kenya, and wherever they went, they set up Gurdwaras. In time, there was a significant Sikh population in the British East Africa—Kenya, Tanzania, and Uganda—where they worked in police and civil services. The enterprising among them became shopkeepers, businessmen and factory owners.

Sikhs prospered in Africa and made a name for themselves in diverse fields, including business, sports and even local politics. However, rising nationalism and the adoption of "Africanisation" created political problems and an adverse situation for them, which led to an exodus from these African countries in the 1960s. A few decades later, more liberal policies and a promise of restoration of properties, especially in Uganda, resulted in some Sikhs coming back. Over time they have done well.

Today there are Gurdwaras in many African countries, as well as Khalsa Schools and medical facilities run by the Sikhs. Such facilities even exist in places that do not have a significant Sikh presence. Historically, what was set up has been maintained and expanded.

Africa has changed. Many countries have opened up their economies and now welcome foreigners. Apartheid was abolished in South Africa in 1994. New immigrants to Africa have brought in fresh energy and greater engagement with local and community endeavours. As the number of Sikhs increases, there is a need for more Gurdwaras, and we find new ones coming up in various places across the continent.

KENYA
SOUTH AFRICA
Africa

Gurdwara Makindu Sahib

MAKINDU, KENYA

SIKH WORKERS building the Kenya-Uganda railway established Gurdwara Sahib, Makindu, in 1926. British Imperial authorities had brought skilled Sikh workers to Kenya to build the railroad. The immigration started in the early 1900s as the British sought to make East Africa accessible. As expected, the workers moved as the railway line was extended.

Makindu became a significant centre for refuelling the steam-engine locomotives plying between Nairobi and Mombasa, providing water and other provisions, and adding another engine to help climb to Nairobi. This led to more and more people settling in what became a bustling town. By the 1920s, there was a small community of Indians, primarily Sikhs, who soon built their Gurdwara.

A copy of Guru Granth Sahib that had been reverentially carried from India by the devotees was used to pray,[211] and it still has the distinction of being the largest *swarup* in Africa. The Gurdwara, which started in a tin shed, expanded for the next 20 years or so. The key people were connected to the railways—Tara Singh Ahluwalia, a shed master at Makindu; Lachman Das; and Teja Singh, a railway guard. Change is a constant, and through the 1930s and 40s, Beyer Garratt locomotives, with more power, fuel, and water capacities, were introduced, and slowly Makindu's importance as a refuelling stop decreased, and along with it, the population, especially that of the Sikhs.

Sikh workers building the Kenya-Uganda railway established Gurdwara Sahib, Makindu, in 1926. It is among the most significant Gurdwaras in Africa.

211 The original manuscript was printed using stone lithography (*patthar chhap*). It was before the standardisation of Guru Granth Sahib and has around 2,000 pages.

GURDWARA
MAKINDU
SAHIB
1926

The Gurdwara now has several *darbars* where *path* of Guru Granth Sahib is performed.

Gwalo, a Masai tribesman, took care of the Gurdwara and learnt Punjabi. He performed the daily rituals with his son, who also spoke Punjabi. Sikhs who passed by the area would visit the Gurdwara and place their offerings. Even today, a sizeable number of local people serve at the Gurdwara and speak Punjabi with varying degrees of proficiency. In the mid-20th century, Gwalo had a vision of Guru Gobind Singh visiting the Gurdwara Sahib. A painting based on Gwalo's description can still be seen there.

The *sangat* of Nairobi, led by Basan Singh, organised the effort to restore the building, which was a small Gurdwara with blue pillars that were embellished with frescos depicting the Gurus. It was cleaned up by volunteers and he had a genset installed to provide electricity, with Surinder Singh Gujral, a Shell company executive, providing diesel. Families from Nairobi would regularly undertake the two-hour drive to Makindu to perform *sewa*.[212] Sant Puran Singh of Kericho also felt drawn to the Gurdwara and encouraged the *sangat* to frequent the shrine.

Hari Singh Bansal,[213] who had emigrated from Jalandhar in Punjab, was engaged to re-design the Gurdwara building in 1971. A signature Darshani Deori was built along the road, and this Gurdwara was the only one in Africa with this feature typical of historical Gurdwaras of India. Along with it, the traditional style of architecture with domes and arches was used for the main building. Some of the original mirror work on the *chhatris* atop the Gurdwara remains intact, as do some frescos executed then. Hari Singh Bansal maintained the tradition of keeping four doors in four directions. The new Nishan Sahib rose to the height of 40 metres.

The Gurdwara has space to park 150 vehicles and is just off the main highway. Since Sikhs believe that prayers offered here are answered, there is a constant demand for *akhand path* services, and there are four *darbar* halls for devotees. The latest one is Guru Tegh Bahadur Darbar.

The Gurdwara now owns seven acres of land, and thus has ample space to expand. A hospital was built in 1999, and it even has a dairy farm which caters to the *langar*. A larger hospital is being made to provide medical care. It is worth noting that there is practically no Sikh or Punjabi population outside the Gurdwara premises, so the facilities are aimed at and used by the local people.

As expected, given the influx of visitors, special attention is paid to *langar*. A modernised kitchen with cold-storage rooms and gas cookers provides fresh food to the devotees. Complimentary rooms are available for up to two days, and a borehole on the site provides a free water supply, used for horticulture and dairy activities, and shared with neighbours. Over a dozen *granthis* and *pathis* are employed by the Gurdwara. They are provided with free accommodation. The local staff is said to be around 60 people.

A serene place with shady trees and peacocks roaming around the premises, Gurdwara Makindu Sahib is an important cultural and religious landmark in Kenya, so much so that it is called "Harmandir Sahib of East Africa."

It has over 200 rooms and on major festivals it can accommodate thousands of devotees. It is a symbol of the Sikh community's resilience, and contributions to the East African story.

212 Dina Singh, who is now in Chandigarh, remembers that the first wedding was performed there in 1978, since it was equidistant for both the families.
213 He has been described as an "architect-mason-carpenter-sculptor-painter all rolled into one." He executed various Gurdwaras, mosques, temples, ornamental gates, fountains, etc., in Kenya.

Gurdwara Sahib Johannesburg

JOHANNESBURG, SOUTH AFRICA

BEAUTIFUL residential area of the largest city in South Africa hosts Gurdwara Sahib, Johannesburg. It serves as a hub for the local Sikh community, offering religious services, educational programmes, and cultural events.

The first Sikh immigrants arrived in South Africa in the late 19th century, and they were brought from India with other Indians to work on sugar plantations in Natal. Later, they moved to the Transvaal.

The Gurdwara in Pretoria, built in 1911, is considered the oldest Gurdwara in South Africa.

Indian expatriates returned to South Africa after 1994, when the more than four-decade-old apartheid-era ban on immigration from India ended. The Sikhs were not in any significant number among the 1.2 million South Africans of Indian origin at that time. However, since then, their number has increased. Now, there are several Gurdwaras in South Africa, including recently opened ones in Durban and Cape Town.

The Gurdwara was inaugurated in November 2015 and stands out with its distinctive architecture and the *khanda-chakkar* insignia.

STOP

The *palki* is illuminated by natural light from the dome, and two chandeliers hang on the side. The *parkash asthan* has a golden ceiling.

The economic and financial hub of South Africa, and its largest city, however, did not have a dedicated Gurdwara. Looking at it now, it is difficult to imagine the long struggle it took for the Gurdwara to come forth in its present form. Initially, 109 4th Street, Parkmore, Sandton, Johannesburg, was a residence in an upscale suburb. It was donated to the Gurdwara by the Sethi family, led by Harbinder Singh Sethi. Baisakhi was celebrated at the Gurdwara in 2006 for the first time. Until then, Sikhs in Johannesburg held congregations by rotation in the homes of expatriate Sikhs.

Besides the descendants of the original immigrants, Sikhs from various parts of Africa also came to Johannesburg, as did new immigrants from India. The increase in the size of the congregation fed the demand to convert the house into a modern Gurdwara. The local community objected, and it took eight years to get permission to build the Gurdwara in 2014, with plans from Misel Cizek Architects, a leading South African firm. Construction started soon after. The new 2,500-square-metre building was inaugurated on 22 November 2015, and has served the community since. It is a major place of worship for Sikhs in South Africa.

While the building has visible elements of Sikh architecture, including the traditional domes and arches, it also reflects local sensibilities. It is a modern edifice sensitive to the neighbourhood's concerns. Being a corner plot with distinctive architecture, it stands out with the domes gleaming against the blue sky and the Nishan Sahib standing tall. The steel *khanda-chakkar* sign against a blue background is prominent at the corner of the building. The protruding windows with domes at the top reflect the traditional design but also have a modern touch in their detailing—the golden embellishments are executed with finesse and sophistication. The exterior is white, and scalloped arches are widely used. Underground parking is available.

As you enter the *parkash asthan*, you see the light streaming from the sides through traditional scalloped arches. The *palki* is illuminated by natural light from the dome at the top, which has windows at the bottom. Two lovely chandeliers hang to the side of the *palki*. The golden ceiling of the *parkash asthan*, with contrasting insets featuring geometric and botanical designs, stands out.

With the aid of regular staff, *path*, *kirtan*, and *katha* are performed every day. Many local people also join in for the *langar*. The Gurdwara has donated items of daily need, including eatables, clothing, and medicine, to various organisations, institutions, and individuals.

Punjabi and Gurbani teaching classes are held for younger generations, and a Khalsa Club also provides training in performing *kirtan*. Children trained there have performed at various religious and community functions.

One of the most significant events at the Johannesburg Gurdwara is the celebration of Guru Nanak Dev's birth anniversary. The *nagar kirtan* procession starts here and is a big draw with the local people, and civic and political leaders. The event attracts Sikhs from all over South Africa, who come to participate in the celebrations and pay their respects to the founder of Sikhism.

Oceania

Sikhs have made Australia their home since the mid-19th century. The first reference of Sikhs is as labour which was needed for agricultural work, and in sheep rearing. Some Punjabis were part of what was known as 'Afghan cameleers'. The introduction of the Indian Coolie Act in 1862 brought in more Punjabis as farmhands. By then, some older immigrants had found success as hawkers. The farming community in Woolgooga is considered an early significant presence in Australia, and in time they became prosperous. By 1961, following a relaxation in rules, women could emigrate and they raised their families with them. The first Gurdwara on the continent was built in Woolgoolga in 1968.

The White Australia policy made immigration for Sikhs difficult until the Immigration Restriction Act was modified in 1966 to ensure that the same rules and restrictions about acquiring visas were applied to all candidates for migration and citizenship. The change resulted in more Sikh immigrants. The Racial Discrimination Act, 1975, gave further impetus to professionals and students to make Australia their home. Most of the Sikh immigrants now focused on Australian cities. While an overwhelming majority were from Punjab, others were from Asian countries such as Malaysia, Singapore, and Fiji, as well as African countries such as Kenya and Uganda.

Since the 2000s, many new immigrants have studied in Australia and stayed on, raising families. A large number have risen to significant positions in various professions, including civil and foreign service. Some Sikhs have also been successful in local politics.

The Sikh presence in New Zealand dates to the 1890s, when a few Sikhs came to work on sheep and dairy farms. Since the mid-1960s, the number of Sikhs has increased significantly. The New Zealand Sikh Society was formed in 1964, with the first Gurdwara inaugurated in 1977 in Hamilton.

Oceania

Sikh Temple Blackburn

MELBOURNE, VICTORIA, AUSTRALIA

HERE HAS been Sikh presence in Australia for almost two centuries now, but the initial migration, which is traced to the late 1830s, was of only a few who ventured this far. They found agricultural work on farms, sheep stations, and later also as hawkers. Many of the Sikhs came to New South Wales, which included Queensland and Victoria.

Today the province of Victoria has the largest population of Sikhs,[214] and the Gurdwara is located at 127 Whitehorse Road, Blackburn, in Melbourne. It was inaugurated on 5 December 1993, and along with the Sikh *sangat*, it was the local councillor who supported the cause.[215] A big yellow sign on the road announces, "Sikh Temple Blackburn". It is also known as Sri Guru Nanak Satsang Sabha.

The building was originally a mail sorting centre for the eastern suburbs of Melbourne. Even as the exterior was left unchanged, the interior was converted into a large *darbar* hall, a *langar* hall, a library, and a Punjabi language school. Since no significant exterior changes were envisaged at the time, no architect was engaged. An elected committee manages the day-to-day operations of the Gurdwara.

Since 2023, a major renovation of the Gurdwara has been undertaken, which is on even as this book goes to print. The exterior, which is a squat brick building with a *khanda-chakkar* atop, will be made to look more like a traditional Gurdwara. Emergency accommodation is being built to assist vulnerable members of the community, especially women and children in need, as well as others who need temporary housing.

The building was originally a mail sorting centre for the eastern suburbs of Melbourne. This is how the Gurdwara is expected to look after the renovation.

214 New South Wales has the second-largest population of Sikhs.

215 Since 1977, families met in private homes, then Rathdowne Primary School, and later Box Hill Primary School. In 1984, the pioneering families purchased the Uniting Church in Fern Tree Gully and set up the first Gurdwara in Melbourne.

ੴ ਸਤਿਗੁਰ ਨਾਨਕ ਪ੍ਰਗਟਿਆ ਮਿਟੀ ਧੁੰਧੁ ਜਗਿ ਚਾਨਣੁ ਹੋਆ ॥ ੴ

The richly appointed white *palki* has the *Ek Onkar* symbol displayed behind it.

Even as the renovation work is on, the Gurdwara functions in a regular manner. The richly appointed white *palki* dominates *darbar* hall. It has the *Ek Onkar* symbol displayed behind it and is flanked by two *khanda-chakkar* symbols. The hall is well-lit and has a wide-open space for the *sangat*. The *langar* functions with a modern kitchen.

Regular programmes where visiting *ragi jathas* perform *kirtan* are held on Wednesday evenings and Saturday and Sunday mornings. The main programme is always on Sunday morning. There are also additional *kirtan* performances on other significant occasions. Weddings too are organised on the Gurdwara premises. The number of people seeking *Anand Karaj* at the Gurdwara has steadily increased to the extent that weekends are fully booked, and often ceremonies take place on weekdays.

Given the large population of Sikhs, it is not surprising that the number of devotees that visit the Gurdwara every week is between 5,000 and 8,000. The largest crowds are seen on special occasions such as Baisakhi, Diwali, and Gurpurbs. Diwali is the occasion when most people show up because it is celebrated by not just the Sikh *sangat* but also other religions, and non-Sikh Punjabis and Sindhis join in the celebrations at the Gurdwara in significant numbers. *Langar* is served daily and is, of course, open to all. It has proved to be effective in attracting local people to the Gurdwara and familiarising them with the Sikh ethos.

The Gurdwara has several outreach initiatives for the community and beyond. Khalsa Punjabi School holds classes for teaching the Punjabi language each Sunday. It is also offered as a Victorian Certificate of Education (VCE) subject,[216] for which classes are held on Wednesday evenings. The school is active in the community programmes to promote cultural diversity. Students regularly take part in multicultural activities and win prizes. Classes for Gurbani, *kirtan*, and musical instruments are held on Saturdays and Sundays.

Sri Guru Hargobind Library was opened in 1995, and it has been steadily upgrading its collection through donations and acquisitions. It focuses on books on Sikhism and Punjab, both in English and Punjabi. It has an extensive children's section and books on poetry, literature, and fiction in Punjabi. It also subscribes to newspapers and magazines from India. The audio-visual collection at the library includes *kirtan* and *katha* renderings on various types of digital media that members can borrow.

Since many Sikh students opt to take Punjabi as a subject for the VCE, the library puts in extra effort to provide the required support for such students. There is a regular group of senior citizens who come together and participate in activities like Gurbani recitation, picnics, or free health check-ups.

The Sikh *sangat* takes out a *nagar kirtan* to commemorate the birth anniversary of Guru Nanak Dev every year. Over the past few years, this procession has been organised in Melbourne CBD, with Sikhs from across the city joining in. It is a colourful affair with participants in their traditional attire and delegations of different organisations taking part. From starting out as people with meagre resources to building institutions that serve the community and people of the region in times of need, the Sikh community in Melbourne has come a long way indeed.

216 The Victorian Certificate of Education (VCE) is a senior secondary qualification in Victoria, Australia. The VCE is undertaken by most students in Years 11 and 12.

Gurdwara Sahib

GLENWOOD, NEW SOUTH WALES, AUSTRALIA

A LOVELY alabaster building that stands out against the sky, with the words "Gurdwara Sahib Glenwood, Sydney," written across the arched entryway, represents not only the prominent place of worship for the Sikhs in the city but also the realisation of their aspirations arising from the formation of the Sikh Cultural Society in 1969 as part of the worldwide initiative to celebrate the 500th birth anniversary of Guru Nanak. Another organisation, the Australian Sikh Club, merged with it to form the Australian Sikh Association in 1983. In 2016, to comply with government requirements, the association changed its legal structure from an incorporated association to a company limited by guarantee.

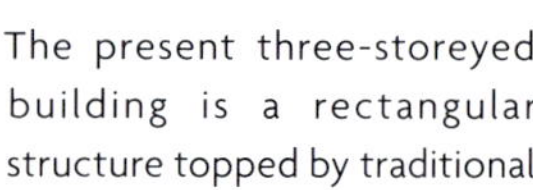

The present three-storeyed building is a rectangular structure topped by traditional domes and *chhatris*. The entryway is arched.

The Gurdwara, run by the association, is located at 18 Meurants Lane, Glenwood, in the Blacktown Council Area in the western Sydney Metropolitan Area. The building has evolved over time after it started with land being purchased in 1981.[217] The Sikhs initially used a two-bedroom cottage on the site for religious and community gatherings. More land was purchased in 1986, but it took another 10 years for work to start on the new building, which was completed in 1998.[218]

Further renovations were done in 2006 when the golden domes were added. Today, the Gurdwara complex stands on about 5 acres of land. It is a short ride from Blacktown train station, and on Saturdays and Sundays, a free bus service is provided from the station to the Gurdwara complex at specified times.

---

217 The pioneering leadership of Dr Gurdarshan Singh Sidhu, Kirpal Singh Pannu and Ajaib Singh Sidhu is remembered fondly by old-timers like Giani Santokh Singh, who was *granthi* at the Gurdwara for an extended period. It is said that they even mortgaged their homes at some point to take loans for building the Gurdwara.

218 Kartar Singh Thakral, the Singapore-based billionaire, contributed a total of Australian $5,01,000 in various tranches for building the Gurdwara.

GURDWARA SAHIB GLENWOOD SYDNEY
GOD IS ONE

ੴ

A golden *palki* is placed on a platform. It has a railing with golden *khanda-chakkar* and *Ek Onkar* symbols.

The present three-storeyed building is a rectangular structure topped by traditional domes and *chhatris*. The entryway is arched, and it leads to the well-appointed *darbar* hall. A golden *palki* is placed on a white platform, which has golden *khanda-chakkar* symbols all around it. A decorative brass railing demarcates the sacred area. The stage for the *ragi jathas* to perform *kirtan* is on a side, and it has a large display screen behind it, where relevant Gurbani couplets are displayed as they are sung.

The Gurdwara attracts *ragi jathas* from all over the world for *kirtan* and *katha*. Many of the well-known *ragis* from India have performed at the Gurdwara. While it started with only volunteers, it has now been supplemented with staff who are on the rolls, including a manager, a *granthi*, two *ragi jathas*, and some kitchen workers for the *langar*.

The spacious *langar* hall can serve over 450 people at a time. The kitchen was extended recently and new equipment for large-scale cooking provided. A room built on top of the kitchen has become a hall for *kirtan* and special functions. The Gurdwara takes pride in providing accommodation for people in need, and there are plans to increase the capacity.Bhai Gurdas Ji Library on the premises has over 2,500 books, audio-visual material, and a librarian.

A catalogue is available online for easy reference. As expected, the focus is on Sikhism, spirituality, translation of Guru Granth Sahib and books on Sikh Gurus. Reading areas, audio-visual projectors, etc, make it attractive. It is open on Saturdays and Sundays. The Gurdwara organises training in *kirtan*, turban-tying, *gatka*, and classes in Punjabi. For senior citizens, there are computer classes. Guru Nanak Punjabi School, located within the Gurdwara complex, is a community language school run by the Australian Sikh Association.

Registered with Community Languages Schools, Department of Education, New South Wales, it also provides teachers for Special Religious Education (SRE) classes in local public schools to teach about Sikhism and promote multiculturalism. The school also has online courses. Outdoor activities for young Sikhs include the Baisakhi camp and the annual athletics carnival, which encourages outdoor sports.

The Gurdwara is a venue for wedding ceremonies and other functions, for which a recent renovation has made additional space available. Apart from being a space for spiritual solace, the Gurdwara serves as a cultural centre for the Sikhs of the area. Given its prominence among Australian Sikhs, it also plays a significant role in the political realm.

The Australian Sikh Association, which runs the Gurdwara, elects its Board of Directors biennially. An expansion was detailed in a master plan for Glenwood Gurdwara Complex, which received support from local government officials. The plan is to build an aged-care facility, child-care facility, short-term accommodation, multi-storeyed car park, auditorium, heritage museum, gymnasium, and new classrooms for its language school at the site. Certain other renovations would also be undertaken.

The Gurdwara is open daily. From a time when it was a weekend gathering of a few, the *sangat* has burgeoned, primarily since the beginning of this century when the student population around Sydney increased dramatically. As the numbers increase, so do the activities and responsibilities of the largest of the six Gurdwaras in the Sydney Metropolitan Area.

Glossary

Ardas: is the Sikh prayer. Literally a petition, it is performed individually or in a congregation at the end and often at the beginning of religious functions in Gurdwaras and homes. A Sikh starts the day by reciting the assigned hymns in the morning, followed by the *ardas*, which is not inscribed in Guru Granth Sahib but is a supplicatory "evolute of the community's heart in prayer over the centuries."

Baoli: A well, often deep, with steps leading down to the water level. Gurus built towns with *baolis*. The *baoli* at Goindwal Sahib, built by Guru Amar Das, has great historical significance.

Baisakhi: A festival celebrated on the first day of the Baisakh, the second month in the Indian calendar, generally corresponding to April 13 or 14. A popular festival associated with harvest and thus happiness and abundance, it gained religious importance when Guru Amar Das started celebrating it at Goindwal Sahib. It is also the day of the formation of the Khalsa by Guru Gobind Singh, which is commemorated by Sikhs worldwide.

Darbar: The Persian word for court is used in various spiritual contexts in Sikhism. The place where Guru Granth Sahib is ceremonially placed is often called *darbar* or *darbar* hall. Certain historical Gurdwaras are also reverently called Darbar Sahib. This term is used, particularly by the local people, for Harmandir Sahib in Amritsar and Gurdwaras in Tarn Taran, Khadur Sahib, and Dera Baba Nanak.

Darshani Deori: Literally the most beautiful doorway, it is often the dominant entrance. In the Sikh context, it is the entrance gateway to the causeway leading to Harmandir Sahib.

Diwan: High official or courtier in historical contexts. The word also means congregation. Thus, a *diwan* hall is where the *sangat*, congregants, gather in Gurdwaras.

Gatka: A Sikh martial art in which participants use 'stick-fighting' instead of swords to polish defensive skills. It is part of the broader *shastarvidia*, or weapons training curriculum, that dates to 14th-century Punjab and was promoted by the Gurus. *Gatka* performances form part of many a *nagar kirtan* parade.

Gurbani: The words of the Gurus as enshrined in Guru Granth Sahib, the central religious scripture of Sikhism.

Guru Granth Sahib: The central religious scripture, first compiled by Guru Arjan Dev, and scribed by Bhai Gurdas, the final recension of which was declared Guru by Guru Gobind Singh. Primarily comprising compositions of Guru Nanak Dev, Guru Angad Dev, Guru Amar Das, Guru Ram Das, Guru Arjan Dev, and Guru Tegh Bahadur, it also has writings of 15 saints, some Hindu, others Sufi, and Sikh bards.

Gurmukhi: The script used to write the Sikh scripture. Literally, the script of Gurmukhs, i.e. Sikhs, traces its origins to Sharda and Takri. Guru Nanak Dev's Bani *Patti Likhi* comprises 35 stanzas, each introducing a letter of the Gurmukhi alphabet and giving a spiritual message. Later, his successor, Guru Angad Dev, devotedly spread the Guru's word by formalising and popularising the script and creating literature for the Sikhs.

Gurmat sangeet: Sikh devotional music that uses appropriate *ragas* to sing Gurbani. It is a major part of formal worship.

Gurpurb: A compound word of Guru+Purb, it marks the birth or death anniversary of any of the Gurus, and its observance forms a prominent part of the devotional calendars of Gurdwaras. Prominent Gurpurbs commemorate the birth of Guru Nanak and Guru Gobind Singh, the installation of Guru Granth Sahib and the martyrdom days of Guru Arjan Dev and Guru Tegh Bahadur. The occasions are marked by religious, devotional, or festive activities that bring the devotees together.

Har-ki-Pauri: The steps leading to the *sarovar* at the eastern end of Harmandir Sahib.

Hukamnamas: Edicts or orders to the Sikhs issued by Gurus. Hukamnamas are now issued by Akal Takht Sahib and the other four Takhts.

Ishnaan: Sacramental ablutions, a purifying bath, usually in a *sarovar*. Humility and prayer are essential to *ishnaan*.

Kar sewa: Altruistic service with one's own hands is of special significance to the Sikhs. *Kar sewa* is a voluntary physical service for any cause, often focused on various tasks at Sikh shrines.

Khalsa: Literally pure, sans impurities. The word Khalsa appears in a *Hukamnama* of Guru Hargobind, who described the *sangat* in the east as Guru-ka-Khalsa. Guru Tegh Bahadur's *Hukamnanas* also use the term. With the administration of *Amrit* by Guru Gobind Singh, the word acquired a specific connotation for the collective body of initiated Sikhs who had "excellent moral qualities, spiritual fervour and heroism."

Kimkhwab: A rich brocade silk fabric, often woven into rich floral patterns with metallic, gold, or silver threads.

Kirtan: Devotional singing of religious texts to appropriate musical notes. *Shabad kirtan* is the singing, in proper *ragas*, of the *shabads* in Guru Granth Sahib, most often in a congregational setting.

Langar: A community kitchen run in the name of the Guru, and thus formally *Guru ka langar*. Free meals are served to all visitors in a Gurdwara, regardless of their faith. *Langars* in Sikhism date back to Guru Nanak. *Sangats* were seated in *pangats*, or rows, without distinction of caste or status. They shared a common meal. *Langar* is served in all Gurdwaras and even outside them on various festivals. The word *langar* is used for the institution, the meal, the kitchen where this food is cooked, and the hall where it is served.

Nagar kirtan: A Sikh procession singing hymns held in a particular city area, especially during festivals. Lately, the tradition has been adopted in distant lands worldwide.

Nishan Sahib: The tall triangular Sikh religious flag seen at all Gurdwaras. It originated from the time of Guru Har Rai, the Sixth Guru, who hoisted the flag over Akal Takht Sahib in 1606. Nowadays, it has the *khanda-chakkar* symbol on it. Akal Takht Sahib on 15 July 2024 decreed the official colours as *basanti* (mustard yellow) or *surmai* (greyish blue).

Nisan: A distinctive mark or symbol, a seal, in a temporal and spiritual context. For the Sikhs, a *Nisan* is the seal or signature of the Gurus, especially seen in *Hukamnamas* issued by them. These days, the *khanda-chakkar* symbol is considered the *Nisan* of the Khalsa.

Parkarma: Circumambulation or the act of moving around a Gurdwara and/or Guru Granth Sahib. *Parkarma* reflects the humility and surrender of the devotees as they seek a connection to the Divine.

Pietra dura: is an inlay technique that uses cut and fitted, highly polished coloured stones to create images. Although the term is Italian, this technique is cross-cultural. In India, Harmandir Sahib and many Gurdwaras were embellished in the early 19th century with *pietra dura* work.

Parshad: Distributed among the *sangat* after *ardas* as a mark of Akal Purkh's grace, *karah parshad* is a soft, sweetened food made of flour or semolina and ghee, cooked while hymns are recited.

Sangat: Literally a fellowship or company, *sangat* is a congregation/ assembly of devotees who meet for prayer, listen to *kirtan* or religious instructions, or take part in a ceremony in the presence of Guru Granth Sahib, especially in a Gurdwara. *Sadh sangat* is thus a congregation of seekers of truth, and the term has been used since the time of Guru Nanak.

Sarovar: A sacred pond, tank or lake whose sanctity is often related to where it exists. This is where the devotees perform *ishnaan*. While bathing in the *sarovar* is an established Sikh religious practice, the real *sarovar* for the Sikhs is the Guru's *bani*, which alone can wash away sins.

Sewa: Literally, to attend upon, honour or worship. Practically, it is selfless service to strangers, often expressed through volunteering for common noble causes. *Sewa* is imperative for spiritual life, and three forms of *sewa* are accepted in Sikh practice: *tan* (physical), *man* (mental), and *dhan* (material).

Sikh: Literally, a learner or disciple of the Gurus, a follower of Sikhism. A Sikh believes in the unicity of God and follows the teachings of Guru Nanak and his successor Gurus as enshrined in Guru Granth Sahib.

Sindhi: People and language related to the Sindh region. Guru Nanak preached in this region and had many devotees there. Many Sindhis identify themselves with the founder of the Sikh religion, are often called Nanak Panthis and are Sehajdhari Sikhs, i.e., they believe in Sikh tenets but are not Amritdhari Sikhs. In the early 1900s, thousands became Amritdhari Sikhs. After Partition, they were widely dispersed, and even in distant lands, they played a prominent role in developing Gurdwaras for the Sikh diaspora.

Singh Sabha Movement: A movement for religious and social reform among the Sikhs in the late 19th century. Concerned Sikhs in Lahore and Amritsar reacted to the common perception of the dangers of dilution of the community's precepts and practices and undertook reforms that found widespread acceptance. The Singh Sabha Movement's assertion of the Sikhs' distinctive identity and its lead in reforming the Gurdwara management practices had a long-standing impact on the Sikhs.

Takht: A Persian word for throne, in the Sikh context, it is a spiritual seat of authority. There are five Takhts, which have equal authority, although Akal Takht Sahib is preeminent. The Sikhs follow the edicts issued by Takhts.

Udasis: The followers of Guru Nanak's son, Sri Chand, are called Udasis. They had a close relationship with the Sikhs, even though they were a distinct sect. During Mughal oppression, Udasis administered Gurdwaras. Separately, Guru Nanak's four spiritual journeys/ preaching tours are also called *Udasis*.

Acknowledgements

GURDWARAS. So much has been written about them, and I am grateful to all those who have worked on this subject before me. The bibliography gives a more detailed list of the books that I found valuable in my research.

A large number of people helped in gathering the information about Gurdwaras I could not visit, and I am grateful to them. Indeed, the book would not have happened without their active participation in this project. I have tried my best to gather and present accurate information. Even as I give their names and express my gratitude to them, I accept the responsibility for any mistakes that may have crept in and offer my sincere apologies.

Jaspreet, my wife, keeps my creative juices flowing and organises my life so that I can work on what I am most passionate about. She is the woman behind this man, and is also the person I bounce ideas off and give the first proofs to read. Jansher pitched in, accompanying us and driving us to Gurdwaras in Canada and in India, as well as in assisting with reading proofs and providing the assistance needed in many other ways while the book was being written.

The knowledgeable eye of Bhayee Sikandar Singh and Manjit Singh Khera improved the book. The manuscript also benefitted from reading of the draft and suggestions given by Amandeep Kaur, Gurpreet Bhattal, Naninder Dhillon, Harpal Singh, Simranjit Singh, Drishinder Singh Sandhawalia, and Davinder Singh.

Kuljit Bains has edited most of my books, including this one. I have often leaned on his professional knowledge, and meticulousness. He has also been the person who evolves the style sheets and looks at the final proofs.

Amardeep Singh has documented Gurdwaras in Pakistan extensively, through both, books and videos, and he was generous in sharing his contacts, as was Amandeep Sandhu, who is now working on Sikhs outside Punjab. K V Prasad, Sumit Seth, Nikhil Swahney, and Karan Garg's help arrived at crucial moments.

People who helped with specific information on the Gurdwaras that they knew about included Kulwant Singh, Mumbai; Raj Kamal Singh, Balbir Singh, and Satvinder Singh Gunsi, Bengaluru; Surinder Singh and Sajjan Singh, Hyderabad; Rajinder Singh, Chennai; Jagmohan Singh Gill, Kolkata; Ravinder Singh Sethi, Kathmandu, Nepal; Dr. Surender Singh Kandhari, Dubai, UAE; Balwant Singh Kumar, Manila, Philippines; Gulbir Singh Batra, Hong Kong SAR China; Manmohan Singh, Singapore; Ranmit Singh, Kuala Lumpur, Malaysia; Iqroop Sandhawalia, Baljit Bahrey, and Jujar Singh, London, UK; Ranjit Singh, Bhai Chain Singh, and Bhai Kashmir Singh Gosal, Paris, France; Naginder Singh Sehmi, Geneva, Switzerland; Jaitej Singh Anant, Vancouver, BC, and Ajit Singh Sahota, Toronto, ON, Canada; Jaswinder Singh Gunsi, Satnam Gunsi, Mountainview, and Pritam Singh Grewal, San Jose, CA, USA; Harpreet Singh Toor, New York, Rajwant Singh, Potomac, MD, USA; Swaran Singh, Panama; Harminder Singh, Kisumu, Kenya; Rajinder Singh and Anterpreet Singh, Blackburn, and Jasbir Singh Randhawa, Sydney, Australia. 'The Turban Traveller' Amarjeet Singh Chawla's videos on Gurdwaras in India and abroad are informative.

In the years spent researching and writing the book, so many people were generous with their time and knowledge. I appreciate and acknowledge everyone's contributions, and I regret having inadvertently omitted any names.

Publisher Rajiv Daswani's personal involvement and the level of support that he has extended to me has been beyond expectation. He has gone the extra mile in ensuring a unique publication. Allan Jay Quesada's eye for architectural detail and artistic skill is reflected in his magnificent illustrations. Danyel Maxin Santos, Gentry Press' Senior Graphic Designer, has superbly executed the book's stunning design. Ultimately, they have shaped my words into the book that is in the readers' hands.

Select Bibliography

Singh Amardeep. 2016. *Lost Heritage: The Sikh Legacy in Pakistan*. New Delhi. Nagaara Trust, Himalayan Books.

Singh Amrik. 2003. *Sikh Shrines in Delhi*. New Delhi. USPD and National Institute of Punjab Studies.

Randhir GS. 2016. *Sikh Shrines in India*. Delhi. Publications Division India.

Banerjee Himadri. 2023. *Beyond Punjab: Sikhs in the East and North-East India* Oxon, New York. Routledge.

Bhatti S S. 2013. *Golden Temple: Marvel of Sikh Architecture*. Pittsburg. RoseDog Books.

Pal M K. 2013. *Historical Gurdwaras of Delhi*. New Delhi. Niyogi Books.

Bance Peter, Paul Sukhbinder Singh, Anand Gurpreet Singh & Sidhu Amarpal Singh. 2008. *Khalsa Jatha British Isles 1908-2008*. London. The Central Gurdwara, (Khalsa Jatha).

Singh Gurmukh. 1995. *Historical Sikh Shrines*. Singh Bros, Amritsar.

Gill Jagmohan Singh. *Exploring the Sikh Roots in East India*. 2024. Singh Bros, Amritsar.

Singh Harbans (ed). 1982. *The Encyclopaedia of Sikhism (Four Volumes)*. Punjabi University, Patiala.

Singh Harbans. 1983. *The Heritage of the Sikhs*. Manohar Publications.

Singh Mohinder. *Punjab Heritage Series*. New Delhi. USPD and National Institute of Punjab Studies.

____ 2002. *Pilgrimage to Hemkunt*.

____ 2002. *Anandpur the City of Bliss*.

____ 2004. *Gurdwaras in India and Pakistan*.

____ 2008. *Takhat Sri Hazur Sahib, Journey into Eternity*. New Delhi. Himalayan Books.

Singh Patwant. 1988. *The Golden Temple*. New Delhi. Times Books International.

____1992. *Gurdwaras in India and Around the World*. New Delhi. Himalayan Books.

Singh Ranjodh. 2012. *Nankana Sahib and Sikh Shrines in Pakistan*. Ludhiana. GS Distribution Inc.

Singh Roopinder. 2004. *Guru Nanak: His Life and Teachings*. Rupa, New Delhi.

------, Singh Bhayee Sikandar. 2012, *Sikh Heritage: Ethos and Relics*. Rupa, New Delhi.

Sidhu Puneetinder Kaur. 2019. *Guru Nanak's Blessed Trail: The Sacred Sites Across Punjab*. New Delhi. Lonely Planet.

Pannu Dalvir S. 2019. *The Sikh Heritage: Beyond Borders*. San Jose. Pannu Dental Group.

Singh Gurharpal, Tatla Darshan Singh. 2006. *Sikhs in Britain: The Making of a Community*. London. Zed Books.

Kahlon Swarn Singh. 2012. *Sikhs in Latin America: Travels Among the Sikh Diaspora*. New Delhi. Manohar.

______. 2016. *Sikhs in Asia Pacific. Travels Among Sikh Diaspora from Yangon to Kobe*. New Delhi. Manohar.

______. 2020. *Sikhs in Continental Europe: From Norway to Greece and Russia to Portugal*. New Delhi. Manohar.

Mitra Swati Ed. 2004. *Walking with the Gurus: Historical Gurdwaras of Punjab*. New Delhi. Eicher Goodearth Limited.

Goswamy B N, Caron Smith. 2006. *I See No Stranger: Early Sikh Art and Devotion*. Ahmedabad. Mapin.

Mann Gurinder Singh, Numrich Paul, Williams Raymond B. 2001. *Buddhists, Hindus and Sikhs in America*. New York. Oxford.

Mann Gurinder Singh, 2004. *Sikhism*. New York. Pearson.

______, Hawley John Stratton (Ed). 1993. *Studying the Sikhs: Issues for North America*. Albany. State University of New York Press.

______, 2001. *The Making of Sikh Scripture*. New York. Oxford University Press.

Singh Nikki Guninder Kaur. 2023. *Janamsakhi Paintings of Guru Nanak in Early Sikh Art*. New Delhi. Roli Books.

Singh Khushwant. 1999. *A History of the Sikhs Vol I and II (2nd ed)*. New Delhi. Oxford University Press.

Lal Brij V., Reeves Peter. 2006. *The Encyclopedia of the Indian Diaspora*. New Delhi. Oxford University Press.

Papers

Rising India and Indian Communities in East Asia. Ed K Kesavapany, A Mani, P Ramasamy. 2008. Institute of Southeast Asian Studies.

The Sikhs in the South. BA Saletore. Indian History Congress. 1939 Session. Reproduced in *The Khalsa and the Punjab*. Ed. Himadari Banerjee. 2002. New Delhi. Tulika. pp. 70-71.

Punjabi

Nabha Kahn Singh. 1981. 4th ed. *Guru Shabad Ratnakar Mahan Kosh*. Patiala. Bhasha Vibhag, Punjab.

Chaihal Patialavi Dhanna Singh. Ed. Chetan Singh. 2016. *Guru Tirath Cycle Yatra*. Walsall. European Punjabi Sath.

Directory

GUR SIKH TEMPLE

Harmandir Sahib

AMRITSAR, PUNJAB, INDIA

Every Sikh prays to be able to pay obeisance at Harmandir Sahib. Devotees come from all over the world and for many in Amritsar, the day starts and ends there. The divine sounds of *kirtan*, serenity, and *sarovar*, all create an ethereal atmosphere, where the sacred permeates the souls of the devotees.

Golden Temple Road,
Atta Mandi, Katra Ahluwalia,
Amritsar, Punjab, 143006,
India

Akal Takht Sahib

AMRITSAR, PUNJAB, INDIA

Akal Takht Sahib is the primary seat of authority for the Sikhs. Situated near Harmandir Sahib, it represents temporal authority tempered by spiritual guidance. Disputes are resolved, eminent Sikhs are honoured, and transgressors are awarded penance. An edict issued by Akal Takht Sahib is considered binding by all followers.

Harmandir Sahib, Golden Temple Rd,
Atta Mandi, Katra Ahluwalia,
Amritsar, Punjab,143006,
India

Takht Sri Kesgarh Sahib

ANANDPUR SAHIB, PUNJAB, INDIA

The birthplace of the Khalsa, Takht Sri Kesgarh Sahib is situated atop a hill. Steeped in history connected with Guru Tegh Bahadur and Gobind Singh, it has a significant collection of weapons and other artefacts of the Gurus that are displayed for the *sangat* on special occasions. Holla Mohalla celebrations at Anandpur Sahib attract hundreds of thousands of Sikhs.

Anandpur Sahib,
Rupnagar District,
Punjab, 140118,
India

Takht Sri Damdama Sahib

TALWANDI SABO, PUNJAB, INDIA

Guru ki Kashi, a centre of Sikh learning from the time when Guru Gobind Singh dictated the *Adi Granth*, which was scribed by Bhai Mani Singh, Takht Sri Damdama Sahib has a rich history of learning. It also has a significant collection of manuscripts, including the *Adi Granth* scribed by Baba Deep Singh.

Talwandi Sabo Road,
Talwandi Sabo,
Punjab, 151302,
India

Takht Sri Harimandir Ji

PATNA, BIHAR, INDIA

Guru Nanak Dev, Guru Tegh Bahadur, and Guru Gobind Singh all visited Patna and stayed there. The easternmost *takht* has a rich history and heritage and has provided leadership to Sikhs in the region. It has an extensive collection of artefacts, including manuscripts and *Hukamnamas*, with Guru Gobind Singh's signatures.

Harimandir Gali Patna Sahib,
Jhauganj, Haji Ganj, Patna,
Bihar, 800008,
India

Takht Sachkhand Sri Hazur, Abchalnagar

NANDED, MAHARASHTRA, INDIA

Guru Gobind Singh's final resting place, Takht Sachkhand Sri Hazur, Abchalnagar, is the southernmost *takht* of special significance to Sikhs worldwide, and especially the Sikhs of the Deccan. A contemporary portrait of Guru Gobind Singh, and several weapons of Sikhs of historical prominence, are among the many important artefacts preserved there.

Gurdwara Road,
Yatri Niwas Road, Nanded,
Maharashtra, 431601,
India

Gurdwara Baba Atal Sahib

AMRITSAR, PUNJAB, INDIA

A towering tribute to Guru Hargobind's son Atal Rai, a monument to the commitment to non-interference with the Divine Will and penance for having done so, and a father's wish to commemorate his devoted and brilliant son, Gurdwara Baba Atal is an octagonal nine-storeyed tower with beautiful frescos.

Clock Tower Building,
Atta Mandi, Katra Ahluwalia,
Amritsar, Punjab, 143006,
India

Gurdwara Baoli Sahib

GOINDWAL SAHIB, PUNJAB, INDIA

A major centre of spiritual pilgrimage developed by Guru Amar Das, who had a *baoli* constructed. Completed in 1559, it has 84 steps. The Guru insisted that everyone partake of the *langar* with the *sangat* before joining the congregation. The tradition still holds, and devotees partake of *langar* and then pay obeisance.

Goindwal Sahib,
Dist. Tarn Taran,
Punjab, 143422,
India

Gurdwara Darbar Sahib

TARN TARAN, PUNJAB, INDIA

Built on land bought by Guru Arjan Dev, the Gurdwara has a massive *sarovar* and is beautifully embellished with *gach* and *tukri* work. It attracts tens of thousands of devotees every *amavas*, or no moon night. It played a major role in the Gurdwara Sudhar Movement.

Adda Bazaar,
Old City, Tarn Taran,
Punjab, 143401,
India

Gurdwara Darbar Sahib (Angitha Sahib)

KHADUR SAHIB, PUNJAB, INDIA

Khadur Sahib was Guru Angad Dev's headquarters where he compiled and dispersed Sikh literature. Eight of the 10 Gurus visited it. Gurdwara Darbar Sahib (Angitha Sahib) marks the spot where the Guru was cremated by his successor, Guru Amar Das. The complex also has Bibi Amro's Khuh and a multimedia museum.

Khadur Sahib,
Tarn Taran, 143117,
India

Gurdwara Paonta Sahib

SIRMAUR, HIMACHAL PRADESH, INDIA

Guru Gobind Singh founded Paonta Sahib. He patronised poets and had Indian classics translated. There he also trained his Sikhs and transformed them into warriors. The Gurdwara has a rich collection of articles connected with the Tenth Guru, including his pens, swords, maces, *chakras*, arrows, and matchlock guns.

Court Road, Devinagar,
Paonta Sahib,
Himachal Pradesh, 173025,
India

Gurdwara Nada Sahib

PANCHKULA, HARYANA, INDIA

A significant Gurdwara in Haryana, Nada Sahib is historically connected with Guru Gobind Singh. Also known as Gurdwara Patshahi 10, Nada Sahib's history, infrastructure, and nodal location make it a major place of pilgrimage. With the exception of Gurpurbs, Puranmashi gatherings draw the largest number of devotees.

Nada Sahib, Panchkula,
Haryana, 134109,
India

Sri Guru Singh Sabha

SECTOR 19, CHANDIGARH, INDIA

The Gurdwara was built in the 1960s and uses the visual metaphor of a turban, transformed into concrete by the original architects of Chandigarh. A traditional dome and entrance were added later. The Gurdwara has accommodation for devotees. It also has many medical diagnostic facilities, a clinic, and runs two schools.

Sector 19-D,
Chandigarh, 160019,
India

Gurdwara Bangla Sahib

NEW DELHI, INDIA

Guru Har Krishan, the Eighth Guru, was hosted by Raja Jai Singh in his house in March 1664. The site is now Gurdwara Bangla Sahib, which has a large *sarovar* and is famous for the healing powers of the water of its well. The *langar*, diagnostic and medical facilities, and a library are noteworthy.

Baba Kharak Singh Road,
Connaught Place,
New Delhi, 110001,
India

Gurdwara Sis Ganj

DELHI, INDIA

A monument to mark the sacrifice of Guru Tegh Bahadur, who gave up his life for the right of others to practise their religion, the Gurdwara is situated in the heart of Mughal Delhi. The Gurdwara is richly appointed. Besides accommodation for devotees to stay, it also has a reference library and an underground parking.

Chandni Chowk Road,
Chandni Chowk,
Delhi, 110006,
India

Gurdwara Rakab Ganj

NEW DELHI, INDIA

Gurdwara Rakab Ganj marks the cremation site of Guru Tegh Bahadur's body. Sacred relics preserved in the Gurdwara include Guru Gobind Singh's swords, a dagger, and two *katars*. The complex houses the Delhi Sikh Gurdwara Management Committee, a large *langar* building, and a big covered space for gatherings. An old well has also been restored.

Pandit Pant Marg,
New Delhi, 110001,
India

Hemkunt Sahib Gurdwara

CHAMOLI, UTTARAKHAND, INDIA

Nestled high in the Himalayas, 15,210 feet above the sea level, Hemkunt Sahib Gurdwara is located next to a crystal-clear lake that reflects white snow-clad mountain peaks. The unique building of the Gurdwara is open only for three months in a year because of the weather.

Chamoli District,
Uttarakhand, 249401,
India

Sri Guru Singh Sabha Dadar

MUMBAI, MAHARASHTRA, INDIA

Central to the socio-religious activities of the Sikhs in Mumbai, Sri Guru Singh Sabha Dadar is a refuge that helped many Sikhs when they first moved into India's commercial capital. The families of many cancer patients who undergo treatment at a nearby hospital are given a place to stay. It also runs a school.

Dr Ambedkar Road,
Opposite Chitra Cinema,
Dadar, Mumbai, Maharashtra,
400014, India

Sri Guru Singh Sabha Ulsoor

BENGALURU, KARNATAKA, INDIA

A shiny new Gurdwara building stands at a site that dates to the 1940s. The new building has a magnificent *darbar* hall, an underground parking, accommodation for visitors, facilities for marriage functions, etc. Right next to the Gurdwara the management runs a school for needy children.

Gurdwara Road, Ulsoor,
Bengaluru, Karnataka, 560008,
India

Gurdwara Baram Bala

HYDERABAD, TELANGANA, INDIA

Gurdwara Baram Bala has great historical and religious significance in the lives of the Sikh community in Hyderabad, where Maharaja Ranjit Singh's Sikh soldiers were deputed to help the Nizam in 1882. The new building was inaugurated in 2018, and it showcases the devotion of the Sikhs in Telengana.

Maharaj Ranjit Singh Nagar,
Sikh Chawni, Huda Colony, Attapur,
Hyderabad, Telangana, 500048,
India

Sri Guru Nanak Sat Sangh Sabha Gurdwara

CHENNAI, TAMIL NADU, INDIA

Madras got its first Gurdwara in the 1950s, and the original building still stands. It has been supplemented by other structures that offer facilities like accommodation for devotees and those in the city to seek medical treatment, a multimedia centre and a library. It is central to Sikh devotional and social interaction in Chennai.

GN Chetty Road,
Gangai Karai Puram, Thyagaraya Nagar, Chennai, Tamil Nadu, 600017, India

Gurdwara Bara Sikh Sangat

KOLKATA, WEST BENGAL, INDIA

Kolkota was blessed by Guru Nanak Dev and Guru Tegh Bahadur's presence. A historical and spiritual landmark, Gurdwara Bara Sikh Sangat is an eight-storeyed white building topped with golden domes. It has a library, a nursery, and classrooms for students of Punjabi language and culture.

Mahatma Gandhi Road,
Near Maa Shitala Mandir,
Block A, Kolutolla, Kolkata,
West Bengal, 700073,
India

Gurdwara Janam Asthan

NANKANA SAHIB, PUNJAB, PAKISTAN

The birthplace of Guru Nanak, Nankana Sahib has a unique place in the hearts of Sikhs worldwide. Although there have been several renovations and improvements, the main building still reflects the essence of the shrine built by Maharaja Ranjit Singh. Some Sikh families from Pakistan live near the Gurdwara and a considerable number of Sikh devotees visit it.

Buchey ki Road,
Nankana Sahib,
Punjab, 39100,
Pakistan

Darbar Sahib Gurdwara

KARTARPUR, PUNJAB, PAKISTAN

Guru Nanak gave material shape to his teachings by gathering a community of his followers at Kartarpur in the last years of his life. This Gurdwara was opened in 2019 to Indian pilgrims who now take the land route to it through the Kartarpur Corridor, which the governments of India and Pakistan built.

Shakarghar Rd,
Kartarpur,
Punjab, 51800,
Pakistan

Gurdwara Sri Rori Sahib

EMINABAD, PUNJAB, PAKISTAN

Guru Nanak Dev meditated at the spot where the Gurdwara is built. The Guru visited the city many times and Eminabad is familiar to Sikhs because the *sakhi* of Bhai Lalo and Malik Bhago. The distinctive brick architecture stood out, before it went into neglect and was damaged due to flooding in a storm in 2024.

Eminabad,
Gujranwala,
Punjab, 39100
Pakistan

Gurdwara Nanak Shahi

DHAKA, BANGLADESH

Guru Nanak Dev and Guru Tegh Bahadur both visited Dhaka, a country that does not have a permanent Sikh presence now. The *sangat* comprises local non-Sikh devotees and Sikhs working in various international organisations who are posted there. The Gurdwara has been steadily renovated and additional facilities created, including a research centre.

Nilkhet Road,
Dhaka University Area,
Dhaka, 1000,
Bangladesh

Guru Nanak Satsang Gurdwara

KUPONDOLE, LALITPUR, KATHMANDU, NEPAL

The primary Gurdwara for Sikhs in Nepal is a double-storeyed building with traditional architecture. It was inaugurated in 1999, along with a large guesthouse for devotees. The Gurdwara was extensively renovated in 2019. It is the only Gurdwara maintained and managed by the community and actively undertakes charitable activities.

Kupondole, Lalitpur,
Kathmandu, 44600,
Nepal

Guru Nanak Darbar

DUBAI, UNITED ARAB EMIRATES

The first 'official' Gurdwara in the Gulf region opened on 17 January 2012. It serves the over 50,000 devotees of the UAE. The three-storeyed grand edifice draws in crowds from around the world. The main hall is magnificently appointed and the *langar* hall can seat 900. Interfaith outreach is encouraged.

PO Box 5576,
3806 Sheikh Zayed Road,
Jebel Ali Village, Dubai,
United Arab Emirates

Khalsa Diwan Society

MANILA, PHILIPPINES

Inaugurated in 1933, the Gurdwara holds congregations daily, with larger ones on Sundays. People come from various cities of the Philippines to celebrate Baisakhi, Diwali, and Lohri. *Nagar kirtan* is organised on Guru Nanak Dev's birth anniversary, in which the local Sindhi community also participates in large numbers.

1350 United Nations Avenue, Paco, Manila, 1007, Philippines

Central Sikh Temple

SINGAPORE CITY, SINGAPORE

Wadda Gurdwara, as it is generally known, is a double-storeyed building with a 13-metre dome, modern though heavily inspired by traditional design. The Central Sikh Temple has the largest *darbar* hall in Singapore and holds daily *diwans*. It is a favoured venue for *anand karaj* ceremonies.

2 Towner Road, 327804, Singapore

Khalsa Diwan Sikh Temple

HONG KONG, SPECIAL ADMINISTRATIVE REGION, CHINA

The new building was inaugurated in 2022, having been rebuilt many times since the original Gurdwara came up in 1902. The new three-storeyed 76,000 sq ft structure serves the 15,000 Sikhs of Hong Kong and has a library and various halls for events. It has active outreach programmes.

371 Queen's Road East, Wan Chai, Hong Kong, SAR, China

Gurdwara Guru Singh Sabha

BANGKOK, THAILAND

Sikh presence in Thailand is over a century old and this complex dates to 1932 when the land was purchased. The rebuilt six-storeyed Gurdwara was inaugurated in 1981, and it has extensive facilities for religious education, including a school, as well as accommodation for visitors, and a clinic that serves the neighbourhood.

571 Chakphet Road, Bangkok, 10200, Thailand

Sri Guru Nanak Darbar Tatt Khalsa Diwan

KUALA LUMPUR, MALAYSIA

Celebrating its centenary in 2018, it is one of the oldest and largest Gurdwaras in Malaysia. It has a rich history of producing literature and teaching Punjabi to expatriates. Free Gurbani classes are held. The new Gurdwara building was inaugurated in 2002 and the *sangat* gathers every day for *path* and *kirtan*.

24, Jalan Raja Alang, Chow Kit,
Kuala Lumpur, 50300,
Malaysia

The Central Gurdwara

LONDON, UNITED KINGDOM

Khalsa Jatha, British Isles, as this Gurdwara is also know, is the oldest in Great Britain and has been associated with many important events and individuals. The building was renovated in 2016 and has a new look, with many additions. Outreach programmes have been undertaken since the time the Gurdwara first came into existence.

62 Queensdale Road,
London W11 4SG,
UK

Sri Guru Singh Sabha

SOUTHALL, LONDON, UNITED KINGDOM

The social life of many Sikhs in London revolves around this Gurdwara. In addition to religious programmes, it organises a Sikh studies course, Punjabi classes for adults, and school visits for non-Sikh schoolchildren. A community clinic provides legal, medical, and well-being advice and essential treatment. Sports, including football, *gatka*, and wrestling, are encouraged.

2-8 Park Avenue,
Guru Nanak Rd,
Southall, UB2 4NP,
UK

Gurdwara Singh Sabha Culte Sikh France

BOBIGNY, PARIS, FRANCE

Sikhs are small in number and a visible minority in France. This Gurdwara opened in 2011 fulfils their spiritual needs. It also provides community support, more so since the implementation of *laïcité* laws since 2004. The Baisakhi parade has been declared "Intangible Cultural Heritage" by the French Government.

16 Rue de la Ferme,
93000 Bobigny,
France

Gurdwara Singh Sabha

NOVELLARA, REGGIO EMILIA, ROMAGNA, ITALY

Opened in 2000, the two-storeyed Gurdwara stands on 17 acres of land. Diwans are held and *langar* served on all days. The Gurdwara has some rooms for short-term stay of devotees. The Baisakhi parade involves local political and civic leaders and is a major event that brings in tens of thousands.

Via Lorenzo Bandini, 7, 42017,
Novellara Reggio Emilia,
Italy

Shri Guru Nanak Niwas

LIER, DRAMMEN, NORWAY

Drawing in *sangat* from the area, and nearby Oslo, the Gurdwara was founded in 1991, and the present new building inaugurated in 2011. A nearby building houses *ragi jathas*. There are daily *diwans*. Turban Day during Baisakhi celebrations raises awareness regarding Sikhs, who have successfully negotiated issues related to their visible identity with the government.

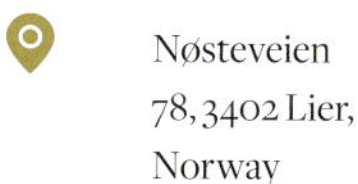

Nøsteveien
78, 3402 Lier,
Norway

Gurdwara Sahib Switzerland

LANGENTHAL, BERN, SWITZERLAND

The white traditional architecture of the Gurdwara makes it stand out, especially its 16-metre-high dome. The Gurdwara was inaugurated in 2006. Much of the traditional work on the *palki* was done in Kashmir and the Gurdwara has two significant old manuscripts. *Nagar kirtans* and interfaith conferences help in awareness and integration.

Dennliweg 31a,
4900 Langenthal,
Switzerland

Gur Sikh Temple

ABBOTSFORD, BRITISH COLUMBIA, CANADA

The oldest existing Gurdwara in Canada was inaugurated in 1912. Its exterior melded with the traditional frontier buildings of the time. It was designated a National Historic Site in 2002 and renovated by 2007. The ground floor has a museum and a new Gurdwara across the road is used by the present *sangat*.

33089 South Fraser Way, Abbotsford, BC V2S 2B1, Canada

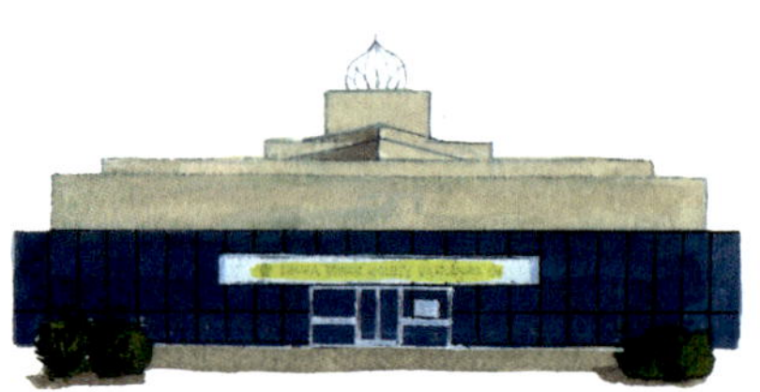

Khalsa Diwan Society

VANCOUVER, BRITISH COLUMBIA, CANADA

Designed by legendary Canadian architect William Henry Archer, the Gurdwara building was inaugurated in 1970. Damaged after a fire, it was renovated and reopened in 2018, and proudly traces its history to the original Gurdwara of 1908. Traditional service is held regularly, and many modern facilities for younger Sikhs are also available.

8000 Ross St, Vancouver, BC V5X 4C5, Canada

Ontario Khalsa Darbar

MISSISSAUGA, ONTARIO, CANADA

The first Gurdwara in Ontario was inaugurated in 1989. It is now a large complex that has evolved with the needs of the community. Besides religious activities, it encourages sports and has a large gymnasium hall. Kiratpur Park in the complex provides a unique water body to immerse the ashes of the deceased.

7080 Dixie Rd, Mississauga, ON L5S 1B7, Canada

Sikh Temple

STOCKTON, CALIFORNIA, UNITED STATES OF AMERICA

The oldest in the USA, this Gurdwara was built in 1915. It was intimately involved with the Ghadar Movement, visual history of which is showcased there. It sponsored Indian students to UC Berkeley in the early 1900s, and now runs a Sunday Khalsa School, holds sport contests and cultural activities.

1930 S. Sikh Temple St,
Stockton, CA 95206,
USA

Sikh Gurdwara

SAN JOSE, CALIFORNIA, UNITED STATES OF AMERICA

Located on a hilltop, the biggest Gurdwara in North America was originally located on White Road, San Jose. The Gurdwara's stunning architectural elements and range of services stand out, as does its collection of original commissioned art. A Sunday school teaches requisite skills in Gurbani and Punjabi language.

3636 Gurdwara Ave,
San Jose, CA 95148,
USA

Gurdwara Sikh Cultural Society

NEW YORK, UNITED STATES OF AMERICA

New York's oldest Gurdwara was housed in a converted Methodist church building till a fire destroyed it in 2002. The new building was built a few years later. The most prominent gurdwara on the East Coast holds the Annual Sikh Parade in Manhattan around Baisakhi. Gurdwara Street was named in 2020.

9530 118th St,
South Richmond Hill,
NY 11419,
USA

Guru Gobind Singh Foundation

ROCKVILLE, MARYLAND, UNITED STATES OF AMERICA

A 60-mile drive from the White House, this Gurdwara was inaugurated in 2005. It provides traditional services to the local *sangat*, with a special focus on children. It has undertaken interfaith events that also involve general students. The *sangat* has shown great involvement in broader community issues.

13814 Travilah Rd,
Rockville, MD 20850
USA

Gurdwara Guru Nanak Sahib

PANAMA CITY, PANAMA

With its traditional architecture and five domes, the Gurdwara stands out in Panama, where Sikhs were engaged in the construction of the Panama Canal. It is a bastion of the Sikh *sangat* in the country and hosts major *samagams* on each *sangrand*. Many third-generation Sikhs of Panama connect with their roots through this Gurdwara.

Iglesia, 5 Quebrada De Piedra,
Panama City,
Panama

Gurdwara Makindu Sahib

MAKINDU, KENYA

Sikh railway workers established the Gurdwara in 1926, and it has been rebuilt many times since. Woven into the history of Sikh diaspora in West Africa, it is considered the most important Gurdwara of the Sikhs in Africa. The complex also houses a large *sarai*, a hospital, and a dairy farm.

Mombasa Road, Makindu,
Eastern Province, 90138,
Kenya

Gurdwara Sahib Johannesburg

JOHANNESBURG, SOUTH AFRICA

The first Sikh immigrants arrived in South Africa in the late 19th century. This Gurdwara is new and was inaugurated in 2015. The building has visible elements of Sikh architecture, blended with local sensibilities. Sikhs from Johannesburg and neighbouring areas gather in large numbers for Guru Nanak Dev's birth anniversary every year.

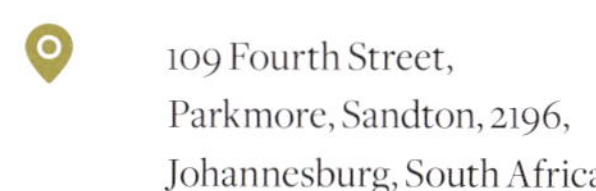

109 Fourth Street,
Parkmore, Sandton, 2196,
Johannesburg, South Africa

Sikh Temple Blackburn

MELBOURNE, VICTORIA, AUSTRALIA

Catering to the largest population of Sikhs in the province of Victoria, the Gurdwara's outreach initiatives for the community and beyond include Khalsa Punjabi School for teaching the language. Punjabi is a subject for Victorian Certificate of Education, and the Gurdwara holds classes.

127 Whithorse Road,
Blackburn, Victoria 3130,
Australia

Gurdwara Sahib

GLENWOOD, NEW SOUTH WALES, AUSTRALIA

Located on five acres of land, and completed in 1998, Gurdwara Sahib, Glenwood, is run by the Australian Sikh Association. The three-storeyed building is a rectangular structure topped with traditional domes and *chhatris*. It has a well-appointed library and plays an important role in providing teachers of Sikhism for local schools.

4/18 Meurants Lane,
Glenwood, New South Wales 2768,
Australia

The Author

Roopinder Singh is an experienced journalist and accomplished author with a deep passion for Sikh history, religion, and heritage. With a career spanning several decades, he has contributed as a journalist, writer, and photographer.

A graduate of St. Stephen's College, University of Delhi, with a BA (Hons) and MA in Philosophy, he began his writing journey in school, crafting short stories that he initially shared within his family. His passion for storytelling led him to a career in journalism, working for over 36 years.

Roopinder served as a reporter-editor in New York and Chandigarh, and retired as Senior Associate Editor of The Tribune, Chandigarh, in 2020. Notably, he was on the editorial board for 20 years and launched the Internet Edition of *The Tribune* in 1998. He played a key role in the newspaper, overseeing weekly supplements, including the Sunday magazine, and serving as the book reviews editor.

Roopinder has been an editorial writer, feature writer, and columnist. He wrote his first article on computers for *The Tribune* in 1991, which led to his column *Computer Chat*, introducing readers to the emerging cyber world. He also headed *Log In Tribune* (2001–2004), a supplement on information technology. Over the years, he contributed hundreds of opinion pieces and articles to *The Tribune*, covering international affairs, information technology, and Sikh history and culture. His interviews and contributions to *The Last Word* column were particularly well-received. Roopinder continues to write for newspapers and magazines, including *The Tribune*, *The Indian Express*, and *Taj* magazine.

An accomplished author, Roopinder has written, co-authored, and edited numerous books, most of which focus on Sikhism and its rich cultural heritage. He was a consultant for *Sikhs: The Story of a People, Their Faith and Culture* (2023), which explores the spiritual journey and global impact of Sikhism. His significant works include *Delhi '84* (2014), a poignant novel about the 1984 anti-Sikh violence; and *Guru Nanak: His Life and Teachings* (2004), a widely regarded biography of the founder of Sikhism, later published in Hindi as *Guru Nanak Jeevan Aur Shikshayen* (2007). His book *Sikh Heritage: Ethos and Relics* (2012), co-authored with Bhayee Sikandar Singh, in collaboration with the Smithsonian Institution, Washington, D.C., explores Sikh culture and relics in private collections, and has been published multiple times. His debut book *MIAF Arjan Singh DFC* (2002) is a biography of the distinguished Marshal of the Indian Air Force.

He has also edited bilingual works such as *An Inspiring Journey: Inderjit Kaur Sandhu* (2021), a biography of a pioneering woman educationist, who was his mother, and *Giani Gurdit Singh 1923–2007* (2008), a festschrift honouring his late father, a noted scholar.

A keen photographer who learned darkroom techniques in school, his photographs have featured prominently in his books and are part of private collections in India and abroad.

The Illustrator

Allan Quesada is a talented illustrator with a rich background in architecture and a deep passion for ecclesiastical art. A graduate of the Pamantasan ng Lungsod ng Maynila, he earned his bachelor's degree in architecture and spent over a decade honing his skills as an architect. During this time, he developed a keen understanding of perspective and refined his artistic abilities, which laid the foundation for his career as an illustrator.

Inspired by the works of Renaissance masters such as Leonardo da Vinci and Michelangelo, Allan's art is defined by its realism and intricate details. His illustrations vividly capture the beauty and essence of architecture, with a particular focus on places of worship. His passion for ecclesiastical art dates back to his childhood, when his first drawing—a basilica—was created at the age of five. Over the years, his travels across the world provided opportunities to sketch places of worship, each imbued with the spirit and character of the structures he admires.

Primarily working with watercolour, Allan also employs mediums such as oil, pastel, ink, and acrylic to bring his creations to life. Among his notable achievements is the illustrated book, Simbahán, which celebrates Philippine churches.

Allan shares his creative journey and art expertise on his YouTube channel, Watercolors by Allan Jay Quesada. Beyond illustration, he is pursuing architectural photography and revisiting his passion for oil painting, showcasing his versatility as an artist.

The *khanda-chakkar* symbol with the double-edged *khanda* in the centre, and a *chakkar* flanked by two single-edged *kirpans*.

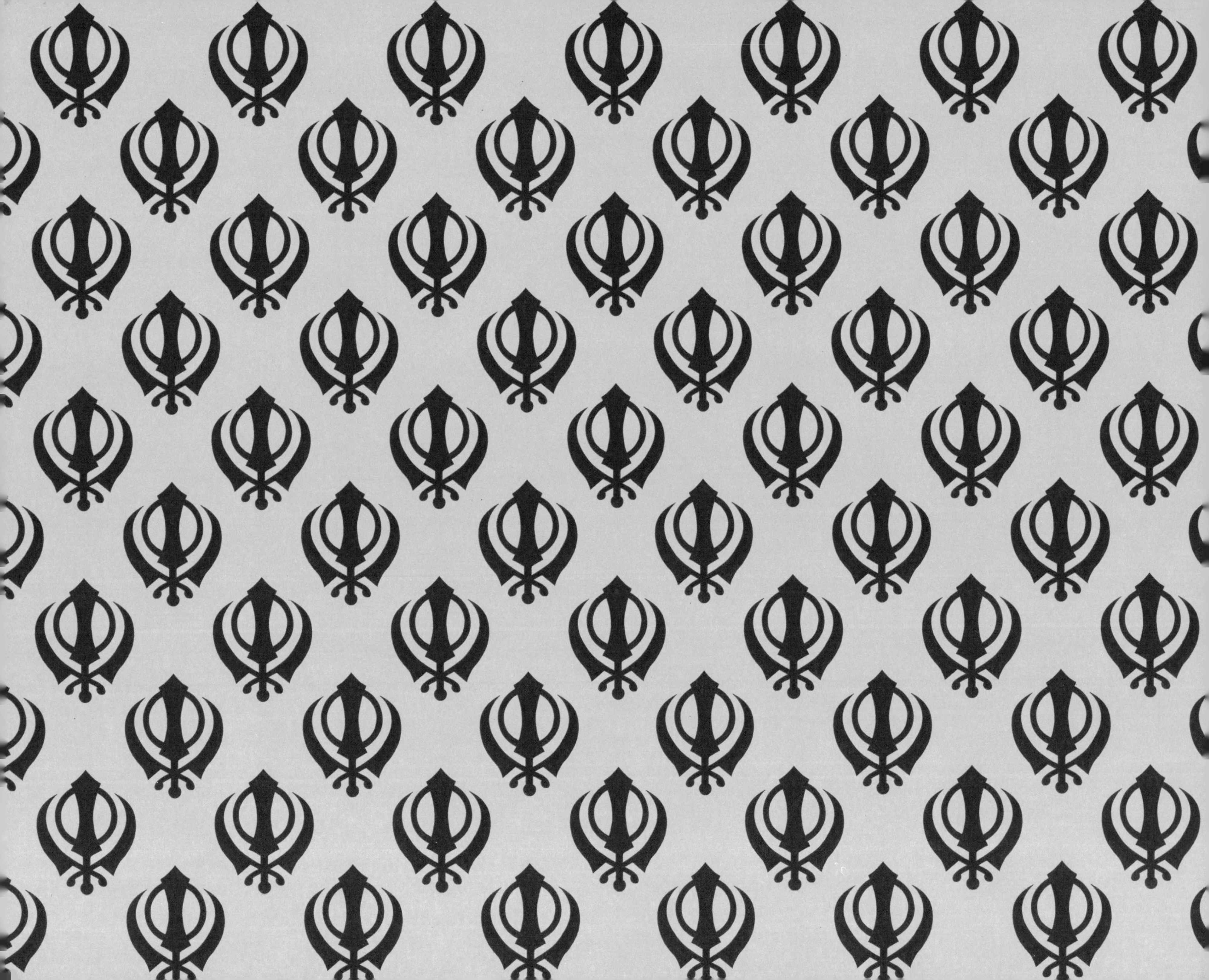